INDUSTRIAL RELATIONS IN PLANNED ECONOMIES, MARKET ECONOMIES, AND THE THIRD WORLD

As a working person – or unemployed at one stage or another – have you ever wondered in which direction industrial relations are moving in the world at large? Is it as bad – or as good – in this country as elsewhere? Can we learn anything useful from the solutions and failures of other countries? This book may not provide all the answers to these and other perplexing questions of our times, but it goes a long way in that direction.

This study identifies and discusses contrasts and unexpected similarities between all the major spheres of industrial relations in the three world divisions – the developed capitalist market economies, the socialist planned economies and the less-developed countries of the Third World. Employment, unemployment, work discipline, organized labor, industrial democracy, technological change, wages, incentives, inflation, industrial disputes and international migrations of workers under different social systems are the major fields of analysis.

Special attention is given to the conditions and recent developments in the social countries – both European and Asian, plus Cuba. Amongst specific questions examined are such topical issues as the role of labor in the social system, women and employment, alienation, the humanization of work, collective bargaining, independent unionism, workers' participation in ownership and management, technological redundancy, differences in personal earnings, strikes, the settlement of disputes and the Marxist view of "guest workers." The significance of the emergence and activities of Solidarity in Poland is considered in a broad context, together with dissident trade unions and work stoppages in other socialist countries. References for further reading are provided at the end of each of the ten chapters, including original socialist sources available in English.

By the same author

The Economics and Politics of East–West Trade

The Economics of Socialism
  Das sozialistische Wirtschaftssystem (*German translation*)
  Economia de socialismo (*Portuguese translation*)
  Economia del socialismo (*Spanish translation*)
  Elm al-eqtssad al-eshtraki (*Arabic translation*)
  L'economia dei paesi socialisti (*Italian translation*)
  Samajvadhache arthasastra (*Marathi translation*)
  Socialistische economie (*Dutch translation*)

Towards Multilateral Payments in Comecon Foreign Trade

Socialist Economic Development and Reforms
  Desarollo y reformas en los paises socialistas (*Spanish translation*)

Prospects for the Export of Australian Farm Products

Profit, Risk and Incentives under Socialist Economic Planning

Technology in Comecon

The Multinationals and East–West Relations

Comparative Monetary Economics

An Encyclopedic Dictionary of Marxism, Socialism and Communism

INDUSTRIAL RELATIONS IN PLANNED ECONOMIES, MARKET ECONOMIES, AND THE THIRD WORLD

A Comparative Study of Ideologies, Institutions, Practices, and Problems

J. Wilczynski

St. Martin's Press New York

© Jozef Wilczynski 1983

All rights reserved. For information, write:
St. Martin's Press, Inc., 175 Fifth Avenue, New York, NY 10010
Printed in Hong Kong
First published in the United States of America in 1983

ISBN 0-312-41513-3

Library of Congress Cataloging in Publication Data

Wilczynski, J. (Jozef), 1922-
Industrial relations in planned economies, market economies, and the third world.

Includes bibliographical references and index.
1. Industrial relations. I. Title.
HD6971.W6   1983   331   82-20551
ISBN 0-312-41513-3

Contents

v

Preface

Industrial relations are no longer a matter of isolated employer–employee dealings, but a question of wider economic, social and political consequence – and they are becoming increasingly complex under the impact of technological and social change. But in these developments, however progressive (or regressive), the basic problem has essentially remained – the conflict of interests between employers and employees. This generalization is valid in application to any social system.

For a long time it was officially claimed in the Marxist-ruled countries that under socialism basic industrial conflict did not exist, as the interests of the socialist state and of the workers were identical. As is demonstrated in this book, these countries also have the problem of conflicting industrial relations – they have always had it, however suppressed it might have been. The industrial upheavals in Poland 1980–2 bear dramatic witness to this inexorable reality.

As is well known, industrial conflicts lead not only to immediate losses to the parties directly involved, but also to other entities and in many cases to the public. To minimize these adverse effects and the cost to society, it is important that industrial disputes are reduced to a minimum, or are at least settled speedily and in a manner fair and reasonable to the parties concerned (and society in general).

Industrial relations differ in detail from one workplace to another, but in each country they conform to, or are at least exposed to, the same political, legal, economic and social set-up. There are, of course, considerable differences in these set-ups. Nevertheless meaningful generalizations can be made as to capitalism and socialism. The focus of attention in this study is to examine the differences between these two rival systems of our times.

Comparative industrial relations is a relatively new field of study. Although the International Labour Organization recognized the value of this field long ago, and in 1960 established the International Institute for Labour Studies in Geneva, it is surprising how little interest had been aroused until recently. There are now many specialists in the field who believe that the comparative study of industrial relations on a more systematic basis is long overdue.

This discipline holds great promise for theoretical writers, policy makers and practitioners on both sides of the Iron and Bamboo, or Strategic and Technological curtains. The increasing internationalization of economic relations, the expanding activities of the international trade union movements, the international repercussions of technological change on work relations and the growing assertiveness of the workers under both systems further enhance the need for this study in the international setting. A knowledge of industrial relations under different social systems may not only be helpful to a better understanding of different countries, but may also suggest new solutions to domestic problems. The reader will be surprised at how much mutual (mostly subconscious) transplantation of ideas and practices has taken place between the two systems – to the chagrin of parochial diehards, but to the delight of the believers in the convergence thesis.

In this book the author examines all major facets of industrial relations in capitalist market economies and under socialist economic planning. The usual approach is in each case to first outline the principles and practices prevailing in capitalist countries. Against this backdrop, the contrasting elements in the socialist set-up are examined in greater detail and striking, unexpected similarities are pointed out. Special attention is given to the role of ideology and political factors which, in the author's view, were largely neglected in the past treatment of industrial relations (especially in the West). Differences amongst capitalist nations as well as amongst the socialist countries are indicated where warranted.

The author's well-meant intention is to be honestly informative and neutral. He does not, however, steer away from critical evaluations of both sides, still in a detached and constructive spirit.

Much of the research for this book was carried out at the University of Manitoba where the author was Visiting Professor in the Department of Economics in 1980. He wishes to thank the University for the facilities provided and the fruitful atmosphere for research. He profited from the ideas and counter-ideas of Professors C. L. Barber, N. E. Cameron, C. W. Gonick, J. Loxley, D. Mole, P. Phillips, H. Rempel, W. Simpson, R. H. Vogt, A. M. C. Waterman and Mr R. Grynberg, but in no way implies their responsibility for any shortcomings of this book.

University of Manitoba,   J. Wɪʟᴄᴢʏɴꜱᴋɪ
Winnipeg, and *University*
of New South Wales at Duntroon,
Canberra

1 Labour and the Social System

A. THE SOCIAL SYSTEM

The social system can be briefly described as a network of relations amongst individuals and groups regulated by beliefs and institutions. Social systems can be viewed in historical ('vertical') perspective or in the contemporary ('horizontal') scene. In this study we are primarily concerned with the comparative setting prevailing in the world today, although we shall be occasionally referring – still for comparative purposes – to historical antecedents.

Capitalism and socialism[1] are the two major social systems confronting each other today – competitively and antagonistically. To generalize, capitalism is noted for a multi-party system of government, the predominantly private ownership of the means of production, the operation of the market mechanism and the freedom of enterprise spurred basically by the private profit motive.

On the other hand, socialism is characterized by the mono-party system of government exercised (or dominated) by the communist party, the social ownership of the means of production (land and capital),[2] and economic planning guided by social interest as interpreted by the ruling party.

From the above fundamental elements other related features derive, such as those pertaining to personal freedom, economic management, the allocation of resources, prices, developmental strategy, income distribution and external economic relations. The contrasts between the two rival social systems are summarized under 20 criteria of comparison in Figure 1.1.

Capitalism is best developed in the 'Western countries' (numbering 25), viz. in Western Europe, North America, Japan, New Zealand, Australia and South Africa. On the whole, they have reached high income levels and most are highly industrialized.

FIGURE 1.1   *Contrasting features of capitalism and socialism*

Capitalism	Socialism

1. Government

| Democratic multi-party system of government | Mono-party system of government (exercised by the communist party) |

2. The State

| Relatively small, rather residual | Dominant, ubiquitous |

3. Personal freedom

| Democratic, civil liberties | Restricted human rights |

4. Society's locus of interest

| Individualism (persons, households, firms) | Primacy of social interest |

5. Ownership of the means of production

| Predominantly private | Predominantly socialized |

6. Economic mechanism

| Market mechanism, competition | Economic planning and orderly development |

7. Mainspring of economic activity

| Private profit | Planned directives, material and moral incentives |

8. Economic administration and management

| Mainly decentralized | Basically centralized, hierarchical and directive |

9. Enterprises

| Predominantly privately owned but operated by professional managers; freedom of enterprise | Chiefly state or collectively owned operating within the planned bureaucratic framework |

10. The allocation of resources

| Mostly by private firms in response to market demand | Almost exclusively by the state in the economic plan |

11. Consumption

| Consumer's sovereignty, strong emphasis on private consumption | Planned consumption, freedom of consumer's choice, social consumption favoured |

FIGURE 1.1 *(Contd.)*

Capitalism	Socialism

12. Investment

Chiefly private and motivated by profit | Almost completely by the state motivated by long-run social interest

13. Money and banking

Very important in economic development and social structure | Reduced to a passive role, accommodating planned economic and social development

14. Prices

Basically determined by the market, fluctuations, inflation | Mainly planned and controlled by the state, reasonable price stability

15. Development strategy

Mostly left to free enterprise and private capital, uneven industrial development | Accelerated planned development emphasizing all-round industrialization

16. Agriculture

Private farming, subsistence as well as advanced large-scale | Collective and state farms, planned neglect, inefficient

17. The service sector

Highly developed | Poorly developed, planned neglect

18. Organized labour

Independent trade unionism, protecting workers and championing their claims | State dominated trade union establishment preoccupied with fulfilling economic plans

19. Distribution of national income

Wide differences accentuated by non-labour income | The ideal of equality, but considerable differences 'according to work'

20. Foreign trade

Mainly in private hands for profit, spurred by comparative advantage | State monopoly, carried on by large foreign trade corporations, insulation from foreign markets

Socialism has been best established in the 14 'older' socialist countries where the communist regimes had come to power before 1960, viz. (the year of the formal communist accession to power in brackets): Albania (1946), Bulgaria (1946), China (1949), Cuba (1959), Czechoslovakia (1946), the [East] German Democratic Republic (1945), Hungary (1945), the Democratic People's Republic of [North] Korea (1946), Mongolia (1924), Poland (1947), Romania (1946), the USSR (1917), Vietnam (1954, 1976) and Yugoslavia (1945). In addition there are 11 other 'new' socialist members, viz. Afghanistan (1978), Angola (1975), Benin (1975), Congo (1970), Ethiopia (1974), Guinea-Bissau (1972), Kampuchea (1975), Laos (1975), Mozambique (1975), Somalia (1976) and the People's Democratic Republic of the [South] Yemen (1970). The remáining countries, nearly 100 in number, can be described as the 'Third World'. Almost all of them are economically under-developed, with low per capita income levels. Although for the sake of neatness and simplicity these countries are generally classed as part of the capitalist ('free') world, their capitalism is mostly of an earlier rudimentary type, where traditionalism, custom and several elements of socialism (indigenous or transplanted) are also present or even predominant. They are less dynamic, partly non-monetized and largely engaged in subsistence activities, but they are committed to modernization, accelerated economic development and social transformation.

The relative place of the three divisions in the world scene is summarized in Table 1.1.

In this book, the focus of comparison rests primarily on the industrialized capitalist countries and the well established socialist countries. Social systems are, of course, not static, but are usually

TABLE 1.1   *The West, the Socialist Bloc and the Third World: percentage shares in the world and* per capita *incomes in 1979*

	Developed capitalist countries	Socialist countries	Third World countries	World
Area	24	27	49	100
Population	18	34	48	100
National income	56	30	14	100
Industrial output	57	35	8	100
Foreign trade	67	11	22	100
Per capita income (in US $)	6 600	1 700	800	1 900

Sources. Based on Western and socialist sources and the author's estimates.

subject to transformation in one way or another in response to such factors as ideas, the discovery of new resources, inventions, technologies and exceptional personalities. But the extent and degree of changes in these conditions differ from one part of the world to another. Both capitalism and socialism have passed through several stages and developed into a number of variants. From the point of view of the operation of the economic system most relevant to our enquiry, the spectrum of the variants are represented in the following list – the extremes being found at the upper and lower ends.

Variant	*Example of countries*
Competitive laissez-faire capitalism	19th century Britain and the USA
Oligopolistic capitalism	Contemporary Japan and USA
Corporatism	Nazi Germany, Fascist Spain
Managed capitalism	France, the Netherlands
Liberal capitalist socialism (mixed economy)	Austria, Britain, Sweden
Market socialism	Hungary, Yugoslavia
Moderately revisionist planned socialism	Bulgaria, Czechoslovakia
Economically less-developed and moderately decentralized planned socialism	China, Vietnam
Reformed, centralized directive planned socialism	German Democratic Republic, the USSR
Stalinist command model	The USSR 1928–62

It can be concluded that, in general, both capitalism and socialism have been departing from their original extreme models, tending in several respects to become increasingly similar to each other.

A variant system which, although never put fully into operation, warrants special mention in this study is syndicalism. It aims to solve the problem of social conflicts (including that of industrial relations) by the socialization of the means of production, the reassertion of democratic freedoms and by the fusion of labour organizations with the organs of social administration.

The theory of syndicalism was developed in the wake of the Industrial Revolution in the second half of the nineteenth century by such thinkers as P. J. Proudhon and G. Sorel (of France), G. D. H. Cole (Britain) and

A. Labriola (Italy). The different models that have emerged range from the peaceful evolutionary scheme of guild socialism to militant radical versions of anarcho-syndicalism and revolutionary syndicalism. Syndicalism emphasizes personal freedom, equality, industrial co-operation, social security and continuous full employment. It is opposed to both capitalism and communism – in particular to capitalist private property, big business, the wage system, nationalism, political parties the state power, authoritarianism and the dictatorship of the proletariat. It advocates the organization of all workers into powerful all-inclusive unions, the creation of producers' and consumers' co-operatives, owning and controlling the means of production, and the enhancement and development of the working class culture. In the syndicalist vision of the ideal society, administrative power would be assumed by trade unions under self-government, mildly co-ordinated by a central trade union federation.

Syndicalism reached the peak of its popularity in the latter part of the nineteenth, and in the first quarter of the twentieth, century (especially in France, Spain, Italy and Russia) and several experiments were attempted. In the USSR at first anarcho-syndicalists gained control of many plants, but their zeal and excesses soon antagonized most trade union officials. But more importantly, the Soviet Government could not tolerate the syndicalist anti-authoritarian and anti-Marxist–Leninist stance, and syndicalism was ruthlessly suppressed and eliminated in the early 1920s.

There were efforts to rally syndicalist forces on the international scale by the creation in 1922–3 of the International Workers' Association, also known as the 'Berlin International of Trade Unions', to rival the Communist International – but without significant success. Although the movement is still in existence its influence is negligible, and, curiously enough, most trade unions are hostile to it. The nearest practical implementation of syndicalism can be found in the Yugoslav system of workers' self-management, although syndicalist links are officially disclaimed.

So much for the past and the present. But what about the future of capitalism and socialism? This question has been a subject of controversial debates and doctrinaire speculation. Some thinkers envisage capitalist countries reaching a 'post-industrial stage,[3] with high levels of affluence where technological progress will solve all major social problems. The traditional higher and lower classes will disappear, leaving a virtually classless middle class society.[4]

The future of socialism is conceived by Marxists to be 'full communism'. This ultimate 'socio-economic formation' is vaguely assumed to embody the following ideals.

(1) The complete socialization of the means of production.
(2) The abolition of money.
(3) The elimination of market relations.
(4) All-round affluence.
(5) Work and distribution based on the principle 'from each according to his ability, to each according to his needs'.
(6) A classless society.
(7) The 'withering away of the state'.
(8) The disappearance of political and economic boundaries on the world scale.[5]

It is helpful to bear these idealistic Marxian goals in mind, as they largely explain the policies and practices of the socialist countries today.

The relations between capitalism and socialism are envisaged in different lights by various thinkers. Some maintain that in the long run there is room for only one system – the less viable will be eliminated or 'submerged' (the 'submergence thesis'). Some believe that the two systems will continue to co-exist, but they will be developing increasingly divergent ideas, methods and ways of work and life (the 'divergence thesis').

But according to an impressive number of observers, the two systems will 'converge' in the future. They argue that this outcome is inevitable, considering the converging trends in the past two decades or so, whereby each system has been shedding its extreme features and borrowing some of the best elements from the other system (the 'convergence thesis').[6] Although this proposition has met with considerable interest and support in the West and to some extent in the socialist countries, officially the communist leaders reject its validity. In their view, the Marxian thesis and postulate of the 'breakdown of capitalism', giving way to socialism and eventually evolving into full communism, is historically inevitable. This view is in fact a version of the submergence thesis, and it assumes that socialism and communism will emerge as the triumphant social systems.

B. THE ROLE OF LABOUR

The term 'labour' has several connotations. It can mean 'human activity directed towards the satisfaction of individual or social wants' (in the form of goods and services), or a 'factor of production' (as distinct from land, capital and enterprise), or 'organized employees' (as opposed to the employer or management).

The question of labour cannot be viewed meaningfully in isolation, but must be considered in the context of the existing philosophy and the political, legal and economic set-up in force. Historically, in almost all societies labour was associated with toil, affliction, poverty and bondage. It was regarded as a necessary evil, morally inferior and assigned to individuals and social groups who were in a weaker position and could not defend themselves, viz. children, women, prisoners of war, slaves, serfs.[7]

In ancient and medieval societies, with some minor exceptions, labour and the working class (especially hired workers) were treated with pity or contempt and were humiliating to a well-born person.

The Christian church had a rather ambivalent attitude. On the one hand, work was looked upon as a punishment for the original sin and a necessity conducive to humility and the cultivation of virtues. But on the other, its ranking was second only to prayer and contemplation (as indicated in St. Benedict's maxim *ora et labora*).

Capitalism, whatever Marxists may otherwise say about it, to some extent rehabilitated labour as a highly desirable resource capable of creating wealth. But on the whole, labour has been regarded rather as a means, and the working class as the lowest social class (below the upper and middle classes).

It is only Marxism and the communist regimes in the socialist countries that have raised the significance and prestige of labour to the highest and unprecedented levels. Marx stressed that all labour is social in character, as it involves more than one person, in addition to the means of production, and it further necessitates the division of labour, co-operation and exchange. Marx disagreed with Adam Smith's view that work was a 'sacrifice' and a 'scourge' for the labourer.[8]

In the Chinese Constitution of 1978 (under Article 10) it is stated:

> The state applies the Socialist principle: 'He who does not work, neither shall he eat' and 'from each according to his ability, to each according to his work'. Work is an honourable duty for every citizen able to work.

The present socialist view on labour is in fact more profound, as is reflected in a recent Polish study on the subject:

Work is a necessity in a Socialist society, as indeed in any society . . . a condition of economic existence of society and of its existence in general. But in addition, coextensively, work is a moral category, a source of moral value and of individual satisfaction, a basic factor in the development of personality . . . In the Socialist economy, labour has been raised to the highest pedestal, being regarded as a right, obligation and a question of civic honour, and the planned economy ensures the implementation of these principles.[9]

It was further pointed out that:

Work enables the acquisition of discipline and organized pursuits, it cultivates strength of will, firmness, courage, systematic conduct, rational thinking, perfection, confidence and it teaches the properties of objects, the laws of nature and how to adapt one's actions to the existing principles and regulations.[10] . . . In industrialised and urban society, the traditional neighbourly ties weaken or disappear . . . instead work links and labour relations assume increasing importance.[11]

The crucial role of labour under socialism stems from its very Marxist philosophical foundations, viz. several labour theories.

(1) *The labour theory of humanization.* The evolution of humans from apes is attributed to work processes, involving the making and use of tools and weapons, including the changeover to the upright posture, the freeing of fore-limbs and transforming them into work hands and the development of work teams and social organization.[12]

(2) *The labour theory of language development.* It is held that speech developed in the process of making and using tools and weapons and the associated organization of productive activities necessitating thinking, verbalization, sentence construction, explanation and the co-ordination and delegation of work tasks.[13]

(3) *The labour theory of value.* Value is attributed to the 'socially-indispensable labour time' incorporated in the product, whilst the contribution of other factors of production (land, capital, enterprise) is disregarded. Thus only workers are real producers while capitalists deriving income from property ownership (rents, interests, profits) are exploiters of the proletariat, the only respectable social class.[14]

(4) *The labour theory of social morality.* This proposition rejects

religious ethics as the basis of morality, and instead it emphasizes that man's moral values are shaped by, and reflected in, the process of work, viz. the feeling of responsibility, honesty, reliability, creativity and solidarity, in relations involving individual workers, and the working classes of different nations.

The development of democracy and parliamentary institutions have led in most capitalist countries to the emergence of labour or socialist parties. But although some three-quarters of income earners are employees (in the industrialized nations), left-wing parties usually score only from one-third to one-half of the votes at elections. Class consciousness is quite strong in some countries (Britain, France, Italy, Spain) but less so in others (such as Japan and Sweden), and in the USA a mass working-class political party has failed to emerge. Where working-class parties do exist, since the Second World War they have become less class-oriented and revolutionary, and in fact labour movements have tended to develop into very broadly based social movements.

In the socialist countries, only the working class is politically represented, viz. essentially by the communist party. Although in some of them (viz. Bulgaria, China, the German Democratic Republic, the Democratic People's Republic of Korea, Poland and Vietnam) non-communist parties are still tolerated for one expedient reason or another, they are insignificant and they accept the communist leadership.

Labour as a social group or class has traditionally been dominated in non-socialist societies by upper classes privileged in one way or another. Marxists trace this subordination to the existence of private property which, in their view, emerged only after the initial social system, viz. primitive communism. The ownership of the means of production by the elitist groups – masters, feudal lords and then capitalists – placed them in a strong position in relation to the slaves, serfs and the proletariat. The propertied classes, using their wealth and better training, soon developed the state as an institution for the protection of their interests and the domination and oppression of those whose only source of subsistence was working for the property owners.[15]

Later Marxists and other radical writers pointed out that the market mechanism and individualism under capitalism have further subordinated labour to capital. R. Hyman concluded that the market itself is both a medium of power and a reflection of the distribution of power in society.[16] Colin Crouch further explained:

The market relation itself . . . imparts a degree of power on the employer . . . Purely capitalist domination is dependent on the worker being treated as an individual. This relationship is distinguished from other commercial contracts in that the worker accepts a role of subordination . . . Capitalist doctrines are sometimes reinterpreted to define as fair that which is rational according to the laws of the market.[17]

An American economist, D. D. Martin, considers the faulty operation of the market mechanism as a sufficient justification for nationalization in the USA.[18]

As is well known, in the industrialized capitalist countries the actual control over the means of production is no longer exercised by the capitalist owners, but rather by professional managers. However, to the Marxist thinkers this has not changed the exploitative and socially unjust essence of capitalism. The corporate assets are still private property and their ultimate use is determined not by the workers but by shareholders, or, if not, by managers who are recruited mostly from the propertied or middle classes. 'Managers', as two Polish economists pointed out, 'do not make decisions in the name of the whole society, but in the name of capital. Managers employ delegated powers in the interest of the *capitalist* owners, if not they could be sacked'.[19]

In the socialist countries, with some minor exceptions (mainly in agriculture, and only in some countries), there is no property-owning class. Although labour falls into three 'classes', viz. industrial workers, peasants and intelligentsia, they are considered officially to be vertical (non-stratified), non-antagonistic divisions, which will disappear anyway under full communism.

However, the above assertion belongs more to theory and wishful thinking than to the actual situation and practice. In most socialist countries (other than Yugoslavia) state capitalism simply replaced private capitalism and as far as the workers are concerned they have merely exchanged one type of employer for another – in fact a much more powerful master than the private capitalist (see Chapter 4C). Furthermore, new elites have emerged and there is indisputable social stratification in terms of income, power and prestige.

The workers' role in their workplace and to some extent in society can be judged by the degree of 'workers' sovereignty' (a concept parallel to consumers' sovereignty and the state sovereignty). It involves not only the freedom of choice of occupation and of place of employment, but also the ability of the workers to influence the terms of their employment and the conditions of their work. Workers' sovereignty can be considered at different levels – individual, occupational, industrial, regional, national and international. It depends, of course, on the extent to which the workers are organized to be influential industrially and have access to state power to be influential politically.

Workers' sovereignty in its highest form could exist only under syndicalism or full communism. Industrialization in capitalist countries has with some occasional setbacks, enhanced the power of workers – virtually nil before the Industrial Revolution to quite impressive levels in the case of some organized groups. Some exclusive professional associations (such as medical practitioners, engineers, pilots, air traffic controllers), dockers, metal workers, some transport workers and power supply workers are amongst the most powerful groups, whilst textile and catering workers (mostly women and unorganized) are amongst the weakest.

The increasing specialization and interdependence in the economy and the large financial resources accumulated by many trade unions have strengthened their power in recent years and in extreme cases have led to the so-called 'labour monopolies'. The accession of a left-wing political party to power usually strengthens workers' sovereignty. But some unions (particularly those associated with nationalized enterprises, public services and vital industries) often prefer to negotiate with a non-labour government.

The question of workers' sovereignty in the socialist countries is more elusive. Officially, it is asserted that a socialist country is a workers' state controlled by the working class for its own benefit. Although in a general ideological sense this is true, most workers view their position in a more restricted horizon and are preoccupied with their practical and immediate problems. In the working class movement, revolutionary Marxists accord precedence to politics over the economic interests of the workers. The state power is exercised by the communist party elite which on many occasions proved to be insensitive and even vindictive to popular demands for better working and living conditions. In general, trade unions are dominated by the Party and are merely tools of the state (see Chapter 4C). This, together with the mono-party system of government, the over-developed police system, the violations of civil liberties and the virtual prohibition of strikes have in several respects restricted workers' sovereignty to levels below those prevalent in capitalist countries.

C. THE PROBLEM OF INDUSTRIAL RELATIONS

The scope and content of industrial relations have been a subject of many a controversy. In its narrowest and popular usage, the term has been employed synonymously with collective bargaining in industry,[20] or, slightly wider, with labour–management dealings, or personnel relations or human relations in industry. In its wider connotation, it covers relationships between employers (owners and top management) and employees (white and blue-collar workers).

In its still wider meaning, the concept encompasses relations affecting work in the whole economy and involving not only employers and employees but also the state; it thus embraces relations between individual employees and between individual employees and the employer, between unions and between unions and employers, between employers, between the state and unions and between the state and employers. Wages, incentives and other benefits, hours and other conditions of work, recruitment and dismissal, job training, work discipline, safety, health and various amenities and workers' participation, are the most important facets of industrial relations.

Industrial relations may involve links and dealings in two directions: horizontal – between different individuals, groups and institutions, and vertical – between different individuals and entities within each group or institution at different levels of seniority, standing, authority and the like.

There are two related terms which are sometimes used coextensively with 'industrial relations', but in fact are not identical in scope. *Labour relations* involve a network of relationships within the labour movement and actions and responses in relation to other factors (employers and the state) in the labour market, with an emphasis on the institutional set-up and equity. On the other hand *labour economics* is wider in coverage, embracing all aspects of economics relevant to labour and the accent is on economic rationality and efficiency.

Industrial relations are a 'problem' because the interests of employers (maximum efficiency and/or plan implementation) and of labour (maximum income and leisure) are in conflict with each other – the pursuit of one usually appears to be at the expense of the other. In this conflict, historically labour was typically the dominated side and on the defensive. Officially, it is claimed in the socialist countries that the social ownership of the means of production removes this basic conflict, as the owners and workers are the same persons – so that what is of advantage to the employer is *ipso facto* of benefit to the employees.

But experience has shown only too clearly that this claim is not necessarily supported by the facts of life in practice, as demonstrated, for example, by the industrial upheavals in Poland in the early 1980s. The state employer in reality usually behaves not unlike a private capitalist, insisting on work discipline and maximum performance (planned targets and/or the effectiveness or production). The success of managers depends on their ability to pursue these objectives successfully, which usually involves the extraction of the maximum feasible effort from labour, not necessarily remunerated *pari passu*. The adoption of profit as the only or an important criterion of enterprise performance has added to the management's determination along these lines. The link between the accrued gain to the state and even the enterprise concerned on the one hand, and the individual workers' benefit on the other is too remote to be convincing enough.[21]

A special comment is warranted on the role of the state in industrial relations. In capitalist market economies, these relations are characterized institutionally by a tri-partite set-up – labour (represented by independent trade unions), owners (or management) and the state. The state is, as a rule, a neutral institution, endeavouring to mitigate industrial disputes between the other two parties and create better conditions for the avoidance or settlement of the conflicts. Admittedly, it may be biased, once to capital, once to labour, largely depending on the democratically elected political party in power. The state as the holder of public authority is a separate entity from that as an employer, and in its latter capacity it is not much different from a private employer. Higher wages and other improved conditions of work have to be won from the state in bargaining and industrial actions as tough as with private firms. State enterprises are subject to industrial disputes and the state has to defend its position before industrial courts or arbitration tribunals, which are independent from the governmental machinery, and the state can be sued. The state does not claim that there is an identity of interests between the public enterprise and its employees.[22]

On the other hand, the socialist set-up is noted for dualism – the state and the employees (excepting the Yugoslav self-management system and the insignificant co-operative and private sectors). The state is the owner and manager – the enterprise 'director' is appointed by the state and he answers to it under the one-person managerial responsibility prevailing in all the socialist countries. Although the enterprises generally have a legal status and in some cases can be sued (for example, in the case of dismissals), the general rules for management, wage scales, bonuses and prices and the provision of amenities are fixed by the state which – however remotely – is a party to industrial disputes. Moreover, the same state is also the central planner, the mouthpiece of the mono-party in power, the legislator and the law enforcer aided by an over-developed police force (uniformed and secret).

Historically, it may be generalized that from labour's standpoint industrial relations have been marked by increasing humanization and democratization. Under early capitalism (roughly up to 1825–70, depending on the country) employer authoritarianism, private profit maximization and the absence of legal labour organizations were the facts of industrial life. Then came the legalization of trade unions which, in some countries (such as Britain), established labour or socialist political parties. The humanization of industrial relations has received increasing attention since the Hawthorne experiment beginning in 1927, although still dictated essentially by microeconomic efficiency.[23]

The increasing democratization since the Second World War has emphasized negotiations, collective bargaining and workers' particip-ation in management and even ownership. There has also been a similar trend in the socialist countries. The regimentation of labour and forced labour camps in the USSR were largely abandoned after Stalin's death in the 1950s. Since the economic reforms of the 1960s in the European socialist countries (of the 1950s in Yugoslavia), the centralized, directive system of planning and management has been partly or largely liberalized in favour of decentralization and incentives. Under the new economic system local trade unions have been assigned a more active role in plan implementation and giving protection to workers against the state bureaucracy and management. In Poland on two occasions striking trade unions brought about changes in Party leadership and won a number of concessions of not only economic but also political content.

With the growing complexity of the economic and social processes in the modern world, industrial relations are becoming increasingly intricate. There is a proliferation of new situations and alternative ways and means of handling them, in which the availability and electronic processing of data can play a most useful role. Some specialists envisage a new scientific approach to handling industrial relations in the future, viz. by the application of control systems. A control system is a formal means by which organizations select goals and ensure their optimal achievement (as practised, for example, in management accounting). In the view of two British management specialists, control systems could be applied for the benefit of management or of trade unions, or jointly:

Control system may be used to bolster either management or union control over aspects of work relations, or may be used as the basis for extending the scope of joint regulation by both management and unions . . . The development of worker participation and continuing attempts at integrative bargaining is likely to accelerate the use of control systems in industrial relations, as well as opening management control systems to union influence and use.[24]

Although control systems in industrial relations may be first introduced in the industrialized West, the socialist centrally planned economies lend themselves better to their systematic development and comprehensive application.

RECOMMENDED FURTHER READING

1. W. Bienert, L. Bress and C. D. Kernig, 'Labour', in C. D. Kernig (ed.), *Marxism, Communism and Western Society: A Comparative Encyclopedia*, (New York: Herder & Herder, 1973) vol. 5, pp. 33–47.
2. A. B. Evans, Jr, 'Developed Socialism in Soviet Ideology', *Soviet Studies* (Glasgow) July 1977, pp. 409–28.
3. I. Fetscher, 'Socialism', in Kernig (ed.), *A Comparative Encyclopedia*, (1973) vol. 7, pp. 422–31.
4. W. Lazonick, 'The Subjugation of Labor to Capital: The Rise of the Capitalist System', *Rev. of Radical Political Economics* (New York: Spring, 1978) pp. 1–31.
5. L. H. Legters, 'Syndicalism', in Kernig (ed.), *A Comparative Encyclopedia*, (1973) vol. 8, pp. 110–21.
6. H.-J. Lieber and H. G. Bütow, 'Ideology', in Kernig (ed.), *A Comparative Encyclopedia*, (1972) vol. 4, pp. 199–211.
7.* J. Pajestka, 'Conscious Shaping of Socio-Economic Processes in a Socialist Economy', *Oeconomica polona* [Polish Economics] (Warsaw) 1/1977, pp. 1–25.
8. M. Shalev, 'Industrial Relations Theory and the Comparative Study of Industrial Relations and Industrial Conflict', *British Jl of Industrial Relations*, March 1980, pp. 26–43.
9. J. Schregle, 'Comparative Industrial Relations: Pitfalls and Potential', *Int. Lab. Rev.* (Geneva) Jan.–Feb. 1981, pp. 15–30.
10.* Teng Wensheng and Jia Chunfeng, 'How to Evaluate The Socialist System', *Beijing Rev.* (Peking) 19 Jan., 1981, pp. 16–18.

* *Indicates contributions by writers from the socialist countries.*

2 Employment, Unemployment, Mobility

A. MANPOWER, THE LABOUR MARKET, PLANNING

In its broadest sense, the supply of labour encompasses the actual and potential working population and it is known as *manpower*. It is usually understood to include persons of 15 years of age and over, consisting of the following categories: (1) employees (working for wages or salaries), (2) self-employed, (3) persons living entirely off the income derived from the ownership of assets, (4) persons supported by others, and (5) unemployed persons. The *working population* embraces categories (1), (2) and (3), whilst the labour *force* or the *economically active population* (the term used by the United Nations) includes only (1) and (5).

The proportion of the labour force in the total population is known as the *labour force participation rate*, or to be more precise the *crude labour force participation rate* or (in the terminology of the International Labour Organization) the *crude activity rate*.[1] Although the concepts of the participation rate are clear in the abstract sense, the international comparability of the actual figures produced in different countries is limited.[2] Nevertheless these figures provide interesting comparisons, however rough.

Thus according to the International Labour Office (ILO), the average crude activity rate in the world as a whole in the late 1970s was about 43 per cent, the developed regions having averaged 47 per cent and the less-developed areas 30 per cent.[3] The relatively low rates applicable to the latter countries are largely explained by the fact that persons engaged in part-time economic activities in agriculture, especially women, are not included in statistical returns as either 'employed' or 'unemployed'.[4]

The degree of labour force participation in different capitalist and socialist countries is indicated in Figure 2.1. It will be noted that, on the whole, at a given stage of economic development the rates prevailing in the socialist countries are almost consistently higher than in the case of

FIGURE 2.1 *Labour force participation rates in selected capitalist and socialist countries in the late 1970s**

Non-socialist countries		Socialist countries	
	(Not to scale)		
		52	Bulgaria
Denmark, Sweden	51	51	German Democratic Republic, Poland, USSR
		49	Czechoslovakia
Finland, Japan	48		
Canada, Switzerland, UK	47	47	Hungary, Romania, Vietnam
Hong Kong, Portugal	46		
Australia	45		
Federal Republic of Germany	44	44	China, Democratic People's Republic of Korea
France, Indonesia	43	43	Albania
World average	43		World average
New Zealand	42	42	Yugoslavia
		40	Angola, Kampuchea
Argentina, Italy, Uruguay	39		
Republic of Korea	38	38	Mongolia
Netherlands	37	37	Congo
Spain	36		
Chile, Israel	33		
Bolivia, Peru, Philippines	32		
Pakistan	30	30	Cuba
Mexico	28		
		27	Democratic People's Republic of Yemen
Iraq	26		
		25	Afghanistan
Upper Volta	23		

* Crude activity rates as defined in ILO publications (percentage ratio of the total economically active population to total population).
Sources. Based on *Year Book of Labour Statistics 1980* (Geneva: ILO, 1980) pp. 15–31; *Rocznik statystyczny 1980* [Statistical yearbook 1980] (Warsaw: Central Statistical Office of Poland, 1980) p. 507.

the capitalist countries and, in general, the more developed they are the higher the rates. The rates have tended to increase in the last two or three decades. Thus in the USSR, the labour participation rate of working-age manpower (women 16–54 years and men 16–59 years) rose from 74 per cent in 1951 to 91 per cent by 1970.[5]

The higher socialist rates can be explained by the following facts and circumstances. First, there is social pressure for all able-bodied persons in the working-age bracket to work (see Chapter 1B). Second, owing to the prevalent shortages of labour, people are encouraged to continue working beyond the usual retirement age. Third, high targets allocated by central planners and shortages of capital impel enterprises to labour-intensive solutions, and the strictly controlled wages (depressed below the levels otherwise warranted by the stage of economic development achieved) make the employment of labour relatively cheap. Fourth, for a variety of reasons relatively high proportions of women take up outside work (see the following section). Fifth, owing to the social ownership of the means of production, the proportion of people classed as self-employed, employers and capitalists is relatively small, and consequently the category 'employees' is correspondingly larger.

We shall now turn to the examination of the processes associated with the supply of, and demand for, labour. The labour market may be defined as a network of dealings between buyers and sellers of labour. Different kinds of labour may be involved according to sex, age, qualifications, occupation and experience, and the size of the market may be local, regional, national and even international.

In the capitalist market economy, the labour market is part and parcel of the overall economic mechanism, in particular of the factor market (in addition to land and capital), where the forces of supply and demand operate with varying degrees of competition influencing wages and other terms of employment. The demand for labour derives from the demand for the goods and services which the workers can produce, and their remuneration is basically dependent on the marginal productivity of the different kinds of labour. It may be generalized that in the confrontation of the supply of and demand for labour, it is rather the former that adjusts itself to the latter.

On the whole, the distribution of labour is shaped by profit, on the one hand, and wages and other terms of employment, on the other. There is normally freedom of the choice of occupation and of the place of employment.

A perfectly functioning labour market would require the following five conditions.

(1) The freedom of entry and exit of the existing and potential employees into and out of a particular workplace and occupation, provided he or she satisfies the required relevant physical, mental and skill requirements.

(2) The freedom of entry and exit of the employers into and out of a particular sphere or place of activity.
(3) The absence of monopolistic and monopsonistic power on the part of the employees and employers.
(4) Perfect knowledge amongst the existing or potential employees and employers of the availability and nature of jobs, workers and conditions of employment.
(5) Rationality of behaviour of the employees and employers, that is, each endeavouring to maximize their wages and other advantages and their profits, respectively.

Although much is said about the operation of the market mechanism and competition in capitalist countries, in reality there is little of either in the labour market. The five conditions listed above hardly ever prevail, except perhaps in some local markets. In general, departures from perfect labour markets increase as the capitalist country advances to higher stages of economic development. The distortions stem from the pressures applied by organized labour, employers and the government.

Most workers, in fact, are not 'in the market' looking for or taking advantage of better alternatives, as the mobility of labour is more or less limited occupationally and geographically. The labour market is noted for what has come to be known as 'segmentation', that is, the existence of separate sub-markets within each of which there is a distinct set of supply and demand schedules. Entry into particular markets is not necessarily free, owing to qualifications or 'closed shop' conditions, and exit may be hampered by superannuation, seniority and other accumulated benefits, plus the uncertainty of finding similar employment elsewhere.

In several respects, labour market segmentation is more accentuated in less-developed countries where, in addition to the urban–rural dichotomy, four segmentations can be typically distinguished. In the urban sphere they are: (1) the public sector – employing skilled and unskilled labour, with the salaries of the former being usually disproportionately high; (2) the modern large-scale industrial and commercial sector, often dominated by foreign interests; (3) the medium and small-scale, fairly skilled labour-intensive sector; and (4) the small-scale labour-intensive sector, mostly embracing unskilled labourers and helpers.

In the countryside, also, four major segmentations prevail: (1) large farms employing wage-labour, in some cases also engaging in financial and commercial ventures; (2) self-employed peasants owning small holdings and occasionally working for others; (3) agricultural labourers permanently attached to rich farmers and earning their living entirely from wage-labour; and (4) seasonal, migratory and casual workers, usually under-employed.

The imperfect operation of the labour market, whether due to restrictive practices by organized labour, monopsonistic employers or even by the government and rigid custom, is largely blamed for otherwise unjustified differences in wages for the same type of job, low income levels, unemployment, under-employment and slow economic growth. This problem, now described by some economists, as the 'labour market failure', is particularly serious in less-developed capitalist economies. However, some economists maintain that the economic problems of these countries are not due so much to the faulty operation of the labour markets, but rather to the maldistribution of land and capital ownership, the economically irrational pricing of resources (including certain types of labour) and unsatisfactory education and vocational training. Some others believe that the labour markets there are functioning as well as might be expected.[6]

Largely because of the increasing complexities of labour needs and persistent unemployment, many large enterprises (private companies as well as public utilities) and governments have turned to some kind of 'manpower planning'. However, it is not as comprehensive and systematic as under socialism. Under capitalism it is pursued at two levels. At the microeconomic level, it is an element of management and administration. At the national level, it is associated with budgetary policies, concern over employment and social welfare programmes, but it is usually of a mild and non-mandatory nature.[7]

In the socialist centrally planned economies, there are no conventional markets, either of the perfect or imperfect type. First of all, the very concept of the labour market is rejected on ideological grounds. The accepted postulate of the dignity of the working class demands that labour must not be treated as a commodity subject to buying and selling according to supply and demand. Instead, it is emphasized that in a socialist society the development and distribution of manpower are not left to the whimsical market or to chance, but are embraced by economic planning like the rest of the economy.

Manpower planning was first introduced on a systematic basis in the USSR in 1928, with the first five-year plan. It has been subsequently developed into an elaborate and a rather sophisticated instrument of economic policy and management, also adopted by other socialist countries. Employment targets are set at the national, ministry, industrial branch, regional and enterprise levels, as well as (in the more developed socialist countries) by major objectives – modernization, computerization, decentralization and the economization of labour.

More specifically, manpower plans encompass the following spheres.

(1) Enrolments in all educational and training institutions.
(2) Job placements after the completion of general education or vocational training.
(3) Transfers of labour from labour-redundant to labour-deficient industries.
(4) Organized *ad hoc* recruitment drives, particularly for outlying areas and shifts of labour from agriculture to industry and construction.
(5) The creation of new jobs in existing and new workplaces.
(6) Wages and other forms of personal income.

Manpower plans for enterprises and institutions include ceilings on the number of employees, mandatorily-expected increases in labour productivity and perhaps labour releases, wage funds, incentive funds and average wages. These plans at all levels are co-ordinated with investment plans to support educational and vocational training schemes and the maintenance of full employment (including the creation of new jobs).

Whilst in a capitalist market economy demand for labour is the critical side and the supply of labour adjusts itself to the demand, under socialist central economic planning the availability (supply) of labour receives the initial focus of attention, and total demand for labour is then adjusted accordingly to ensure full employment.

Although the administration and management of manpower are essentially pursued on the basis of central economic planning and in accordance with social interest, to some extent the market mechanism and private interest also play a role in the actual distribution of labour. First of all, the available supply of labour has to be reconciled with the demand for labour, to avoid unemployment or labour shortages. Basically, there is no direction of labour and the authorities prefer to achieve their planned employment targets by incentives and disincentives. The individual freedoms of choice of training, occupation and of the workplace are respected in principle. But there are some exceptions (for details, see section D of this chapter).

Although manpower planning in the socialist countries may look impressive and tidy on paper, the situation *ex-post* is rarely, if ever at all, as orderly as central planners would like to see it. Errors of judgement by central planners are inevitable. This can be a consequence of erroneous or incomplete information received, or the originally correct data at the planning stage being rendered erroneous by subsequent developments in the course of plan implementation. In effect, surpluses of labour in some workplaces coexist with shortages in others. This may be due partly to dishonest data supplied by enterprises to central planners or, more importantly, to structural changes in the economy. Central planners may also overestimate or underestimate non-labour resources necessary to give support to the manpower available.

Manpower planning has been hampered by poorly developed demographic studies. In the past, population projections were in many cases little better than guesswork. It is well known that the Chinese central planners and even demographers have never really known the precise figure of China's total population, and much less its age structure. According to Margaret Schroeder, in the Soviet five-year plans the actual percentage increases in the labour force turned out to be, compared with the planned figures (100), as follows: 1928–32: 238, 1933–7: 68, 1946–50: 186, 1951–5: 164, 1956–60: 145.[8]

In Poland, where population studies are probably better developed than in any other socialist country, the predicted manpower figures have differed widely, even in recent years. This is illustrated in Table 2.1 showing increases in the labour force in recent and prospective five-year plan periods as predicted by different institutions and researchers.

A Hungarian economist pointed out that although a multiplicity of manpower plans were prepared in Hungary and were becoming increasingly detailed, they had proved to be unreliable. He bluntly conceded that the plans did not answer the needs of the economy which, in his view, stemmed largely from the faulty programmes followed by educational and vocational training institutions.[9] Similarly, a Soviet specialist in the field concluded that manpower planning did not work well in the USSR, even under a single authority – the State Committee for Labour (created in 1966). He explained:

Planning and other economic agencies usually have no comprehensive and suitably synchronized schemes for personnel training . . . The result is that newly established enterprises suffer from acute shortages of appropriate personnel . . . Thus new industrial enterprises with up-to-date equipment, which could be very efficient, suffer from labour shortages . . ., whilst old inefficient ones hoard labour and highly skilled and experienced specialists.[10]

TABLE 2.1 *Projected increases in the Polish labour force over the five-year plan periods, 1971–2000*

Five-year periods	By W. Kowalec*	By Z. Schulz†	By Z. Schulz‡	By the Institute of Labour and Social Affairs§	By the State Planning Commission¶
1971–75	1 706 000	2 000 000	1 800 000	1 300 000	1 800 000
1976–80	1 481 000	1 300 000	1 100 000	1 200 000	1 300 000
1981–85	705 000	370 000	490 000	430 000	400 000
1986–90	373 000	260 000	300 000	160 000	300 000
1991–95	463 000	(not available)	(not available)	(not available)	(not available)
1996–2000	552 000	(not available)	(not available)	(not available)	not available)

Sources.
* *Nowe drogi* [New Paths] (Warsaw) 8/1972, p. 30.
† *Gospodarka planowa* [Planned Economy] (Warsaw) 5/1976, p. 268.
‡ *Rada Narodowa, Gospodarka Administracja* [Local Economy and Administration] (Warsaw) 25/1978, p. 27.
§ *Nowe drogi*, 2/1978, p. 123.
¶ *Nowe drogi*, 10/1976, p. 56.

B. WOMEN AND EMPLOYMENT

(a) Ideological and historical background

The employment and treatment of women to a large extent reflect not only the stage of economic development, but also the social system in force. In general, the less developed a society is economically, the lower the proportion of women in outside employment and the greater are the differences in the conditions and terms of employment for men and women – usually, but not necessarily, to the economic disadvantage of women. To illustrate this by reference to the USA (the country in which economic development and the feminist movement have reached the highest stage): the proportion represented by the economically-active women in the total female population of over 14 years rose from 18 per cent in 1890 to 37 per cent in 1963 and in 1979 it stood at 39 per cent.[11]

Marxists attach greater importance to the social system as a determinant of the position of women. They emphasize the inferior economic and social status of women in pre-socialist societies, seeing it as a form of class oppression and exploitation, and insist that only communism is capable of achieving complete emancipation and equality of women. The (female) Secretary of the All-Union Central Council of Trade Unions in the USSR recently argued in a journal meant for Western consumption:

> The ideologists of the exploiting classes have always sought to justify and legalize the submissive position of the woman in society, a position where she is completely without rights . . . Her biological peculiarities and maternal functions which allegedly make her dependent on the family are given as the objective hindrance to her being man's equal in social life. The founders of scientific communism subjected these reactionary conceptions to merciless criticism. They proved that women's inequality was based on socio-economic reasons and came to the conclusion that the struggle for women's real emancipation was an integral part of the common struggle to reshape the world.[12]

In his most controversial work, Engels maintained that:

> The first class antagonism appearing in history coincides with the development of the antagonism of man and wife in monogamy, and the first class oppression with that of the female by the male sex . . . In the family, he is the bourgeois, the woman represents the proletariat.

In the industrial world, however, the specific character of the economic oppression weighing on the proletariat appears in its sharpest outlines . . . The supremacy of man in marriage is simply the consequence of his economic superiority and will fall with the abolition of the latter.[13]

Some later Marxist writers have focused their attention on other causes. Shulamith Firestone singled out child-bearing as basically responsible for women's inferior role and status, and to end women's oppression it would be necessary to produce children artificially in laboratories.[14] Paddy Quick's contention is that the oppression of women is based on their role in the exploited class society, that is, labourers who are the 'performers of exploited surplus labor'.[15]

The main body working towards the emancipation of women on a world scale, 'regardless of race, nationality, religion and political opinion', is the Women's International Democratic Federation, founded in Paris in 1945. It embraces 129 organizations in 114 countries, totalling about 200m members. It makes appeals to governments and parliaments and other institutions for the improvement of women's position, it has a consultative status with the ILO, International Red Cross and the UNESCO, it conducted the International Women's Year (1975), it has sponsored the International Women's Decade (1975–85), and it publishes a bi-monthly, *Women of the Whole World.*

Although both capitalist (mostly) and socialist[16] countries are represented in it, the WIDF is dominated by left-wing ideology and communist regimes, and it is commonly regarded in the West as one of the 13 international communist front organizations. It was founded on socialist initiative in Paris, but it was expelled from France in 1951 and its Secretariat was moved to East Berlin. It co-operates closely with the World Federation of Trade Unions (see Chapter 4F) and its President and Secretary-General are represented on the Presidential Committee of the World Peace Council.

Most Marxists envisage a disappearance of the traditional family household under full communism in favour of communal living and consumption which, in their view, will constitute the final stage in the emancipation of women. An American radical feminist, Batya Weinbaum, expressed her vision of the future in the following words, citing Mao Tse-tung's ideas on the subject:

Clearly women have the most to gain from this form of transition to communism based on the abolishment of the household as the unit of consumption, and the consequent breakdown of sexual division of labour in production . . . Mao said: 'Under the present system of 'to each according to her/his work', the family is still of use. When we reach the stage of communist relationships of 'distribution according to his/her need', many of our concepts will change. After maybe a few thousand years, or at the least several hundred years the family will disappear'.[17]

(b) Discrimination against women

Traditionally women in almost all societies have experienced discrimination in outside employment in the form of greater difficulties in finding jobs and lower remuneration. In a recent study of collective agreements between employers and trade unions in Austria, systematic discrimination against women was found in six respects relevant to remuneration.

(1) Concentration of job classifications in the lower wage groups (seamstresses, milliners, embroiderers).
(2) The differentiation of skills and job requirements, where dexterity is rewarded less than heavy physical labour.
(3) The differentiation of rating of nominally identical occupations (for example, homeworkers paid less than factory workers for identical work).
(4) The differentiation of provisions for bonuses, fringe benefits, long service payments, severance pay, death grants (generally available to male, but not female employees).
(5) The differentiation of qualifying periods for promotion, and so on. (usually longer for women than for men).
(6) Restrictions on the exercise of an occupation (for example, a relatively low age limit for air hostesses).[18]

Other examples of discrimination against women in capitalist countries as publicized in Soviet sources include:

(1) In the EEC, women constitute 50 per cent (in Belgium 60 per cent) of the unemployed, although they make up only 37 per cent of the labour force.[19]
(2) In the USA in the leading professions, women account for only 1 per cent of engineers, 3 per cent of lawyers, 7 per cent of physicians and 9 per cent of scientists; in the USSR, it is claimed, 33 per cent of

engineers are women and women account for 59 per cent of specialists.[20]

(3) Women's wages in the EEC are 20–40 per cent (in Italy 50 per cent) lower than men's. In Britain, manufacturers exploit women to the tune of £600m. annually (in underpaid wages). The USA has refused to ratify the Convention on Equal Remuneration for Men and Women Workers for Work of Equal Value.[21]

(c) The economic emancipation of women

The tendency towards the economic equality of women and men today is well known, but of the two social systems socialism appears to be more genuinely interested in it, both in theory and in practice. Lenin reasoned that for the emancipation of women to be really effective, it must first of all be based on solid economic foundations. He stressed that: 'The total liberation of women and their true equality on a par with men require the socialization of the means of production and women's participation in production activities.'[22]

The most dramatic improvement in the position of women has occurred in the USSR and China, where their subjection had been firmly entrenched before the communist accession to power. Before the Bolshevik Revolution, few women in Russia had opportunities of earning income from outside employment, and of those who did work, 80 per cent were employed as domestic servants or farm workers.[23] But now women represent the following proportions in professional employment in the USSR: scientists – 40 per cent, industrial managers – 50 per cent, doctors and teachers – 70 per cent; 60 per cent of university graduates are women; every second factory, works or local trade union committee is headed by a woman; 59 per cent of all specialists in the country are women and 40 per cent of women work in engineering.[24]

In China, the communist regime immediately embarked upon a campaign to eliminate footbinding, forced marriages and restrictions on political and economic rights and responsibilities. One-third of professional research workers in China are now women, they are increasingly represented in other professions and they actively participate in production campaigns.[25]

One of the noteworthy developments in this respect in China is the 'Iron Girls' Movement. It started in the Tachai Commune during a devastating flood in 1958, when girls between the ages of 13 and 18 organized themselves into a team to rescue crops and reconstruct buildings under extremely difficult conditions. Their perseverance and success captured the admiration of the local community and public fancy further afield. Similar teams have been mushrooming all over the country, and their ideals are not the traditional virtues of fragility, beauty, reticence and humility, but those of strength, hard work, self-assertion and leadership. Many older women have also participated in ambitious ventures, including the construction and operation of factories.[26]

Similar developments have taken place in other socialist countries. The state, to enable married women to take up outside employment, gives priority to the production of labour-saving devices for household use and also provides child-care facilities in workplaces (four-fifths of their costs are typically met by the state).

However, in reality, the equalization of women with men has not gone as far as is often claimed officially and by other enthusiastic champions of socialism. A Soviet feminist trade union activist complained of the exclusion of women from certain professions and specializations on the grounds of psychological differences, of continued sexism at school, men's avoidance of housework and, in general, of the Soviet lag behind the developed capitalist countries in uplifting the role of women.[27]

A Western feminist who lived in China complained that the old Confucian doctrine of the inferiority of women ('women are worthless people who are difficult to keep') is still prevalent in China and she concluded that 'one revolutionary change does not solve all the problems at once'.[28] Another Western feminist made the following generalization based on the Chinese experience:

the strategy for liberating women based on socializing the means of production and getting women into production needs a few more tactics, due to the reciprocal relation between division of labor by sex in socialized production and the organization of consumption through the household.[29]

Paddy Quick pointed out that women are exploited also under socialism, even though there 'the ruling class is on their side'.[30] It is conceded that women still work in largely unskilled, monotonous and arduous jobs and reports indicate that, for example, in China and the USSR, in many cases women are not considered by managers to be capable or trustworthy to operate machines.[31]

(d) Special protective legislation for female workers

One of the important ways of improving the employment position of women is by special protective legislation, which is now common in both socialist and capitalist countries. It usually regulates three areas of women's employment, with the following aims.

(1) Protecting women against a harmful working environment, considering their weaker physique and psychological and moral peculiarities.
(2) Ensuring women's equality of working opportunity and remuneration.
(3) Safeguarding women's interests associated with child-bearing, child-care and family responsibilities (maternity leave, facilities for working mothers, exemption from night work).

The legislative measures along these lines are, on the whole, more comprehensive and systematically applied in the socialist countries than either in the West or the Third World. But in fact there are now two views on the need for special protection of female workers. Those who support it, justify it on the grounds of women's lower physical strength and their special responsibilities as mothers and homemakers, which tends to disadvantage them compared with men. They quote historical evidence of the prevalence of discrimination against women. This view is officially adhered to in the socialist countries and widely (but not universally) held elsewhere, too.

The opponents of special protective legislation fall into two categories. On the one hand, some male groups point out that if women are to be accorded equality, there should be no legal favouritism of female workers, as in the final analysis such privileges are borne by male workers or society in general. Special legislation, they argue, merely confirms that women are not men's equals in employment and it underlines their inherent inferior capacity. Others add that technological advances and increasing affluence are eliminating heavy, hazardous and unhealthy jobs. Furthermore, families are now smaller and there are many labour-saving devices at home and child-care facilities outside.

On the other hand, some feminist groups believe that special protective legislation is not only contrary to the principle of equality, but it also results in economic loss for individual women if they are excluded from jobs. It is emphasized that, in effect, such legislation narrows down job opportunities for women making them 'second-class' citizens, and in fact constitutes a 'smokescreen for protecting jobs for men'.[32]

The Scandinavian countries are noted for their early protective legislation which reached its peak in the first quarter of this century. But it has been largely dismantled since, leaving women virtually in the same position as men. This practice may very well spread to other countries, too, as they reach higher stages of economic and social development. At present the attitude of the ILO is that only those jobs and working conditions should be subject to special regulation which present a threat to women's social function of motherhood.[33]

(e) Women's participation in the labour force

Female participation in the work force can be measured in different ways, depending on the definition of work and the coverage of the labour force. Although the comparability of the available statistics of different countries is limited, the following generalizations can be made. The lowest rates are typically found in the less-developed countries of the Third World, and the highest in the socialist planned economies, whilst the industralized capitalist countries are in the middle (closer to the socialist rates, though).

Using the economically active female rate (female labour force as a percentage of the total female population) as a measure, the range applicable to the less-developed countries is mostly 2–40 per cent and the industrialized West is 36–45 per cent.[34] The ILO is not usually supplied with figures by the socialist countries, except Ethiopia, Hungary, Poland and Yugoslavia.[35] But using the same basic calculation, the rates for the socialist countries mostly fall within the range of 35–50.

If calculated on the basis of the female labour force as a percentage of working-age women, the comparative rates given in a Soviet source were as follows: the USA – 40 per cent, France – 43 per cent, the Federal Republic of Germany – 52 per cent, Japan – 53 per cent, Poland – 63 per cent, the German Democratic Republic – 72 per cent, Hungary and Romania – 73 per cent, Bulgaria – 74 per cent, the USSR – 82 per cent and Czechoslovakia – 83 per cent.[36] In the USSR, 93 per cent of able-bodied working-age women (16–54 years) are working or studying.[37] The female workforce constitutes 43 per cent of the total labour force in Poland,[38] 48 per cent in Czechoslovakia[39] and over 50 per cent in the USSR.[40]

The relatively high proportion of women in the socialist countries working outside the home is attributed by A. P. Biryukova to five circumstances.

(1) Full political and economic emancipation.
(2) The state guarantee of equality for women in education, vocational training, the provision of jobs and assistance in child-care.
(3) Full employment in the economy.
(4) Women's desire to achieve economic independence within the family.
(5) The desire to augment family income.[41]

Although in the socialist countries the high female participation rates are regarded with pride, in some respects this fact may be considered a reflection of weakness. The high participation has been partly prompted by the low technological levels and inefficient methods of production, where (cheap) labour is being used as a substitute for capital equipment and labour-saving innovations in workplaces. Women are commonly found in arduous occupations, in many cases involved in heavy manual labouring, as in farming and on building sites. It is also reflective of the continued depressed level of wages, impelling wives to earn extra income to meet family expenses. There has been a noteworthy decline in the birth rate in the European socialist countries, which will only accentuate labour shortages in the future. The deterioration of family life, the assertiveness and even militancy of women, rising divorce rates, the neglect of children and increasing juvenile delinquency have caused a good deal of concern to the authorities and some experts have been advocating women's return to their traditional responsibilities.

C. UNEMPLOYMENT AND SHORTAGES OF LABOUR

Unemployment exists when able-bodied job-seekers cannot find suitable employment. It is customary to distinguish six categories of unemployment according to its origin: (1) *seasonal*, (2) *frictional* (occurring in the case of persons seeking their first job or those changing their jobs), (3) *structural* (caused by changes in the composition of the supply of or demand for labour, brought about by technological change and changes in the structure of population tastes and government policies), (4) *cyclical* (caused by the periodical decline of total spending in the economy), (5) *chronic* (caused by perennial aggregate deficiency of effective demand, insufficient to employ all available labour even if all other causes were removed), and (6) *other causes* (monopolistic restrictions, raw material crises, excessive real wages, generous social benefits, flexible exchange rates, a low mobility of labour).

In addition to open registered full-time unemployment, there may also be hidden unemployment or under-employment. As a rule, it is not reflected in official statistical returns but some countries now distinguish in their labour statistics between fully employed and under-employed persons. Under-employment occurs where persons work for shorter hours than they are prepared to, or where they work below their qualifications. This type of unemployment occurs particularly in agriculture and it is widespread in less-developed countries.

The market mechanism has proved to be incapable of ensuring continuous full employment. Seasonal and frictional unemployment are considered in capitalist market economies to be virtually unavoidable and may range from 1 per cent (in smoothly operating developed countries) to 7 per cent (in urban areas of some less-developed countries).[42] But of greater concern are the deficiency-of-demand and structural-maladjustment causes of unemployment. Up to the early 1970s, it had been widely believed that insufficient spending caused by inadequate monetary and fiscal policies was at the root of the problem. But since that time it appears that rapid technological change and lack of or faulty manpower planning have been basically responsible (see Chapter 6C).

Total open registered unemployment in the non-socialist world stood at 46m in 1960, 67m in 1973 and by 1990 it is predicted it will reach 105m, or 4.7, 5.5 and 6.3 per cent of the labour force respectively.[43] The official unemployment rates in some of the capitalist countries in mid-late 1981 were as follows: Australia – 5.6 per cent, Austria – 1.4 per cent, Belgium – 14.4 per cent, Canada – 6.4 per cent, Denmark – 7.9 per cent, the Federal Republic of Germany – 5.5 per cent, Italy – 8.1 per cent, Japan – 2.2 per cent, the Netherlands – 9.6 per cent, Sweden – 2.6 per cent, the United Kingdom – 12.4 per cent and the USA – 7.2 per cent.[44]

The situation is more serious in less-developed countries. According to the calculations carried out by Y. Sabolo, in 1973 the Third World accounted for four-fifths of the world's registered unemployed, viz. 54m of the 67m, to which some 250m under-employed must be added; the combined unemployment and under-employment rate was 29 per cent.[45]

To Marxists, unemployment is an inherent and inevitable element of the capitalist social system. Marx argued that capitalist development inexorably bred unemployment and, in fact, the 'industrial reserve army of workers' was indispensable to the functioning of the capitalist economy. He further reasoned that competition and the 'declining profit rate' constantly prodded capitalists to replace labour with capital, leading to the increasing 'organic structure of capital' (capital–labour ratio). He attributed the insufficiency of spending in the economy to the uneven distribution of personal income, whereby the incomes of the masses are depressed for the benefit of the bourgeoisie; while the former are deprived of sufficient spending power – appropriate to the level of economic development – the latter enjoy incomes well beyond reasonable consumption levels resulting in large savings.[46]

In view of the above, a Soviet economist concluded:

> Historical experience has demonstrated that the apparent excess of labour under capitalism can disappear only with the breakdown of the rule of capital and the creation of a social system where the basic means of production and distribution are in the hands of the people.[47]

The social cost of unemployment is not widely appreciated to the full. In addition to the direct economic loss in forgone potential production by the unemployed, there are adverse psychological, social and political consequences. It produces demoralizing effects on the retrenched workers, young entrants to the labour market and those undergoing (and perhaps giving up) training; it generates a loss of self-respect and insecurity and it breeds anti-social attitudes, which are all likely to leave long-lasting scars on society and the economy.

As a rule, the state in capitalist countries does not guarantee employment to its citizens. But the governments are naturally concerned, and in the Keynesian spirit they endeavour to varying degrees of determination to promote higher levels of employment, mainly by monetary and fiscal policies and public works. In addition, in some countries, governments may resort to more specific measures in response to various pressure groups.

(1) Employment subsidies.[48]
(2) The nationalization or subsidization of electorally sensitive firms suffering from large losses and threatened with large labour retrenchments (as illustrated by British Leyland).
(3) Subsidized schemes for increasing the occupational, industrial and territorial mobility of labour (re-training, travel, removal).
(4) In some developing countries, a turn to employment-oriented policies, in preference to the traditional obsession with microeconomic profitability and high rates of economic growth.[49]
(5) Other measures experimented with or advocated include:

(i) increase in shiftwork (so that employment is expanded even if there is insufficient capital equipment);

(ii) the utilization of second-hand machinery (especially if labour-intensive);[50]

(iii) the reduction or abolition of investment subsidies (or allowance);

(iv) the detection and prevention of monopolistic restrictions on output and employment;

(v) the reduction of the payroll (or labour) tax;

(vi) the reduction of the compulsory retirement age and facilitation of earlier voluntary retirement;

(vii) the reduction of standard working hours;

(viii) limitations on overtime and on retired persons paid employment;

(ix) job sharing (where, for example, one full-time job is shared by two or more workers);

(x) feather-bedding (the retention of unnecessary workers, as a result of a feeling of paternal obligation by the employer or of union pressure).[51]

Consultation or negotiation with workers' representatives, on the extent of dismissals and possible ways and means of minimizing or avoiding them, are now obligatory either by explicit legislation – as in the EEC, Algeria, Gabon, Mauretania and Sweden, or by collective agreements, as in Finland, Morocco, Nigeria, Norway and Trinidad and Tobago. Workers' representatives are usually, but not necessarily, trade union officials. In some countries, such as the Federal Republic of Germany and Luxemburg, the authorities may postpone the date on which a workforce reduction is to take place. In the Central African Republic, Colombia, France, Greece, Iraq, Kenya, Mali, Mexico, Morocco, the Netherlands, Panama, Peru, Spain, Sri Lanka, Venezuela and Zaire prior sanction by a public authority or a tribunal is required before a major dismissal can take place.[52]

But the measures applied in capitalist countries have obviously proved insufficient, judging by the unemployment figures (see above, p. 33). The inflationary tendencies which have also intensified since the early 1970s, have impelled most governments to counteracting the price–wage spiral, and unemployment has in many cases been, at least implicitly, accepted as an anti-inflationary remedy. The determination with which inflation is fought to the detriment of employment in a sense reflects the governments' greater sensitivity to the interests of the wealth-owning groups than to the (lower) working class.

Although capitalism has a theoretical solution to the problem of unemployment in the form of Keynesian methodology, Marxists are doubtful of the practical capacity of the democratic capitalist countries to ensure continuous full employment. Michal Kalecki, a distinguished Polish Marxist economist (who independently in 1933 had discovered the essential theoretical elements of what after 1936 became known as 'Keynesianism'), was the first thinker who highlighted this problem. He pointed out that democracy would prevent the implementation of full employment policies, as with trade unions in a strengthened bargaining position, wages and consequently prices would rise. The really effective way of counteracting inflation in a capitalist market economy is the deliberate creation of unemployment.[53] There is no better confirmation of Kalecki's prediction than the developments since the early 1970s.

In the socialist centrally planned economies, there is virtually no unemployment. Although frictional and seasonal unemployment exist, its level can be reduced to the minimum unavoidable by economic planning. On the grounds of social ethics and practical economic ambitions, these countries officially subscribe to the policy of continuous full employment and to the twin principles of the 'right to work' and the 'duty to work'. Unemployment had been eliminated in the USSR by 1930, in Eastern Europe by 1950 and in China by 1960. Under capitalist regimes, unemployment in these countries had reached 25 per cent.

Continuous full employment is ensured by planning output targets at such levels as to employ all available manpower in the economy. The socialist state is in a position to ensure continuous full employment, because it has the power to fix relative levels of wages and prices, thereby solving the crucial twin problems of sufficient total effective demand (and its broad composition) and the required level and distribution of investment.

In the traditional dilemma between deficiency or excess of total demand, the communist regimes prefer to err on the side of the latter, opting for over-full rather than under-employment. There is a widely held view that the growth of personal income should outstrip the production capacity of the economy, a view which had been raised by Stalin to the rank of one of the 'economic laws of socialism'. In effect, the socialist countries have experienced perennial inflation – of the suppressed type, owing to comprehensive price controls. If necessary, especially in the case of loss-incurring and new plants or enterprises, production is financed independently of current sales.

In their comprehensive and detailed manpower planning, which covers periods of up to 20 years ahead, releases of labour together with new entrants to the workforce as well as retirements are laid down in detail or are estimated. The figures are then progressively corrected or revised in the light of current, expected or desired developments. The shorter the plan period, the more dis-aggregated, detailed, localized and firm the employment commitments become.

In practical terms as far as an individual worker is concerned, he is protected not only by the general state guarantee of employment, but also by the fact that management cannot dismiss an employee without the consent of the trade union, or a workshop or factory committee. The trade union, or committee, can veto a dismissal or apply to the court for an order for reinstatement. If a worker is discharged (not on his own initiative) management is under obligation to find him alternative employment.

Some socialist economists have at one stage or another advocated the creation of a small pool of unemployment as a means of improving labour discipline and efficiency. This question was widely debated at the Comecon conference on the 'Use of Resources' in Budapest in September 1968, but it was strongly repudiated by the majority of the delegates; a Hungarian economist pointed out: 'Planned economy offers us other means and methods for this purpose'.[54]

Shortages of labour in the socialist countries

Shortages of labour can occur in any type of economy, even if there is unemployment. This applies to particular types of labour with required skills (such as computer programmers), particular regions (on account of climate, remoteness) or even unskilled labour (if no one wants to perform it). These are familiar occurrences in capitalist countries – both developed and less-developed.

But in the socialist centrally planned economies, the shortages of labour have been much more prevalent, persistent and acute, especially those in Europe. The shortages have in fact been increasing, especially since the early 1970s. By 1960 the pools of under-utilized labour in agriculture, domestic service and the private sector had been exhausted. Although in the following 10–15 years the postwar birth bulge and the increased participation of married women yielded substantial additions to the labour force, after the mid-1970s these windfalls began to diminish. The decline in the actual and projected additions to the labour force in the CMEA (Council for Mutual Economic Assistance) countries[55] is illustrated below (percentage increases over the five-year plan periods):

1971–75	–	by	8.0 %
1976–80	–	by	6.0 %
1981–85	–	by	2.3 %

Source. Magyar hirlap [Hungarian Bulletin] (Budapest) 6 Sept. 1977, p. 7.

The natural increase has settled at fairly low levels, especially in the CMEA countries owing to declining birth rates. Thus over the period 1960–79, the birth rates fell as follows: Bulgaria – from 17.8 to 15.3, Cuba – from 30.1 to 14.7, the German Democratic Republic – from 17.0 to 14.0, Mongolia – from 43.2 to 37.2, Poland – from 22.6 to 19.5, Romania – from 19.1 to 18.6 and the USSR – from 24.9 to 18.3 (but in Czechoslovakia the rate rose from 15.9 to 17.8).[56] The projected growth of population in the European socialist countries over the period 1980–2000 is only 16 per cent and in the socialist bloc as a whole (Cuba and the Asian socialist countries included) it is 25 per cent. This compares with 17 per cent in the developed capitalist countries as a whole and 63 per cent in the Third World.[57]

The degree of the labour shortage in the socialist countries is indicated by the following examples (from the late 1970s). The percentage represented by unfilled vacancies was 2 in the USSR, 3 in Bulgaria and 4 in Czechoslovakia. In Poland there were some 10–20 vacancies for every job seeker.[58]

The reasons for the shortages are many and complex. The standard working hours have been declining (see Chapter 3B) and annual holidays as well as periods of education have been rising. But more serious are the systemic peculiarities. There are errors in planning (and central planners prefer to err on the over-full employment than unemployment side), including erroneous forecasts (see Table 2.1). The introduction of capital charges in the 1960s[59] has unwittingly encouraged enterprises to substitute labour for capital. It may be noted here that there are corresponding paradoxes in capitalist countries but in reverse – payroll taxes and investment allowances in effect encourage the substitution of capital for labour.

Another peculiarity of the socialist centrally planned economies impelling enterprises to be extravagant with labour are the artificially depressed wages. This policy is pursued for two reasons: firstly, to restrict overall current consumption in favour of maximum feasible investment, and secondly, to expand social consumption (social benefits in cash, kind and services) to the neglect of private consumption. Socialist economists concede that the generous social benefits alone (provided by the state) reduce the microeconomic cost of labour to enterprises by some 15–25 per cent below the social cost of labour.[60] Shortages of labour lead to various forms of waste, such as under-utilized production capacities, bottlenecks, disinclination to advance the division of labour and poor labour discipline. In spite of the claimed full employment, there is in fact an under-employment of the existing means of production, and the factors of production are not combined in optimal patterns, with consequent adverse effects on labour productivity.

Although shortages of labour are a rule in the socialist countries, the following exceptions must be noted. In Yugoslavia, since the reinstatement of the market mechanism and the de-emphasis of central planning (after 1950 and especially since the mid-1960s), unemployment has reached serious proportions. Over the period 1965–80 total unemployment never fell below 265 000, and in 1981 it reached the record level of 820 000 or 12 per cent (and if the 700 000 or so Yugoslavs working temporarily abroad are included, the overall unemployment rate in the latter year was 22 per cent).[61] The pursuit of the highest possible profitability under market conditions in Yugoslavia (or in capitalist market economies) leads to the restriction of output by enterprises below socially optimal levels and it is in the interest of the remaining personnel to dismiss workers.

There is considerable hidden unemployment in China – different estimates place the figure within the range of 20–26m (2–3 per cent of the working population).[62] It also exists in other socialist countries. Owing to precautionary considerations on the part of management, and constraints on dismissals, many redundant workers are 'hoarded'. This amounts to under-employment which, although expedient or un-avoidable in individual cases, is wasteful in the macro-social sense. According to a recent Soviet estimate, hidden under-utilized labour reserves in the CMEA countries range from 5 to 20 per cent of the total labour force.[63]

D. THE MOBILITY AND TURNOVER OF LABOUR

The mobility of labour involves movements of workers between different localities, industries or occupations and is described as 'regional' (or 'territorial'), 'industrial' or 'occupational', respectively. The 'turnover of labour' is a narrower concept, denoting job terminations and acceptances in different workplaces as a percentage of total employment in a year on the micro, industrial or national scale. As a rough approximation, under normal conditions labour turnover is within the range of 10–25 per cent.

There are two aspects of the mobility of labour, positive and negative. On the one hand, it is a highly desirable process, and indeed necessary in a non-stagnant economy, whereby the supply of labour adjusts itself or is adjusted to the demand for labour under varying conditions. As such, it is conducive to a greater job satisfaction, a better utilization of labour and other resources, higher productivity and higher social welfare in general. On the other hand, if labour turnover is excessive, it leads to loss of working time, at least an initial reduced work efficiency and weakened work discipline.

The mobility of labour may be spontaneous, permissively managed or directive. Spontaneous mobility exists only in a capitalist free market economy, whilst directive mobility is usually resorted to in wartime or other national emergencies both in capitalist countries and under socialism. Permissively managed mobility exists under normal conditions in any type of economy, whereby movement of labour may be steered by the authorities by means of incentives, disincentives and propaganda, but with the final decision still being left to the parties involved.

Directive or quasi-directive measures are present under both systems, even under normal peacetime conditions. In democratic capitalist societies, trade unions may distort the mobility of labour in the negative sense, viz. by preventing the hiring of non-union labour under 'union shop' or 'closed shop' conditions. In many less-developed countries, the state utilizes trade unions in its labour–management policy. In some undemocratic capitalist countries, such as South Africa, black workers' movements are strictly controlled and labour passbooks are used as an instrument of enforcement (which is not applicable to white workers).[64]

As a rule, there is no direction of labour in the socialist countries. However, in the context of central planning the socialist state cannot remain indifferent to the movements of labour. Consequently, the authorities endeavour to achieve the desired distribution of labour by material and moral motivation and some disincentives and penalties, still on the whole consistent with individual choice of occupation and workplace. In this process, the well developed state administrative machinery and media are utilized to great effect.

Although rather exceptional, the direction of labour existed and still exists in socialist countries, especially in the USSR, Albania, China, Cuba and Vietnam. In the USSR there was conscription of labour in 1919–20 and Trotsky was in favour of the 'militarization of labour'. In 1928 the assignment of graduates from tertiary educational institutions was introduced and ten years later the system of permanent labour books was instituted. Over the period 1940–56 there was a prohibition on leaving one's employment without the management's permission, under the penalty of forced labour. The development and location of the forced labour camps, in existence up to the late 1950s with up to 20m inmates, were partly conditioned by labour needs in remote areas (see Chapter 3A).

The direction of labour in the USSR and other socialist countries occurs today in the following cases.

(1) Young graduates from tertiary and secondary vocational institutions are usually directed to work for at least one year at workplaces specified by the authorities.
(2) Members of the communist party and the communist youth organization may be assigned to particular jobs for certain periods of time.
(3) There may be compulsory transfers of highly skilled workers and experts to designated positions.
(4) There may be coercive recruiting in rural areas for work in specified industries or locations.
(5) Occasionally in some countries there may be temporary transfers of labour to rural areas for ideological or practical reasons, especially of youth and the armed forces at harvest time.

However, in spite of the various motivational, coercive and directive measures administered, the mobility of labour is far from the pattern and degree desired by central planners. Thus in the USSR in 1970, only 2.6 per cent of the total labour turnover in industry was shaped by the State Labour Organization (*Orgnabor*), which means that over 97 per cent of the labour turnover was not initiated by it, but shaped by the labour market processes.[65]

According to a survey carried out in Poland, there are eight specific reasons for the excessive mobility of labour in a socialist country like Poland (in descending order).

(1) Lower earnings in the abandoned workplace.

(2) Poor prospects for promotion.
(3) Unsatisfactory working surroundings.
(4) The lack of interest on the part of management in workers and their problems and aspirations.
(5) Dissatisfaction with the occupation.
(6) Poor work organization.
(7) Bad relations with superiors.
(8) The absence of facilities for upgrading qualifications.

In the USSR labour turnover is particularly high amongst young workers – nearly twice as high as amongst older workers. Up to 60–65 per cent of labour turnover is contributed by those below the age of 30.[66]

A separate note is warranted in a study of this nature on the 'social mobility of labour'. It is a facet of the vertical mobility of labour, that is, involving workers' advancement to a higher occupational group or demotion to a lower occupation or position. In capitalist countries, upward mobility may be restricted by inflexible social stratification enforced by an inflexible distribution of wealth or income, or even by law. This is more common in traditional and old established societies in the Third World, South Africa and to some extent in Western Europe and Japan, but less so in the open societies of North America, Australia and New Zealand.

In the socialist countries, the social mobility of labour is largely shaped by ideological factors. First of all, the communist regimes have embarked upon rapid economic development in order to ensure continuous full employment and sustained technological progress and to uplift the occupational and living standards of the masses. More specifically, state policies favour the occupational advancement of workers and peasants, and in particular their children.

This is done by generous educational and vocational training schemes. A proletarian background is often stipulated as a qualifying condition for party membership and for promotion to higher positions. On the other hand, members of the former bourgeoisie were removed from positions of influence soon after the communist takeover and their children were, and in some cases still are, discriminated against admission to universities and top positions. Similarly, many dissident intellectuals (especially in the USSR and Poland) have been removed from their positions and demoted to menial jobs or even deprived of employment altogether. As a result, the intelligentsia in the socialist countries has been largely 'proletarianized'.

With regard to the difference in the incidence of labour turnover between capitalist and socialist countries, no simple generalization can be made. But the following observations may be of interest.

(1) Labour turnover varies widely from one country to another, irrespective of the social system, the range being from 3 to 35 per cent; in extreme cases it may be outside this range.
(2) It may change from time to time even in the same country. But in general it is higher, the higher the stage of economic development, the more open the social organization, the more rapid the technological and social change, the greater the ease of obtaining alternative employment and the poorer the working conditions.
(3) It is usually highest in construction, transport, trade and industry, and lowest in agriculture, forestry and public administration.
(4) At a given stage of economic development, labour turnover is on the whole higher in the socialist countries.

Disadvantages of excessive labour turnover are widely recognized under socialism. In a capitalist economy, although its private cost is of direct concern to the employer, its social cost is not as clearly recognized as in a socialist centrally planned economy. As a Polish economist pointed out, excessive labour mobility leads to extra recruiting and training costs, additional overtime, idle machinery and equipment, greater wear and tear of productive assets (when handled by new workers), more industrial accidents, slowdowns in the rationalization of work and poorer work discipline.[67] A Soviet writer calculated that in the USSR productivity declines in the jobs affected initially by at least 10–20 per cent.[68] In an East German source it was emphasized that excessive labour turnover 'impairs personality development of the individual worker'.[69]

A broader aspect of the mobility of labour is represented by the international migrations of workers, which is considered in Chapter 10.

RECOMMENDED FURTHER READING

1. R. Edwards, M. Reich and D. Gordon (eds), *Labor Market Segmentation*, (Lexington, Mass: Heath, 1975).
2. K. Engelhard, 'How Arms Manufacture Is Adding to Unemployment', *World Marxist Rev.* (London) Feb. 1981, pp. 123–26.
3. D. Furth, A. Hertje and R. J. van der Veen, 'On Marx's Theory of Unemployment', *Oxford Econ. Papers*, July 1978, pp. 263–76.

4.* Edith Gömöri, 'Special Protective Legislation and Equality of Employment Opportunity for Women in Hungary', *Int. Lab. Rev.* (Geneva) Jan.-Feb. 1980, pp. 67–77.

5.* T. Iugai, 'The Economic Mechanism of the Formation of Employment Structure', *Problems of Economics* (New York) July 1981, pp. 86–98.

6.* B. Khorev, 'Migration Mobility of Population of the USSR', *Problems of Economics*, April 1977, pp. 70–86.

7. V. Kondratiev, 'Employment Patterns and Prospects in European Socialist Countries', *Int. Lab. Rev.*, May–June 1978, pp. 355–68.

8.* L. Köszegi, 'Labour Turnover and Employment Structure in European Socialist Countries', *Int. Lab. Rev.*, May–June 1978, pp. 305–18.

9. D. Lane, *The Soviet Industrial Worker: Education, Opportunity and Control* (London: Martin Robertson, 1978).

10. Gail W. Lapidus, *Women in Soviet Society: Equality, Development and Social Change* (Berkeley: University of California Press, 1978).

11.* Li Yu-heng, 'Labor Planning', *Chinese Economic Studies* (New York: Spring, 1977) pp. 65–80.

12. W. Moscoff, 'Sex Discrimination, Commuting and the Role of Women in Romanian Development', *Slavic Rev.* (Columbus, Ohio) Sept. 1978, pp. 440–56.

13. D. E. Powell, 'Labor Turnover in the Soviet Union', *Slavic Rev.*, June 1977, pp. 268–85.

14. Lydia Sargent (ed.), *Women and Revolution: A Discussion of the Unhappy Marriage of Marxism and Feminism* (Boston: Southend Press, 1981).

15. H. Schubnell, 'Employment Structure', in C. D. Kernig (ed.), *Marxism, Communism and Western Society: A Comparative Encyclopedia*, (New York: Herder and Herder, 1972) vol. 3, pp. 150–61.

16.* Symposium, *Training Systems in Eastern Europe* (Geneva: ILO, 1980).

17.* V. Tesař, 'Training and Incentives to Training in the Czechoslovak Engineering Industry', *Int. Lab. Rev.*, March–April 1981, pp. 201–14.

18.* J. Timar, 'Employment Policy and Labour Economy in Hungary', *Acta oeconomica* [Economic Papers], Budapest, 2/1976, pp. 123–44.

19. Batya Weinbaum, *The Curious Courtship of Women's Liberation and Socialism* (Boston: Southend Press, 1978).

20. Wen Chung-Kuo, 'The Rustication Policy and Youth Movements in Mainland China', *Issues and Studies* (Taipei) 1981, pp. 53–71.

* *Indicates contributions by writers from the socialist countries.*

3 Work Discipline and Conditions of Work

A. WORK MORALITY AND DISCIPLINE

The ethical approach to work has varied historically and still differs today in different countries. In some societies, work has been linked with religion, as symbolized by the medieval Christian maxim, *ora et labora* ('pray and work'), where honest and hard work was considered to be conducive to salvation. A re-emergence of this attitude can be later found in a more materialistic setting during and after the Industrial Revolution in the leading capitalist countries, as most clearly observed by M. Weber and T. H. Tawney.[1]

Similar idealistic attitudes to work can be found in some traditional communities, especially those organized along communal lines, where work is treated as a moral responsibility, establishing a sense of belonging and confirming group membership. Especially high work morality has been associated in most societies with certain professions, in particular medical, judicial, educational, police and military (especially the officer corps).

But these attitudes have not necessarily been shared by all workers, especially those (such as slaves, serfs, hired labourers) who have had to labour not for themselves but for their property-owning employers (masters, lords, capitalists). Work even came to be identified as a curse, as penance for paradise lost, as reflected in ancient uprisings, medieval peasant revolts and strikes and absenteeism since the Industrial Revolution.

The approach to the morality of work in the socialist countries is much more systematic. Economic necessity in the case of individual workers is absent or is less compelling than in non-socialist societies. This, combined with the virtual absence of private enterprise and the possibility of enrichment through hard work, necessitates sustained and wholehearted work response from the population.

After the communist accession to power, efforts were soon made and have been maintained since to develop the *socialist work morality*. It is emphasized that it is a qualitatively new and superior type of ethics of work, based on the social ownership of the means of production and political power exercised by the working class, where workers do not labour for exploiting employers but for themselves – directly or indirectly, in their drive towards an ideal society of full communism.

According to an officially sponsored sociological study carried out in Poland in 1961, the following eleven elements of the socialist work morality were identified (in descending order of importance).

(1) Scrupulous performance of assigned tasks.
(2) Honesty.
(3) Co-operation with fellow workers.
(4) High-principled personal conduct.
(5) Interest in or ability to organize and manage.
(6) High skills.
(7) Willingness to help others.
(8) Resourcefulness in work.
(9) Interest and diligence in work.
(10) 'Fair play'.
(11) Concern for the common interest.[2]

The highest form of socialist work morality is *work heroism*, consisting in the worker's 'capacity and preparedness to undertake risk and sacrifices for the sake of exceptional results, better solutions and efficiency . . . even in peacetime'.[3]

An important co-element of the socialist work morality is *socialist competition*. It is a movement to stimulate workers to better performance such as the fulfilment and over-fulfilment of targets, economies in the use of materials and power, the improvement of quality and higher productivity of labour in general. Socialist competition is based on the premise that rivalry is a natural human instinct, which should be harnessed to social benefit, and constructive rivalry is encouraged amongst individuals, teams, brigades, enterprises institutions and so on. The driving forces in socialist competition are mainly moral incentives, appealing primarily to non-material idealistic convictions and sentiments, social recognition, professional pride, patriotism, the desire to surpass capitalist countries and the like (see Chapter 7B). The responsibility for socialist competition in the economic field is usually entrusted to trade unions, although the state often directly assists in particular campaigns.

Although Marx was highly critical of competition in capitalist society, which he described as 'anarchy in the social division of labour',[4] communist leaders stress that in a socialist planned economy competition is not disruptive, but a healthy and progressive form of emulation. In China, the new legislation on socialist competition considers the latter an integral part of the economic reforms; it takes place in the spirit of economic commonsense, indispensable to modernization and a more efficient operation of the economy in general.[5]

The oldest and best known form of socialist competition is the *Subbotnik*, initiated in Soviet Russia on Saturday 12 April, 1919 and subsequently held every saturday immediately preceding Lenin's birthday anniversary (22 April). It consists in a day's work done on a voluntary basis for public benefit outside normal working hours, usually a designated Saturday (*subbota* in Russian meaning 'Saturday').[6] Another scheme is the *Shock Workers' Movement* (initiated in the USSR in 1926), directed towards the pursuit of critical output and productivity objectives and the rectification of bottlenecks. It was later (after 1936) transformed into *Stakhanovism*, named after A. G. Stakhanov (1905–1977), an outstanding coalminer in the Donets Basin, aimed at radically raising output and productivity in the economy. Other schemes followed along these lines (such as the *Movement for the Communist Attitude to Work*, launched in 1958), and other socialist countries have developed similar forms of socialist competition.

A problem related to work morality is that of *work discipline*. In precapitalist societies, work discipline was usually harsh, imposed and enforced by the employer who had considerable legal authority and economic power, especially under slavery and serfdom. Although capitalism came to remove the employer's legal disciplinary authority, the worker – to varying degrees in different countries – is still subject to various external sanctions of economic content. These include fines, penalties, relocation to inferior tasks, refusal of promotion, demotion and dismissal from the job.

Unemployment, which is a commonly found situation in capitalist market economies, is a powerful disciplining factor in its own right. A determination to get ahead and earn enough to become independent and perhaps an employer may also act as disciplining factors. The disciplining power is particularly strong in relation to immigrant workers (see Chapter 10D and E).

Work discipline in the socialist countries is a sensitive and complex problem. On the one hand, it is officially claimed that in the workers' state the worker is no longer subject to domination by capitalist employers and economic necessity. But on the other, the workers' direct or indirect ownership of their workplaces, continuous full employment (accentuated by shortages of labour), generous social security and the absence of opportunities for private enterprise, all combine towards weakening work discipline. Yet the waste caused by poor work discipline is much more clearly seen as social loss in a socialist planned economy, with its carefully planned commitment of resources, postulated targets, ambitious developmental and social programmes and the 'march to full communism'.

The observance of work discipline is treated seriously and is viewed broadly as a civic responsibility. In each socialist country it is clearly regulated in the *Labour Code*, laid down by the state in co-operation with trade unions. The Labour Code typically specifies the following six crucial conditions.

(1) Punctual attendance at work in a fit work condition.
(2) Active performance of the tasks handed out by superiors in accordance with the existing legislation, work agreements and social interest in general.
(3) Proper maintenance and protection of social property in the workplace.
(4) Strict compliance with safety and sanitary regulations.
(5) Co-operation with other members of the working establishment.
(6) Appreciation of the commonly accepted rule under socialism: 'He who does not work, neither shall he eat'.[7]

There have been efforts to develop enthusiasm for work and self-discipline through the socialist work morality. To this end the state employs all the media and various social organizations, especially the party and trade unions. Large proportions of workers, especially party members and trade union activists, respond positively to the pleadings, exhortations, admonitions and threats. Their response varies from time to time.

However, taking the labour force as a whole, its work discipline has proved disappointing over long periods of time. A Polish economist frankly conceded:

The poor work attitudes . . . are reflected in the treatment of work as a necessary evil to earn one's living, in avoiding work and being contemptuous of it as a means of gaining the material needs of life . . . Slovenliness in work performance, irresponsibility, covering up one's tracks, passing on the job to someone else . . . but these transgressions of work discipline are far from complete.[8]

An investigation carried out in Polish industry showed that 38.5 per cent of the workers did not treat their work seriously and responsibly.[9] A Hungarian official of the Ministry of Labour, P. Banki, recently pointed out that work discipline was in fact poorer in Hungary than in capitalist countries. He at least partly attributed it to bureaucratic planning, the non-arrival of raw materials and spare parts, leading to demoralizing stoppages ('if management doesn't do its job, how can it demand it from us?'). He also concluded that 'capitalist methods of ensuring work discipline, for a long time rejected as incompatible with our socialist principles, would be quite suitable for Hungary'.[10]

Theft of socialist property (in factories, collective farms, trade unions, sport clubs, and so on), speculation in scarce commodities, engaging in illicit private production on the job, selling state products or technical secrets for private gain and bribery have flourished remarkably in the USSR and other socialist countries for years.[11] Corruption, tax-dodging, stealing state secrets, cheating on government contracts, waste and bureaucratic bungling, allegedly committed by former 'capitalist elements', have been occurring even at high levels in government and party organs, as officially admitted.[12] Poor work discipline is further reflected in absenteeism and high labour turnover (see Chapters 2D and 3B).

To tackle the problem of work discipline, the socialist countries have resorted to a variety of methods (in addition to instilling the 'socialist work morality').

(1) *Personal labour books* – showing the worker's basic personal particulars, education, vocational training and a record of employment.

(2) *Barriers to the freedom of movement* – the virtual prohibition of emigration, plus restrictions on migrations from rural to urban areas (in the USSR, there are the so-called 'internal passports' to the latter effect).

(3) *Comrades' (or social) courts* – semi-judiciary committees in larger workplaces for dealing with breaches of work discipline and minor social misdemeanours.

(4) *Financial penalties* – deductions from wages for damages to produc-

tion or socialized property, and the withholding of bonuses and other benefits.

(5) *Corrective and penal labour* – compulsory assignment to outlying workplaces, forced labour camps and imprisonment, resorted to at one time or another in virtually all socialist countries. These measures reached their extreme in the USSR under Stalin, where up to 20m people were held in labour camps (about 20 per cent of the labour force in 1945). In the mid-1950s, 58 per cent of all court sentences involved corrective labour and even poor time-keeping was punishable by imprisonment. Although forced labour camps were formally abolished in 1956, forced labour has remained in one form or another in the USSR since, estimated at 4.0m people in the late 1970s.[13]

(6) *Scientific management schemes* – such as Taylorism, the Saratov Method, Shchekino Scheme, and Do–Ro Method, emphasizing efficient work environment, incentives and appeals to workers' pride.

In general, there has been a tendency in the socialist countries to replace penalties, restrictions, prohibitions and punishment with positive instruments, viz. various types of incentives (Chapter 7B) and workers' participation (Chapter 5).

B. WORKING HOURS

Historically there has been a tendency for the hours of work to decline, at least in the industrialized countries – from around 60 to 40 hours, or less, per week over the past 150 years. In general, working hours are shortest in the West and longest in the less-developed countries of the Third World, whilst the socialist bloc is roughly in the middle. This is demonstrated in Table 3.1.

Although the working hours are shortest in the most 'bourgeois' capitalist countries, Marxists view this in a negative light. Marx pointed out that:

Only by suppressing the capitalist form of production could the length of the working-day be reduced to the necessary labour-time . . . The more the productiveness of labour increases, the more the working-day be shortened; and the more the working day is shortened, the more can the intensity of labour increase . . . In capitalist society

TABLE 3.1 *Working hours and public holidays in manufacturing in selected capitalist and socialist countries in 1970 and 1980*

Country	Average weekly working hours		Paid public holidays 1980
	1970	1980	
Australia	42	41	8
Bulgaria	43	42	7
Canada	40	38	(not available)
Czechoslovakia	44	43	7
Egypt	55	55	17
France	45	41	16
German Democratic Republic	44	43	7
Federal Republic of Germany	44	42	16
Hungary	44	41	8
Japan	43	43	14
Republic of [South] Korea	52	52	16
Norway	33	31	13
Poland	46	44	8
Romania	48	46	6
South Africa	47	47	10
Switzerland	45	44	(not available)
United Kingdom	42	41	7
USA	41	41	11
USSR	41	41	8
Yugoslavia	42	42	10

Source. Based on literature published in Western and socialist countries.

spare time is acquired for one class by converting the whole life-time of the masses into labour-time.[14]

Largely as a means of dealing with unemployment fed by accelerated technological change, in 1977 the European Trade Union Confederation (see Chapter 4B) embarked on a campaign to reduce the working week further to 35 hours. But the campaign has encountered stiff opposition from employers who point out that the reduction in standard working hours in the last decade or two has not been genuinely needed by workers as in many cases it only led to more overtime and thus to higher costs to employers.

There has also been pressure to reduce the retirement age to 60 at full pension and the extension of the compulsory school leaving age (to the uniform level of 16 where it has not been implemented yet). The pressure for shorter working hours can also assume the forms of more paid public holidays (say, in excess of 6–7 days a year), longer annual holidays (for example, over and above the minimum of two weeks a year) and earlier retirement (at 55–60) at full pension. The more affluent West European countries are ahead of the world in these respects. Thus paid 4–5 week annual holidays are now a rule in France, Germany and Norway and the EEC's policy is to extend it to the whole community.[15]

There has also been popular pressure for shorter working hours in the socialist countries, although in general less pronounced than in the West. A more conspicuous drive in this direction was initiated in 1980 by the independent trade union movement in Poland, Solidarity (see Chapter 4D). Although Solidarity later softened its thrust owing to the country's economic difficulties and the imposition of martial law, it has aroused keen interest in other socialist countries. In some of them, the authorities – partly in response to popular demands and partly to forestall the Polish-style upheavals – have initiated or promised reductions in the working week. For example, as announced in 1981, the working week is to be gradually reduced in Romania from 46 to 44 hours by 1983, with two Saturdays free each month.[16]

But it must be pointed out here that in some arduous occupations working hours are quite short. For example, in the USSR miners work only a five-day thirty-hour week.[17] As a matter of interest, it may be mentioned here that Christmas is treated as a working day, not a public holiday, in at least the following socialist countries: Albania, Bulgaria, China, Cuba, Ethiopia, the Democratic People's Republic of Korea, Mongolia, Romania, the USSR, the Democratic People's Republic of Yemen and Yugoslavia.

In addition to the traditional preoccupation with the quantitative aspect of the working time, increasing attention is now being paid in all advanced countries to the 'quality of working life'.[18] It involves such questions as the distribution of work over the day, week, year or a person's lifetime, including flexible hours, shiftwork, staggered working hours or holidays, part-time employment and early retirement.

This aspect has received particular attention in the socialist countries on ideological grounds. In a study sponsored by the official trade union establishment in Poland a few years ago, it was stated:

> under modern conditions, the value of time is increasing – both in terms of work and of life in general. Nowadays time is life, which is much more than the old [bourgeois] maxim, 'time is money'.[19]

In addition to paid worktime, in all countries there are various forms of voluntary or virtually mandatory work. Those which are of comparative interest are institutionalized charitable activities and state-coerced workdays. The former are typical of capitalist countries and are conducted by private or semi-public institutions, mostly for the alleviation of poverty. The voluntary workers for these pursuits mostly come from the upper and middle classes – property owners or pro-fessionals (including non-working wives) – rather than from the wage-earning class.

In a sense surprisingly, Marxists have traditionally despised charity, as in their view it is humiliating to the recipients who are mostly underprivileged and unfortunate members of the proletariat. More importantly, they regard charity as a misguided or cynically engineered attempt to remove the worst symptoms of social injustice in capitalist society, thereby merely delaying the need for a proletarian revolution. [20]

In the socialist countries, the main form of unpaid work is represented by more or less voluntary weekend work on designated dates (for example, *Subbotnik* in the USSR and *Domingo rojo* in Cuba). On the national scale, this work is performed in the usual workplaces, and the proceeds from the unpaid wages are then devoted to well-publicized causes (see Chapter 3A).

But, in addition to the nationwide efforts, there are many locally prompted community projects and, moreover, persons in positions of authority and professionals are expected to actively initiate and participate in various campaigns of a political, civic and cultural nature. Although all this type of work is officially claimed to be 'voluntary', various forms of pressure and even threats are applied to ensure compliance.

C. ALIENATION AND HUMANIZATION

Alienation denotes the estrangement of the worker in relation to the goods he produces and to his employer. Although the concept goes back to ancient times, it is Marx who gave it an ideological and social connotation. [21] He blamed the private ownership of the means of production, mechanization, monotonous specialization, the discrete division of labour and the private profit motive.

In effect, the worker loses interest in the objects he produces as he no longer has the dignity and satisfaction of producing the complete article himself, and he has no control over his labour and the goods he produces. He is also conscious of the fact that he produces the means of labour (capital goods) utilized by the capitalist to replace labour, which leads to unemployment. Consequently, both the goods produced and the capitalist employer become 'alien' to the worker, who thus becomes dehumanized.

The branches of the economy in which workers' dissatisfaction is typically greatest are mining, certain sections of manufacturing (especially textiles, glassworks, stoneware, metal-working, iron and steel), construction and, to a lesser extent, agriculture.[22] Workers' dissatisfaction, and alienation in general, find their expression in prevailing apathy, the waste of materials, damage to equipment, absenteeism, high labour turnover and frequent industrial disputes (especially 'wildcat strikes').

In the official socialist view, alienation has been regarded as a phenomenon of pre-socialist societies and not of communist or even socialist society, where the means of production belong to the workers and there is no class struggle.

However, there is substantial evidence indicating that alienation does reassert itself under socialism. It has manifested itself in the persistence or reappearance of poor work discipline, a high labour turnover, the neglect of and damage to socialized property, pilfering in factories and on farms, the embezzlement of public funds, parasitism, hooliganism, elaborate ways of circumventing laws and regulations, the black market, dissent and (however, suppressed and hidden) conflicts between workers and management, between enterprises and bureaucracy and between the individual person and the monolithic and ubiquitous state. A number of thinkers in Yugoslavia as well as in Czechoslovakia and Poland and even the USSR have conceded that the abolition of the private ownership of the means of production and the disappearance of the class struggle does not necessarily remove alienation.

In a sense, the economic reforms and the drive to greater efficiency (including profit maximization) have exacerbated poor industrial relations. Management is now more determined to maintain stricter work discipline to avoid waste, and dismissals of workers are more likely to occur.

The existence of alienation under socialism, however suppressed for a long time, has been demonstrated in a rather dramatic manner by the industrial upheavals in Poland in the early 1980s, with the independent trade unionism and the Catholic Church commanding widespread support, to the popular rejection of the Party (see Chapter 4C and D). Alienation has been less evident in Yugoslavia, owing to the development of workers' self-management (see Chapter 5B).

A comparative examination of capitalist and socialist countries indicates that the incidence of job satisfaction varies widely from one country to another and there are considerable differences between different workplaces within the same country, so that no simple and significant difference can be established between the two systems. But one fact appears to be certain: the official assertions in the socialist countries in public statements and propaganda posters, showing happy and contented workers, are far from complete.

According to Teckenberg, quoting sample Soviet studies, the proportion of workers dissatisfied with their work in the USSR ranged from 38 to 80 per cent, compared with 37 per cent in the Federal Republic of Germany, the USA, the Scandinavian countries[23] and in Australia.[24] Similarly, an official survey carried out in Hungary in May 1977 showed that 55 per cent of the workforce employed in key industries laboured under difficult and unpleasant conditions.[25]

Alienation may also be reflected in *absenteeism*. This phenomenon has become a problem causing increasing concern, particularly in industries noted for complex and costly equipment and highly advanced occupational specialization. Losses to the enterprise and society are inevitably greater in the case of the modern operation of a huge excavator than of a labourer using a shovel. This problem was highlighted not long ago by L. I. Brezhnev at their Sixteenth Congress, when he took Soviet trade unions to task for not doing enough to counteract absenteeism.[26]

Absenteeism is a worldwide problem, common to both capitalist and socialist countries, and it appears to be on the increase. High absenteeism can be due to two opposite causes – alienation, on the one hand, and high and stable wages and/or comprehensive social security, on the other. Alienation and high wages are more operative in capitalist countries, whilst the relatively generous social benefits and the security of employment are playing a greater part under socialism.

In the industrialized countries about one-tenth of working time is not actually worked due to one reason or another. The percentages given in a Polish source for the late 1970s were (time not worked apparently due to all causes – justified and unjustified): the USA – 7 per cent, France – 10 per cent, Poland – 10 per cent, the Netherlands – 10 per cent, the Federal Republic of Germany – 11 per cent and Italy – 15 per cent; Czechoslovakia, the German Democratic Republic and the USSR had a lower, whilst Hungary had a higher, incidence of absenteeism than Poland (10 per cent).[27]

A Soviet trade union activist noted that in the USSR absenteeism was unwittingly encouraged by the system. Not only is there an inclination to abuse social security, but enterprises also favour it; for example, hospitalized workers are paid their normal wages out of social insurance funds, whereby enterprises may in fact save money.[28]

Largely to counteract alienation and to promote better attitudes to work and more harmonious industrial relations, efforts have been made to 'humanize work'. Various schemes along these lines have been introduced since the early 1960s (and in some cases even earlier), first in the most industrialized and affluent capitalist countries – Western Europe, North America and Japan.

The main directions in the development of the humanization of work are: the elimination of heavy, dangerous and unpleasant work, a more congenial physical and social environment at work, work enrichment (by adapting work tasks to the comfort and interest of the worker), closer management–worker understanding, delegation of initiative and responsibility to work teams, and workers' participation in management and ownership.[29]

Some of the most publicized schemes or experiments geared to the humanization of work have been embarked upon by multinational corporations, notably Bosch (West German), Cadbury Schweppes (British), Fiat (Italian), Friedrich Elbert Stiftung (West German), Philips (Dutch), Volkswagen (West German) and Volvo (Swedish). In a category of their own are many Japanese companies, which have been very active in engrafting and adapting Western schemes onto the unique local tissue of employers' paternalism and workers' loyalty. Schemes of this type have been initiated in virtually all major firms, such as Esu-Esu Segaku, Maekva Manufacturing, Mitsubishi Electric, Nihon Radiators, Seiki and Sony.

The approach to the humanization of work is much more systematic and comprehensive in the socialist countries. This derives from their official idealization of work (see Chapter 1B). and their ideological commitment to the development of a harmonious and contented working class society. Marx and Engels envisaged the transformation of work from an imposition and a curse in class societies to enjoyment and self-fulfilment under communism.[30]

There is vast socialist literature on the subject, but for our purposes the following general lines of thought warrant special attention. Socialist thinkers distinguish between 'big' and 'small' humanization. The former, also known as 'extensive' or 'macro-social', involves the creation of general social conditions for 'the process of complete liberation of labour', especially the guarantee of the dignity of labour, the democratization of management–worker relations and the elimination of excessive differentiation amongst workers. It is stressed that the complete humanization of labour can occur only in a communist society, where the means of production are directly or indirectly owned and managed by the workers themselves and where other necessary conditions are created on a centrally planned basis.

'Small' humanization, also described as 'technical' or 'microeconomic', consists in the improvement of the conditions of work for individual workers, such as the protection of the health and safety of the workers, the reduction of working hours, the minimization of monotonous and uninteresting work, positive measures for making work tasks more pleasant, interesting and creative, the improvement of interpersonal relations amongst workers and the provision of suitable equipment and other facilities for the implementation of these requirements and objectives.[31] Most socialist writers stress that 'big humanization' is possible only under communism, whilst capitalism at best can achieve only 'small humanization'.[32]

In pursuit of the philosophy outlined above, efforts have been made to transform workplaces into social institutions of sorts, with various amenities provided in the spirit of sympathetic understanding of the workers' needs, problems and aspirations. Thus a typical socialist work entity provides the following facilities and services for its personnel (as far as its resources can allow).

(1) Canteens for meals and take-away foods.
(2) Recreation facilities (reading rooms, indoor games, swimming pools, sports grounds).
(3) Holiday and convalescent homes for its employees.
(4) Educational, vocational and cultural programmes.
(5) Child-care.
(6) Emergency housing.
(7) Various incidental services (such as arranging socials, theatre parties, excursions and providing financial assistance in emergencies).

Thus a socialist work entity is much more than a workplace, but rather a community operating in the spirit of co-operation, involving managerial, skilled and unskilled personnel in activities within and outside working hours, conducive to better personal relations in a more relaxed atmosphere.

However, the extent of the implementation of the official ideals has been rather disappointing. The prevalence of authoritarianism, the disregard of human rights, the policies of austerity pursued in the name of accelerated industrialization and the slow growth of productivity have been in conflict with the cause and practical implementation of the humanization of work. From the author's observation of factories in the West and in the socialist countries, many capitalist companies have made greater progress in practical terms at least in the microeconomic sense. Curiously enough, in the socialist bloc greatest progress appears to have been made in the poorest countries, viz. China and Yugoslavia.

D. THE ILO AND ITS STANDARDS

The International Labour Organization, founded in 1919 and based in Geneva, is the international organization most closely concerned with conditions of work in the broadest sense. It aims to improve working and living standards throughout the world.

The ILO's supreme body is the International Labour Conference, holding conferences annually, with four delegates from each member country (two representing the government, one representing the employers and one representing the working people). Other main bodies are the Governing Body (consisting of 56 members representing governments, employers and workers), the International Labour Office (the permanent secretariat), the International Institute for Labour Studies (a research institution created in 1960 for the study of social and labour relations) and the international Centre for Advanced Technical and Vocational Training (established in 1965 for training leaders for vocational and technical institutions and trade unions, as well as middle-level managers, especially from less-developed countries). The ILO publishes the most authoritative sources on comparative industrial relations in three languages (English, French and Spanish), viz.: *International Labour Review* (a bi-monthly), *Legislative Series* (selected labour and social security laws and regulations, also appearing every two months), *Year Book of Labour Statistics* and other periodical and occasional studies such as the important *International Labour Code* (containing ILO's adopted Conventions and Recommendations).

Of the 165 countries in the world capable of joining international organizations, 143 are members of the ILO. Of these, 23 are socialist and 120 non-socialist. Only two countries ruled by communist regimes are not members, viz. Albania and the Democratic people's Republic of

[North] Korea, whilst of the non-socialist countries 22 are not members.

It may be mentioned here that Albania was a member from 1920 to 1967. The USSR joined only in 1934 but withdrew in 1940 and rejoined in 1954; formally Belorussia and the Ukraine (after Russia, the largest Republics in the USSR) are also members of the ILO, but in our figures they are not regarded as separate countries. Yugoslavia suspended her membership from 1949 to 1951. In the case of (mainland) China, after having been admitted to the United Nations in November 1971, she was offered ILO membership (whilst Taiwan's was discontinued). But up to 1977, the Chinese Government had not clearly indicated if China was prepared to participate in the work of the ILO and to honour its standards and her financial obligations; in that year she formally declared that she was not. A similar situation appears to apply to Kampuchea and Laos.

There is a widely held view in the West that the ILO is more sympathetic to the socialist bloc than to the capitalist world. This conviction is particularly strong in the USA, the country which was most instrumental to the creation of the ILO.[33] The USA objected to the ILO allowing its publications to be used for Soviet propaganda.[34] In 1970 the President of the AFL–CIO, George Meaney, called for a review of US links with the ILO owing to its anti-American course prompted by the socialist and many less-developed countries.

In November 1977 the US Government withdrew from the ILO, as a consequence of which the organization had to dismiss some 500 employees (considering that the USA had contributed one-quarter to the ILO's income). At the same time, the socialist countries accused the USA of dodging ILO standards and of endeavouring to dominate the organization and use it for anti-socialist polemics.[35] However, it may be noted here that after the ILO reportedly moderated its stand, the US Government decided in February 1980 to rejoin the organization.

The main role of the ILO from our point of view is to set and promote better labour standards. In general, the emphasis in the industrialized West has been on amenities for the workers, labour relations, the effects of technological change and protection against unemployment, whilst in less-developed countries emphasis has been on the organization of employment, the introduction of protective labour institutions and basic working conditions. In the socialist countries, the official preoccupation has been mostly with the basic social conditions of work and industrial relations consistent with socialist economic planning;[36] unofficially – partly by local initiative and mostly by the pressure of international opinion – the concern has been essentially with the workers' democratic rights and protection against the powerful socialist state.

The ILO's efforts to upgrade the conditions of working life assume the form of Statements, Memoranda, Resolutions, and Recommendations. None of these is formally binding, but their moral pressure is in many cases surprisingly effective.

Of greater formal importance are the Conventions which are put forward at the International Labour Conferences (usually held annually). After adoption, a Convention is submitted to the member countries for ratification. If ratified, the Convention becomes binding and the governments concerned are expected to report on its implementation.

Up to 1981, 153 Conventions had been adopted (of which 147 are still operative), and the total number of ratifications by the member countries had reached 4856. The predisposition to ratify ILO conventions has been about the same amongst socialist and non-socialist countries, with a slightly better average recorded by the latter countries – the respective averages working out at 27 and 30 per country.

Of the socialist countries, Cuba, Bulgaria and Poland have ratified the highest number of conventions (84, 80 and 73 ratifications, respectively), whilst Laos, Kampuchea and Mongolia have ratified the least (4, 5 and 7 ratifications, respectively). Amongst the capitalist countries, Spain, France and the Netherlands have been the leaders (with 105, 102 and 84, respectively), whilst Bahrain, Botswana and Namibia have ratified none (largely because they joined the ILO only in 1977, 1978 and 1978, respectively). Amongst the capitalist countries, the USA is conspicuous for having ratified only 7 Conventions, in fact those which are of lesser consequence.[37]

The Conventions most relevant to this study are as follows.

No.   1. Hours of Work (adopted in 1919).
No.   81. Labour Inspection (1947).
No.   87. Freedom of Association and Protection of the Right to Organize (1948).
No.   98. Right to Organize and Collective Bargaining (1949).
No. 102. Social Security (Minimum Standards) (1950).
No. 105. Abolition of Forced Labour (1957).
No. 119. Guarding of Machinery (1963).
No. 128. Invalidity, Old Age and Services' Benefits (1967).
No. 131. Minimum Wage Fixing (1970).

No. 132. Holidays with Pay (Revised) (1970).
No. 138. Minimum Age (1973).
No. 142. Human Resources Development (1975).

The details of the ratification of the 12 Conventions by the leading socialist (12) and non-socialist (23) countries are presented in Table 3.2. The ILO not only exhorts the member countries to adopt and ratify Conventions, but also insists on their implementation and periodical reporting thereon. It is expected that national norms are raised to the ILO levels, but if local norms are higher, that they are retained to act as models for further improvements elsewhere. In compliance with the undertaken Conventions, the signatory governments take appropriate steps and, if necessary, modify their national legislations accordingly.

The response of the socialist countries has varied. In most cases they have implemented their ratified Conventions, as is illustrated by Bulgaria's full extension of social services to collective farmers. In 1964 the ILO Committee of Experts on Social Security drew the Bulgarian Government's attention to the fact that collective farmers were excluded from workmen's compensation, in violation of Convention No. 12 (of 1921, which Bulgaria had ratified). In 1965 legislation was passed to provide full workers' compensation to all agricultural wage earners.[38] On another occasion, an ILO Committee of Experts questioned the Bulgarian authorities on whether the inspectors to enforce industrial safety were sufficiently independent as stipulated in Convention No. 81 (considering that they are appointed by the state-controlled Central Council of Trade Unions). But after an investigation, the Committee was satisfied of their independence.[39]

In some cases, however, the socialist governments have failed to comply. They have argued that most ILO Conventions were framed on the initiative of capitalist countries, and many of them were inconsistent with the social and economic system in force under socialism.[40]

The most controversial Conventions ideologically are No. 87 (on the freedom of trade unions) and No. 98 (on the right to organize and bargain collectively). The Polish trade union organization Solidarity, in its struggle to gain independence from the party and the state, in 1980 skillfully exploited these two Conventions which had been ratified by the Polish Government (see Chapter 4D).

TABLE 3.2   *ILO Conventions ratified by selected*

Selected ratified

ILO member country‡		No. 1 Hours of Work (44)	No. 81 Labour Inspection (98)	No. 87 Free Trade Unions (93)	No. 98 Trade Unions and Collective Bargaining (110)	No. 102 Social Security (29)	No. 105 Abolition of Forced Labour (107)
Angola	(1976)	X	–	–	X	–	X
Argentina	(1919)	X	X	X	X	–	X
Australia	(1919)	–	X	X	X	–	X
Brazil	(1919)	–	–	–	X	–	X
Bulgaria	(1920)	X	X	X	X	–	–
Canada	(1919)	X	–	X	–	–	X
Chile	(1919)	X	–	–	–	–	–
Cuba	(1919)	X	X	X	X	–	X
Czechoslovakia	(1919)	X	–	X	X	–	–
Egypt	(1936)	X	X	X	X	–	X
Finland	(1920)	–	X	X	X	–	X
France	(1919)	X	X	X	X	X	X
German Democratic Republic§	(1974)	–	–	X	X	–	–
Federal Republic of Germany§	(1951)	–	X	X	X	X	X
Greece	(1919)	X	X	X	X	X	X
Hungary	(1922)	X	–	X	X	X	–
India	(1919)	X	X	–	–	–	–
Italy	(1919–39, 1945)	X	X	X	X	X	X
Japan	(1919–40, 1951)	–	X	X	X	X	–
Mexico	(1931)	–	–	X	–	X	X
Mongolia	(1968)	–	–	X	X	–	–
Netherlands	(1919)	–	X	X	–	X	X
New Zealand	(1919)	X	X	–	–	–	X
Norway	(1919)	–	X	X	X	X	X
Pakistan	(1947)	X	X	X	X	–	X
Peru	(1919)	X	X	X	X	X	X
Poland	(1919)	–	–	X	X	–	X
Romania	(1919–42, 1956)	X	X	X	X	–	–
Spain	(1919–41, 1956)	X	X	X	X	–	X
Sweden	(1919)	–	X	X	X	X	X
USSR	(1934–40, 1954)	–	–	X	X	–	–
United Kingdom	(1919)	–	X	X	X	X	X
USA	(1934–77, 1980)	–	–	–	–	–	–
Vietnam¶	(1980)	–	X	–	X	–	–
Yugoslavia‖	(1951)	–	X	X	X	X	–

* For the identification of the Conventions, see pp. 60–1. The bracketed figures below indicate the total number of countries which have ratified the Convention concerned.

† The maximum possible is 147.

‡ The socialist countries are shown in *italic* print. The year of accession to the ILO is shown in brackets. Total membership was 145.

capitalist and socialist countries as of 1 January 1981

Conventions*

No. 119 Guarding of Machinery (35)	No. 128 Invalid, Old Age (13)	No. 131 Minimum Wage (26)	No. 132 Holidays with Pay (15)	No. 138 Minimum Age (23)	No. 142 Human Resources Development (30)	Other ratified Conventions	Total ratified Conventions†
–	–	–	–	–	–	27	30
–	–	–	–	–	X	54	60
–	–	X	–	–	X	37	43
–	–	–	–	–	–	52	54
–	–	–	–	X	–	75	80
–	–	–	–	–	–	23	26
–	–	–	–	–	–	38	40
–	–	X	–	X	X	76	84
–	–	–	–	–	X	48	52
–	–	X	–	–	–	29	35
X	X	–	–	X	X	61	69
–	–	X	–	–	–	15	102
–	–	–	–	X	X	20	24
–	X	–	X	X	X	55	64
–	–	–	–	–	–	34	40
–	–	–	–	–	X	40	45
–	–	–	–	–	–	32	34
X	–	–	–	–	X	73	81
X	–	X	–	X	–	29	36
–	–	X	–	–	X	54	59
–	–	–	–	–	–	5	7
–	X	X	–	X	X	76	84
–	–	–	–	–	–	50	53
X	X	–	X	X	X	77	87
–	–	–	–	–	–	25	30
–	–	–	–	–	–	54	62
X	–	–	–	X	X	67	73
–	–	X	–	X	–	33	39
X	–	X	X	X	X	95	105
X	X	–	X	–	X	57	66
X	–	–	–	X	X	38	43
–	–	–	–	–	X	70	76
–	–	–	–	–	–	7	7
–	–	–	–	–	–	20	22
X	–	–	X	–	–	57	63

§ Germany was a member from 1919 to 1935.
¶ Republic of [South] Vietnam was a member from 1950 to 1976.
‖ Yugoslavia was also a member from 1919 to 1949.
Source. Based on the ILO's 'Chart of International Labour Conventions' (Geneva, 1981).

RECOMMENDED FURTHER READING

1. S. Andors (ed.), *Workers and Workplaces in Revolutionary China* (White Plains, NY: M. E. Sharpe, 1977).
2. K. E. Bailes, 'Alexei Gastev and the Soviet Controversy Over Taylorism, 1918–24', *Soviet Studies*, Glasgow, July 1977, pp. 373–94.
3. Chiang Hsin-li, 'Alienation and the "Emancipation-of-the-Mind" Movement in Communist China', *Issues and Studies* (Taipei) March 1981, pp. 18–33.
4. F. Gamillscheg, P. Hanau and Mary McAuley, 'Labour Law and Social Insurance Law', in C. D. Kernig (ed.), *Marxism, Communism and Western Society: A Comparative Encyclopedia* (New York: Herder and Herder, 1973) vol. 5, pp. 47–73.
5. ILO, *Bibliography on Major Aspects of the Humanization of Work and the Quality of Working Life*, 2nd ed (Geneva: ILO, 1978).
6. ILO, *The Impact of International Conventions and Recommendations* (Geneva: ILO, 1976).
7. A. Kahan and A. R. Blair (eds), *Industrial Labor in the USSR*, (New York and Oxford: Pergamon, 1979).
8. W. Laqueur and B. Rubin (eds), *The Human Rights Reader* (New York: Meridian, 1979).
9. T. Meron, 'Violations of ILO Conventions by the USSR and Czechoslovakia', *American Jl. of Intl. Law* (New York) Jan., 1980, pp. 206–11.
10. R. Meyersohn and P. Hollander, 'Leisure', in Kernig (ed.), *A Comparative Encyclopaedia* (1973) vol. 5, pp. 165–74.
11.* Á Olajos, 'Changing Expectations of the Working Population towards Work in Hungary', *Acta oeconomica* [Economic Papers] (Budapest) 2/1977, pp. 189–201.
12.* H. Rehtanz, 'The Organization of Occupational Safety in the German Democratic Republic', *Int. Lab. Rev.* (Geneva) Dec. 1975, pp. 419–30.
13.* A. Semenov, 'Industrial Safety Training for Soviet Workers', *Int. Lab. Rev.* (Geneva) July –Aug. 1978, pp. 481–89.
14. I. Wallimann, *Estrangement: Marx's Conception of Human Nature and the Division of Labour* (Westport, CT: Greenwood Press, 1981).
15. J. Zuzansk, *Work and Leisure in the Soviet Union: A Time–Budget Analysis* (New York: Praeger, 1980).

* *Indicates contributions by writers from the socialist countries.*

4 Trade Unions and Collective Bargaining

A. HISTORICAL BACKGROUND

Trade unions are essentially a product of capitalism. Although their beginnings can be traced back to the journeymen's associations of the seventeenth and eighteenth centuries, their real development became associated only with the industrialization of the nineteenth and twentieth centuries. That development began against the background of the breakdown of paternalistic feudalism, the regulated craft guilds and the orderly domestic system, which were replaced instead by the freedom of enterprise, the dispossession of small villagers, the bankruptcy of the craftsmen, the factory system and ascendant capitalists.

The early period of trade union development coincided with a visible impoverishment of the working masses, reflecting their weak bargaining power and the absence of protective state intervention as prescribed by the laissez-faire philosophy. Early unions combined industrial objectives with benevolent functions (mutual self-help, social activities). Unlike medieval guilds, trade unions became purely working-class organizations, many of which turned to militant action and class struggle. At first they were small, isolated and they combined skilled craftsmen according to the workers' occupation ('craft unionism').

It may be mentioned here that originally it was not the most impoverished and desperate labourers who sought the working-class organizations, but rather the skilled artisans who created exclusive unions. They were more interested in improving their own position than in their less fortunate fellow labourers and the class struggle, as was reflected even in their names – for example, the 'Knights of St. Crispin' (in England) and the 'Noble Order of the Knights of Labor' (in the USA). Marxists came to call them the 'aristocracy of labour'.

But in the latter part of the nineteenth century, there was a tendency towards the inclusion of unskilled and even white-collar workers to form 'industrial unions', further accentuated by integration into larger unions and centralization. That tendency was, however, soon weakened by the emergence of syndicalism, opposed not only to capitalism and the wage system, but also to central coercion, state power and nationalism. Instead, it advocated the organization of society in all-inclusive democratic unions and co-operative enterprises (see Chapter 1A). Although in each country a co-ordinating trade union body was developed, its powers have been limited and further weakened by the federative (not unitary) basis of organization, and furthermore some unions are not affiliated with it.

In most capitalist countries, some unions are left-wing and even revolutionary in outlook, some subscribe to religious ideals and some are moderate and even conservative – facts which are reflected in the three international trade union organizations (see section F below). Since the Second World War, most trade unions (especially in Western Europe), whilst rejecting class struggle, have extended their functionality to the political and social sphere, by pressing for comprehensive social welfare and the development of industrial democracy (see Chapter 5) and engaging in co-operative ventures (housing, trade, services) and even vocational training.

The Marxist approach to trade unionism is, naturally, ideological and rather complex. In application to capitalism, revolutionary Marxist thinkers (viz. Marx, Engels, Rosa Luxemburg and Lenin) insisted that trade unions should not be concerned merely with the protection and improvement of the material conditions of their members, but more broadly with the political class struggle, and that industrial disputes should be transformed into revolutionary violence leading to the overthrow of capitalism.[1]

In fact, Lenin went further by rejecting 'economism', the view held by some Russian Marxists at the time that a communist society would develop spontaneously in due time out of industrial disputes, pursued by trade unions alone for material improvements. Lenin stressed that revolutionary class consciousness and proletarian revolution must be brought to the workers from outside, by intellectual professional revolutionaries organized in a disciplined, dedicated and tight vanguard (a communist party elite).[2] He also warned against opportunistic skilled workers and union leaders ('labour aristocracy') who are open to be bribed by monopoly capital to 'win them to the side of the bourgeoisie . . . against all others'.[3]

On the other hand, evolutionary Marxists, such as Bernstein and Kautsky,[4] were opposed to a violent revolutionary function of trade unions (and of even the political labour movement), and instead advocated a 'parliamentary road to socialism'. Unions which give up class struggle in favour of collaboration with employers are described by revolutionary Marxists as 'yellow trade unions'.[5]

The classical Marxist thinkers provided virtually no guidance on the place and functions of trade unions under socialist economic planning. After the Bolshevik Revolution in Russia in 1917, three views soon emerged on the question. Some extremists insisted that unions were no longer necessary and should be abolished, as their activities could interfere with the operation of the socialist centrally planned economy.

Some thought that trade unions ought to be retained but be transformed into an instrument of the state, and further be organized along military lines for the task of implementing production plans and maintaining work and social discipline; M. V. Frunze (a Bolshevik military Commander) and L. D. Trotsky were amongst the supporters of this approach.

There was another group, led by A. C. Shlyapnikov (at that time, the Labour Commissar in the Soviet Government), Aleksandra M. Kollontai and S. P. Medvedev, which was opposed to a bureaucratic domination of the economy by the party and the state. Instead they favoured the development of society along syndicalist lines and they pressed for economic administration to be handed over to trade unions (whilst the communist party should limit itself to the political sphere).

None of those views was acceptable to Lenin, who considered them to be inconsistent with his model of the socialist centrally planned economy under the conditions of the dictatorship of the proletariat. He contended that trade unions should be subordinated to the communist party and their function was to act as 'transmission belts' from the socialist state to the workers. He envisaged the trade union organization as 'a school of administration, a school of economic management, a school of communism' and a link between the vanguard [the party] and the masses'.[6]

Lenin further postulated that unions be tightly organized into a centralized hierarchical system, in accordance with the principle of 'democratic centralism' (as the communist party was). This means that union officials were to be elected democratically, but each union entity was to be subordinated to the next higher level of authority, finally headed by the Central Council. At the same time, he decided that the revolutionary process in the USSR should be in the hands of the Soviets (political councils), not trade unions, and he urged a similar approach to revolution in other countries.

The trade union establishment was finally developed and institutionalized in the 1930s, in the atmosphere of Stalinist authoritarianism and the disregard of human rights. After the Second World War, the Soviet model was adopted in essence in other socialist countries, with only minor national variations. The party and state control of the trade union establishment in each country was assured.

There have been some interesting developments in China. Mao Tse-tung (noted for his fascination with peasants) was highly critical of trade unions and, unlike his rival Liu Shao-ch'i, wanted to reduce them to passive tools of the party and the state. Mao often accused the unions of siding either with the local management or the workers. After 1957 trade union congresses were suspended (in force up to 1978) and during the Cultural Revolution (1966–9) the trade union organization was virtually wiped out. The All-China Federation of Trade Unions, the national co-ordinating body, was disbanded and ceased to exist until 1978. Since April 1973, however, the Chinese trade unions have been gradually rehabilitated and the All-China Federation of Trade Unions re-established (in 1978), and the importance of trade unions has been growing ever since.

The development of trade unions usually, at least in the English-speaking and Latin American countries, preceded the formation of labour or socialist parties and in fact the former were often instrumental in establishing the latter. On the other hand in the socialist countries, trade union establishments have been essentially created, or radically remodelled by the party and the state after the communist seizure of power. A similar sequence has applied to some newly liberated less-developed countries where trade unions were either established by the new governments, or were re-organized to adopt a more positive attitude to the state authority.

Up to 1980, the trade union establishment in each socialist country had been party and state controlled, in one way or another, and there had been no officially recognized independent trade unions free from authority or manipulation. But in that year, an independent union organization emerged in Poland, and some attempts have been made in several other socialist countries along similar lines (for details, see section D of this chapter).

B. TRADE UNIONS' ORGANIZATION AND FUNCTIONS

Under capitalism, trade unions basically operate within the environment of the private ownership of the means of production, the freedom of enterprise, the market mechanism, parliamentary democracy and democratic freedoms. Stemming from the democratic tradition, there is a great variety amongst trade unions not only between different countries but also within each country. In each country there is a national trade union body, but there are many unions which are not affiliated to it and operate independently. Some unions are peaceful, respectable and even plain conservative, and some are unpredictable, irresponsible, disruptive or corruptible. In many countries (especially in Europe and Africa) some unions have come under the influence of religion (the Catholic or Protestant churches in particular).

Although many unions accept the capitalist system and the need for collaboration with employers and the state, others condemn capitalism and work towards its replacement by socialism, communism, syndicalism or anarchism, by evolution or by revolution. Communist influence may be quite strong in some unions (especially in metal-working, on the water-front, in construction), either by virtue of large communist membership or in some cases simply by the infiltration of the unions' administration. Such unions are noted for disruptive industrial disputes, some of which are politically motivated, as has been the case (for example) in France and Italy. A Nigerian labour specialist recently concluded: 'Throughout the history of the Nigerian labour movement Marxists have always contributed to the split, bitterness and division of workers along ideological lines.'[7]

Trade unionism is best developed in Western democratic countries, where it is steeped in a long history and a tradition of clear class divisions and conflicts. Furthermore, unions have a greater scope for their activities in a pluralist society, rather than in a unitary state. As Joan Robinson once explained:

> Unions are not something foreign to capitalism, but are an absolutely essential part of its machinery. Union pressure, which counters monopolistic tendencies and holds profits in bounds, is necessary for the realization of profits. A strong labour movement is required to save capitalism from its 'internal contradictions'.[8]

In some less-developed countries (especially in Africa), where there are no traditionally antagonistic social classes, trade unions are much more closely associated with the state and participate in administration and economic planning.

Trade union membership in the developed West is typically within the range of 50–65 per cent of the workforce, but in less-developed countries the proportion is much smaller and in some primitive agricultural communities in fact negligible. Trade union funds are derived from membership fees and occasionally donations by the employing firms, not from the state or political parties. On the contrary, unions may have to pay fines to the state for violating legislation or court awards, and it is rather the allied political parties that rely on unions for funds.

In the socialist countries, trade unions are qualitatively different organizations from those in the West, so much so that some specialists in the field consider their description as 'trade unions' to be inappropriate.[9] These labour organizations exist in an environment of the socialized means of production, economic planning (which determines directions of development and the distribution of resources), a well-developed police system, restricted civil liberties and the mono-party system of government exercised by the communist party elite. In spite of some national differences, the trade union set-up in each socialist country is similar, patterned on the Soviet model developed between the two World Wars along Leninist ideas (for exceptions to these generalizations, see section C of this chapter).

In each country, the official trade union establishment is organized according to the principle of 'democratic centralism' – a hierarchical structure headed by a single supreme body, the lower organs being subject to the higher ones and all officials being elected. But there is considerable decentralization and local autonomy in China, Poland and Yugoslavia. As a rule, the unions are organized along unitary industrial (as distinct from craft or occupational) lines. Each union embraces blue and white-collar workers, foremen, various specialists and managers.[10] In this respect, the socialist trade unions rather strongly (but paradoxically) resemble medieval craft guilds and fascist and Nazi 'trade unions', which included both employees and employers.

Union membership is not compulsory, but there are some financial and social advantages of belonging to a union and there is usually mild official pressure to join one. A union is supposed to represent the interests of all workers, members and non-members alike. A relatively high proportion of the workforce is unionized, the percentage in the European Comecon countries ranging from 80 to 95 per cent, but in other socialist countries it is lower (in China it is less than 5 per cent).

Union funds are derived from membership fees, regular or occasional contributions by enterprises, cultural and sporting events, publishing and grants from the state, plus substantial state allocations in the form of buildings and finance for cultural, health, recreational and sporting purposes. For example, in China union dues are 0.5 per cent of the member's wage and the enterprise concerned contributes 2 per cent of the wage bill.[11] In the USSR, members pay about 1 per cent of their wages in union dues which yield about two-thirds of the union's income. Workplaces are required to contribute 0.15 per cent of their wage bill and may also make donations, which together represent one-tenth of the unions' income. The balance comes from various social, sporting and publishing ventures.[12]

Socialist unions have a double role. First, they participate in the implementation of policies pursued by the state under the guidance of the party. Second, more akin to the traditional functions in the capitalist world, they represent and protect the interest of workers. A Chinese union official, Ma Chun-ku, described the responsibilities of the socialist trade unions thus:

> The task of trade unions, generally speaking, is to mobilize and organize the workers and staff to consolidate the dictatorship of the proletariat and accomplish the tasks of socialist revolution and construction . . . . They are also indispensable to the workers and staff in furthering their own education. . . . trade unions protect [the] right and interests [of workers] in accordance with the policies and laws of the Party and state, . . . trade unions are a vanguard force in leading the workers in the struggle against bureaucracy.[13]

The unions' specific functions can be summarized under ten headings.

(1) *Plan implementation.* They organize meetings to discuss ways and means of fulfilling and exceeding targets, improving the quality of production and raising labour productivity. They also organize or participate in emulation campaigns in pursuit of nationally important objectives.

(2) *Worker participation in management.* They participate with management in working out the details of output norms, work incentives and the distribution of enterprise funds (especially, for example, the 'Material Incentives Fund' and the 'Socio-Cultural and Housing Fund').

(3) *Industrial legislation.* They participate in initiating laws and regulations on safety and health standards and amenities in workplaces, and supervise the implementation and maintenance of facilities in good condition.

(4) *Workers' grievances.* They take up individual employees' complaints against management concerning such matters as qualifi-

cations, allowances, bonus payments, transfers and dismissals.

(5) *Vocational training.* They facilitate or organize training schemes for workers, make representations to educational and training institutions and advise individual workers on how and in which directions to upgrade their qualifications.

(6) *Social insurance.* They administer old age pensions, disability compensation and sickness benefits.[14]

(7) *Ideological and civic education.* They co-operate in developing keen political and social consciousness in the Marxist spirit, cultivate the socialist attitude to work and the protection of socialized property and devise rules for work discipline.

(8) *Mass cultural activities.* They organize study circles and theatrical groups, operate 'palaces of culture' and reading rooms and engage in extensive publishing activities.

(9) *Recreation.* They organize social, sporting, art, craft and other hobby acitivies, maintain club rooms, cinemas, holiday centres and rest homes, arrange excursions, help organize summer vacations for children and promote tourism.

(10) *Other functions.* They organize co-operative housing construction, help establish and maintain nurseries for working parents, supervise hygienic and amenity standards in restaurants and shops, send workers to sanatoria and convalescent homes, participate in municipal planning and provide or canvas assistance to members in emergency.

From the above discusion it can be concluded, as has been by a Western specialist in the field that 'the rights of trade union members [in the socialist countries] are meagre but their duties are extensive'.[15]

Trade unions may also play a role in workers' participation in management. For details, see Chapter 5D.

C. TRADE UNIONS AND THE STATE

The attitude and relation of trade unions to the state differ widely according to the country and the type of trade union, which may further vary from time to time with changes in government. The ILO has traditionally (especially since the Second World War) sought to reassert or preserve the freedom and independence of trade unions. This is indicated particularly by the following Conventions.

(1) No. 11, The Right of Association (Agriculture), of 1921.
(2) No. 84, The Right of Association (Non-Metropolitan Territories), of 1947.
(3) No. 87, The Freedom of Association and Protection of the Right to Organize, of 1948.
(4) No. 98, Right to Organize and Collective Bargaining, of 1949.
(5) No. 151, Labour Relations (Public Service), of 1978.

In the democratic capitalist countries, trade unions can be freely formed and the state does not normally intervene in their activities, including the election of officials. There may be close links with a left-wing political party, particularly if the latter gets into power. But even then, unions do not necessarily co-operate with the state (and in some countries, such as Britain, it is said that unions prefer to negotiate with a right-wing rather than a left-wing government).

In general, the unions' attitude and practices in relation to publicly owned workplaces are not much different from those to private firms. In fact, the publicly owned entities may be the first target of industrial action, as political pressure may help win the demands, and the concessions can then be used as a model to be extended to the private sector. There are many well-known cases of labour organizations being more aggressive and militant in the public sector, as is illustrated by coalminers in Britain and France, postal workers in Australia, Canada and the USA, air traffic controllers in Australia and the Federal Republic of Germany and teachers in most Western countries.

In some less-developed countries (such as Algeria, Israel, Tunisia and, especially, Mexico), unions are co-opted to the ruling state machinery and participate in economic administration, and even in political activities ('political unionism'). In some countries, unions are re-organized, placed under state control and their leaders either appointed by the government or subject to official approval.

This is particularly so in a number of African states (such as Ghana), where there is no traditional class division along Western lines and there are not enough skilled workers and experienced activists to provide the backbone and leadership for assertive unions. In some other (such as Egypt and many Latin American countries), unions are prohibited from engaging in political activities. In still others, trade unions are virtually banned by the state, as in South Africa.

In some countries communist parties are illegal, viz., Algeria, Bangladesh, Bolivia, Brazil, Burma, Chile, Egypt, El Salvador, Guatemala, Haiti, Honduras, Indonesia, Iran, Jordan, Republic of

[South] Korea, Malaysia, Nepal, Nicaragua, Nigeria, Pakistan, Paraguay, the Philippines, Saudi Arabia, Sudan, Thailand, Tunisia, Turkey and Uruguay. In such countries, the open communist influence on trade unions is impeded. But in practice, in many cases, communists instead infiltrate the unions and use them as their legal front organizations. Some unions, particularly those dominated by communists or anarcho-syndicalists (as, for example, in Brazil, Chile, France, India or Nigeria) may work towards the destruction of the capitalist state and the replacement of it with some form of communism or anarchism.

The relation of trade unions to the state is of a different order altogether in the socialist countries. In contrast to the West, the trade union organization in each country was established or reorganized by the political establishment (the communist party) and has in fact become a state instrument – even though it is officially denied that it is an integral part of the state machinery. It is often stressed that under socialism the interests of the workers and of the state are 'identical', as the exploiting classes have been eliminated, the workers own their workplaces and the government represents the working class. But in practice this system has not worked as idealistically as implied.

In contrast to democratic capitalism (where the multi-party system prevails), in each socialist country there is a mono-party system of government exercised by the communist party through the socialist state, with no legal opposition to unseat the government in democratic elections. Furthermore (again in contrast to capitalism) the effective owner of the means of production is the state, the employer is the state, the manager is the state (through its appointee, the 'director') and the central planner (replacing the free market mechanism) is the state. The state is also the legislator and the enforcer of its own laws, aided by an extensive network of militia (police) and the powerful and over-developed secret police. There are well-known violations of human rights – the freedoms of speech, correspondence, the press, association, peaceful demonstration and of travel. Although these rights are usually guaranteed on paper, there is no machinery for their enforcement, the courts are not independent and in any case there is usually immunity of the socialist state from legal actions by private citizens. The hard facts of life are that, even though the system means well, in reality control over the means of production and political power are concentrated in the hands of a privileged elite which has proved far from perfect.

Officially it is claimed that socialist trade unions are not part of the state administrative set-up but 'independent public organizations'. This claim is of little practical consolation to ordinary trade unionists, as the communist party dominates both. Thus in the new Soviet Constitution (adopted in October 1977) Article 6 clearly states:

> The Communist Party of the Soviet Union is the leading and guiding force of Soviet Society and the nucleus of its political system and of state and public organizations.

Socialist trade unions are not free to strike (with some exceptions, see Chapter 9A) and their officials are not freely elected by workers, but are essentially nominated by the communist party and are likely to be more loyal to the Marxist state than to ordinary union members and workers in general. The unions' responsibilities are extensive and in many cases burdensome, but most of them have nothing to do with the protection of the ordinary workers against their powerful employer. For a long time, at least up to the 1970s, collective farmers were denied the right to form unions, and yet they needed protection more than other sections of the working community.

Crucial economic decision-making is exercised by central planners, and locally by enterprise managers in accordance with the widely accepted principle of one-man managerial responsibility. The ultimate control of trade unions rests with the party which exercises it through the party members (who often are union officials) and the allocation of funds. In many respects, trade unions are closer to management and the state than to the workers.

The official trade union establishments do not protect or help the worker much. A Soviet dissident, V. Bukovsky (now in the West), revealed that, in the USSR, workers' complaints reported to trade unions are in some cases handed over by the latter to the dreaded *KGB*.[16] But even in Hungary – one of the most liberal socialist countries – it was bluntly admitted in the organ of the Central Council of Trade Unions that the 'unions often co-operate with management . . . to identify trouble-makers and recommend their dismissal'.[17]

State authoritarianism in socialist trade unions, and in industrial relations in general, remained for a long time virtually unchanged. But in spite of various forms of suppression, the official establishments have been increasingly subjected to critical reappraisal, especially since the late 1970s. The most dramatic and far-reaching moves towards free trade unionism have so far occurred in Poland, but attempts in other socialist countries have not been lacking either. We shall consider these developments in the following section.

D. INDEPENDENT UNIONISM UNDER SOCIALISM

(a) Solidarity in Poland

Although the beginnings of free trade unionism in Poland go back to at least the late 1970s, its official emergence came in late 1980, following steep price increases (ranging from 20 to 100 per cent) on 1 July, 1980. In August, the Inter-Factory Strike Committee, based in the Lenin Shipyard in Gdansk, formulated 21 demands addressed to the government (not merely to the managements of the enterprises involved). The demands were not only of industrial but also of political content. Those of greatest interest to us can be summarized in ten points.

(1) Free trade unionism, independent from the party and from employers, and the abolition of administrative interference in trade union affairs.
(2) The right to strike and safety for all strikers, including persons who help them.
(3) The appointment of managerial staff according to qualifications, and not party membership.
(4) The abolition of special shops and similar other privileges for the party and security services.
(5) The revision of censorship laws.
(6) The release of political prisoners.
(7) Access for all religious denominations to mass media (including telecasting church services).
(8) Automatic wage increases to compensate for price increases.
(9) Priority to supplying the domestic market over exports.
(10) Other industrial, economic and political demands, including far-reaching economic reforms.

In the face of widespread strikes, the government accepted these demands 'in principle' (and with some qualifications) in the first of the three historic moves, viz. the Gdansk Agreement, on 30 August, 1980. In the following month, the IFSC was transformed into the Independent Self-Governing Trade Union 'Solidarity'. But to be legally recognized, it was required to register with the District Court in Warsaw and submit its constitution for approval.

The Court ruled that the submitted constitution must be supplemented with a clause on the 'leading role of the party' in the union's affairs. However, Solidarity raised objection to the clause and insisted on self-government and independence from any party organization or state institution, and appealed to the Supreme Court.

In the appended supplement, Solidarity referred to the Conventions of the International Labour Organization, viz. No. 87 ('Convention Concerning Freedom of Association and Protection of the Right to Organize', of July 1948) and No. 98 ('Convention Concerning the Application of the Principles of the Right to Organize and to Bargain Collectively', of June 1949). The point is that Poland is not only a member of the ILO (having joined it in 1919), but has also ratified the two Conventions under the communist regime. At the same time, Solidarity recognized the 'leading role' of the party in the state, but not in its own affairs.

In the second historic event, on 10 November, 1980 the Supreme Court upheld the appeal and ruled that the insistence of the party's supremacy in Solidarity's affairs was unconstitutional and inconsistent with international treaties.

But there was also widespread dissatisfaction amongst the 3.2 m private farmers who own and operate over 80 per cent of the farming land in the country. Peasant groups embarked upon a number of sit-ins and strikes, protesting against discriminatory treatment of private farming and favouritism to state farms. An organization was created, called briefly 'Rural Solidarity', which soon applied for registration on the grounds that its members are in effect state employees, as the state sets prices and conditions of delivery contracts. But the Supreme Court did not recognize it as a trade union, as in its view the peasants were self-employed and consequently could not bargain as employees. However, in response to continued pressure from the dissatisfied peasants, in the third historic landmark, the government yielded, and on 17 April, 1981 agreed to recognize the organization as an independent union. It was duly registered as such by the District Court in Warsaw on 12 May, 1981 under the name of 'Independent Self-Governing Trade Union of the Individual Farmers "Solidarity"'.

Solidarity is organized and operates along democratic lines, in contrast to the hierarchical authoritarian establishment in existence before. Local unions are grouped into strong regional fraternities (about 50), which are affiliated to the national body called the National Co-ordinating Commission (consisting of 102 delegates). This is headed by its policy-making Presidium (of 12 members) led by the charismatic figure of Lech Wałęsa (pronounced Lekh Vahwensa). Solidarity's membership is 9.5 m, embracing about 90 per cent of the country's workers. Rural Solidarity is organized along similar lines and its membership is about 1.5 m. Thus between them, they have 11 m members. It may be mentioned that the membership of the Polish United Workers Party (the ruling communist party) in 1981 was 2.8 m, of whom 1 m belonged to Solidarity.

In addition to Solidarity, there are other independent unions grouped into 'Autonomous Trade Unions' (about 650 000 members, mostly skilled workers and professionals), plus a number of small, unit unions. The old union establishment was formally dissolved at the end of 1980, but its orthodox remnants have survived and were transformed into the officially supported 'Branch Trade Unions' organization, also calling itself 'independent', with a membership of about 2 m.

It must be pointed out that Solidarity arose amongst ordinary industrial workers, not necessarily opposed to Marxism but rather to the abuses of the entrenched and privileged communist oligarchy. The spectacular success of Solidarity before martial law was imposed on 13 December, 1981 had been due not only to widespread popular support, but also to expert advice provided by the influential Catholic Church and dedicated dissident intellectuals.

Although formal political power in Poland is still in party hands (even though temporarily exercised by the Military Council, headed by General W. Jaruzelski), Solidarity commands overwhelming popular support. In a public opinion poll conducted at the end of 1980, 89 per cent of the interviewed people said that Solidarity would protect workers' interests better than the old establishment, and only 3 per cent thought that it would not (8 per cent were uncertain); 54 per cent of the Party interviewees conceded that they supported Solidarity.[18] In another poll, in May 1981, the ranking of different organizations in the country according to public esteem and trust was (in descending order): (1) the Catholic Church, (2) Solidarity, (3) the army. On that scale, Branch Trade Unions were ranked 9, and the party 14.[19]

The significance of Solidarity in Poland and in the international arena can be briefly highlighted as follows.

(1) Solidarity arose not amongst former capitalists or even intel-lectuals, but essentially amongst the ordinary industrial workers, supposedly the very mainstay of communist power.
(2) For the first time in the socialist bloc, it succeeded in bringing dissatisfied worker groups together to act collectively on a national scale against tremendous odds.
(3) It represents the first free legal trade union movement under

socialism, independent of the party and the state.

(4) It successfully achieved the legality of strike action in a socialist centrally planned economy.

(5) It won several non-industrial concessions from the socialist state, such as some diminution of censorship, some de-monopolization of the state's access to the media, the release of some political prisoners and some democratization of parliamentary and party procedures.

(6) The official recognition of Rural Solidarity amounts to the admission that under socialist central economic planning even the self-employed are in effect employees of the state, considering the latter's dominant powers over incomes, prices (agricultural *and* industrial) and other terms in mutual dealings.

(7) For the first time in the socialist bloc, a close working relationship has been established between ordinary industrial workers and peasants on the one hand, and intellectual dissidents, on the other – to considerable mutual benefit.

(8) The movement has directly or indirectly succeeded in removing several top party and government leaders from power, not to mention a large number of over-zealous and authoritarian local party, police and bureaucratic bosses abusing their power. This indicates that rulers can be unseated under socialism – not through the ballot in democratic elections by the opposition, but by free organized labour using the instrument of the strike.

(9) For the first time, a major reform of the communist system was achieved by actions 'from below' (whilst in the past major changes were imposed 'from above'). This unprecedented upheaval was an outcome not of reckless violence, but of cautious industrial action and piecemeal negotiations.

(10) Solidarity has received widespread support from individuals, trade unions and international organizations outside the socialist bloc and some suppressed or open sympathy in several socialist countries.

At the beginning of 1982 the future of Solidarity appeared uncertain. Under the Martial Law, promulgated on 13 December, 1981, thousands of Solidarity leaders and sympathizers were 'interned' (including Lech Wałęsa). Normal trade union activities were severely restricted and strikes were declared illegal, but the remnant Solidarity leadership has apparently continued its work underground. Some judges refused to prosecute arrested Solidarity leaders and the Minister for Justice, S.

Zawadzki, threatened (in late January, 1982) to resign if the military authorities continued to intimidate judges.

(b) The situation in other socialist countries

The traditional Leninist trade union establishments still prevail in the remaining socialist countries. But the Polish free trade unionism has caused many a headache to the ruling elites, because workers in these countries suffer from similar problems. Bulgarian, Czechoslovak, East German, Hungarian and especially Soviet leaders have been most eager to issue statements condemning Solidarity. The official organ of the Communist Party of the Soviet Union described Solidarity's activities as follows:

> The strategy of these moves [by Solidarity] is to create conditions for undermining socialist relations and the workers' state, and for instituting dual power leading to political pluralism for the sake of counter-revolutionary objectives.[20]

Nevertheless, in recent years some efforts have been made, in at least such countries as the USSR, China, Czechoslovakia, the German Democratic Republic, Romania and Yugoslavia, to form independent unions, or at least give more power to the existing unions to protect workers. Thus in the USSR two known attempts have been made.

In February 1978 the Free Trade Union Association of Workers in the Soviet Union was created on the initiative of a Ukrainian coal miner (V. Klebanov) and it existed up to June 1978. It produced a Charter and appealed to the ILO for registration (which was rejected, on the grounds that it was not an official national organization). In its Charter, the FTUA declared:

> All high-ranking officials – our servants as they love to style themselves – are guarded against us by policemen . . . . Soviet trade unions do not protect our rights and lack the requisite authority since the key union posts are filled by Communists. . . . . We have decided therefore to organize our own genuinely independent trade union, in order to gain the official and legal status needed for the defense of our rights and interests.[21]

However, the organizers of the FTUA were soon arrested and either committed to psychiatric hospitals, imprisoned or exiled from

Moscow.[22] In October 1978, the Free Interprofessional Association of Workers in the USSR was formed (also known by its Russian abbreviation, *SMOT*). Its declared objective is the defence of the economic, social, religious and political rights of its members, and possibly aid to other workers as well. Its Council of Representatives, representing at least two free trade unions, decided this time not to deal with the ILO, but to apply for affiliation to the International Confederation of Free Trade Unions (based in Brussels).[23] However, the impact of these unions has so far been negligible, limited only to dissident union organizers and intellectuals, numbering only about 200.[24] The mass of the workers has been untouched and is not even aware of these developments.

In early 1981, it was reported that workers in the Chinese,industrial city of Wuhan (on the Yangtse River) attempted to form independent unions, free from party control along Solidarity lines.[25] This attempt was officially condemned and it is not known how successful this or other attempts have been. In Romania after the strikes in Jiu Valley in August 1977, a Free Labour Union was initiated, but in March 1979 its 30–40 leaders and activists were arrested, dispersed or escaped abroad.[26] In Bulgaria and Hungary trade unions have won the right of vetoing management's decisions violating workers' specified interests. In Hungary the unions can also institute legal proceedings against persons or workplaces not observing the labour code and collective agreements.[27]

In Yugoslavia, with the development of workers' self-management since 1950, trade unions have largely lost their function as 'transmission belts' for state policies and have assumed a more detached stand. Tito himself regarded unions as champions of workers' rights and encouraged them to exert pressure on the government and management to protect workers' interests.

As has been pointed out above (p. 77), Solidarity effectively exploited Poland's membership of the ILO and her ratification of Conventions 87 (on the freedom of association) and 98 (on the right to bargain collectively).[28] It must be realized that virtually all other socialist countries (Albania, China and the Democratic People's Republic of [North] Korea being the only exceptions) are members of the ILO. Moreover, up to January 1981 not only Poland but also Benin, Bulgaria, Cuba, Czechoslovakia, East Germany, Hungary, Mongolia, Romania, the USSR and Yugoslavia had ratified Conventions 87 and 98, and Guinea-Bissau, Vietnam and South Yemen, Convention 98. Thus, if in these countries dissident trade unions emerged and applied to appropriate courts for registration, the applications could not be rejected without violating ILO conventions. One wonders in which socialist country this strategem will be tested next?

However, it must be recognized that, in contrast to Poland, other socialist countries have no powerful church establishment, no such well-organized and forthright intellectual dissidents and no such dynamic working class with a tradition of resistance and struggle for independence. On this score, free trade unionism in these countries, if it continues to develop, is unlikely to burst in such a spectacular and pregnant manner as in Poland.

Independent trade unionism has raised not only serious political questions, but also a fundamental economic problem: can a centrally planned economy – with its predetermined targets and wage funds – function effectively in the context of strikes, unplanned wage increases and unscheduled improvements in other working and living conditions? This problem appears to be unresolved as yet. Its resolution would necessitate far-reaching liberal economic reforms to make planning more flexible and perhaps reduce ambitious developmental programmes in favour of substantial improvements in the current standards of living.

E. COLLECTIVE BARGAINING

Collective bargaining consists in negotiations between organized labour and an employer (or a group of employers), involving terms and conditions of employment. The qualification 'collective' applies to labour indicating that an individual worker is in an inferior position versus his employer and only collective action gives the workers bargaining power comparable to their employer's.

The forms, extent and content of collective bargaining differ widely from one country to another, reflecting historical antecedents, the stage of economic and social development and, of course, the political and economic system in force. In general, collective bargaining is most developed in the industrialized West and least in authoritarian or semi-feudal less-developed regions, whilst in the socialist bloc it has a different façade, frame and buttresses.

The beginnings of collective bargaining go back to mid-nineteenth century Britain. But a new era began in the 1930s, when American labour became a successful pioneer in several respects, after the passage of the Norris–La Guardia Act of 1932 and the National Labour Relations Act of 1935; those two Acts made it illegal for an employer to refuse to bargain in good faith with the employees' representatives.

Collective bargaining has also become an important feature of the industrial scene in other industrialized capitalist countries. But on the whole, its scope is wider in the countries where industrial legislation, workers' participation and the social welfare system are less comprehensive and advanced, as is the case in the USA in contrast to Western Europe. More recently, collective bargaining has spread to many parts of the Third World, especially to many Latin American countries since the mid-1970s.[29]

At first collective bargaining was preoccupied with wages and soon after with hours of work. But it has now come to encompass a wide variety of matters associated with work and employment, such as working rules, discipline, promotion, vocational training, rest periods, sick leave, annual leave, pensions, hiring, dismissals and even the employers' investment policies. The recognition and status of organized labour and procedures for negotiation may also be included. Originally, collective agreements typically covered only one year, but now two or three years are more common. In the socialist countries annual agreements are most usual, but in some cases periods of up to five years may be covered.

Most countries in the world (viz. 108 out of 143 ILO members) have ratified the 'Convention Concerning the Application of the Principle of the Right to Organize and Bargain Collectively' (No. 98, of 1949). See Table 3.2.[30] (Only one ILO Convention has received more ratifications, viz. that on Forced Labour, No. 29, of 1930). The percentage of wage-earners covered by collective agreements in the leading countries is as follows: Finland – 50 per cent, Switzerland – 66 per cent, the United Kingdom – 75 per cent, the Netherlands – 80 per cent, the Federal Republic of Germany – 90 and virtually 100 per cent in Austria, Belgium and Sweden. The number of operative agreements at the enterprise level is 200 000 in the USA and 150 000 in the USSR.[31]

In capitalist countries, collective bargaining essentially takes place between representatives of trade unions on behalf of wage (and salary) earners, on the one hand, and private employers or their organization, on the other. These two sides have traditionally been in an adversary position, because the demands of the former can usually be met, at least seemingly, only at the expense of the latter. The state is typically uninvolved in disputes (especially in Denmark, Ireland and Norway). But it may either establish an independent arbitration authority, or it may act as arbitrator detached from the two parties in conflict (for example, in Australia, Canada, Finland and several Asian countries).

Alternatively, the state may choose to support one side or the other. For example, in Brazil the government has often sided with the unions, playing them off against the entrenched, critical, landed aristocracy, whilst in many other countries the authorities often support the employers – mainly to counteract inflation. Sometimes the union and the employer may conclude a 'sweetheart agreement', whereby the cost is then passed on to the public in one form or another (for example, in higher prices, poorer quality), in which case the government may intervene if it has sufficient power and inclination.

The public sector is in a perplexing position. Collective bargaining implies the equality of the negotiating parties. But in this case, the party on the employing side is the government which in the ultimate analysis constitutes sovereign power, traditionally shared with parliament and not with its subordinate public 'servants'. However, in the last three or four decades, there has been a remarkable expansion of the state's involvement in the economy and public authorities now employ up to one-quarter of wage and salary earners (and in some countries even more). This trend has been paralleled by the growth of the power of organized labour, including the rise of white-collar unions.

As a rule, collective bargaining and parity-footing are more common in publicly owned utilities. But as these undertakings usually provide indispensable services to the public at large and the employees' demands may turn into taxpayers' liability, the public authority may utilize its powers and restrict the unions' negotiating capacity or instruct the management to be tough, itself adopting a position of aloofness or of an umpire.

In the case of publicly-owned undertakings operated on a commercial basis, collective bargaining resembles that prevailing in private firms. The government is rather remote and in general it prefers to leave negotiations to management. But the union may resort to political pressure on the government and even negotiate directly with it, particularly if a sensitive large enterprise is involved (as has been demonstrated in the case of British Leyland in Britain, ENI in Italy, Renault in France and Salzgitter in the Federal Republic of Germany). In some authoritarian capitalist countries, collective bargaining is tripartite, that is, representatives of the unions, employers and the state are involved, as in Chile, Costa Rica and Peru (similar to that in fascist Italy and Nazi Germany).

The Marxist approach to collective bargaining is quite complex. In application to capitalist countries, the need for a collective stand is emphasized owing to the inherently weak bargaining power of individual workers versus their capitalist employer. But revolutionary Marxists are basically opposed to it, as in their view it merely leads to a compromise, class collaboration and the preservation of capitalism, thereby only delaying the need for the proletarian revolution.

On the other hand, under socialism or communism collective bargaining is viewed as an essentially co-operative process to serve the needs of the state and society. In the present socialist centrally planned economies the term 'collective bargaining' has been retained, but in reality its affinity to the traditionally understood meaning virtually ends there.

The official view is that workers own the means of production, the socialist state is their government and managers are the workers' indirect appointees. Hence, in negotiations, unions, cannot adopt an adversary stand either against the well-meaning management or the paternalistic state, as otherwise it would amount to a logical contradiction – labour bargaining with, and seeking to soak, labour. A Soviet trade union leader, A. Brailov, in answer to his rhetorical question, 'Against whom are workers to be protected in the USSR?', said: 'against the extraordinary departmental zeal and bureaucracy of certain managers who distort Soviet policies in production democracy, fail to organize production properly and neglect legislation and collective agreements'.[32]

Trade unions officially have the right to enter into collective agreements, either with the enterprise management or (in fact in most cases) with the branch associations covering the whole industry. But these 'collective agreements' (or 'collective contracts' as they are sometimes called) are not negotiated on an equal footing, but rather prescribed within the framework of the largely predetermined economic plan and the existing Labour Code. The 'agreements' are essentially directed towards the most effective fulfilment and over-fulfilment of targets and related tasks.

They typically embody provisions for the organization of work, the norms of output, the introduction of new technology, the improvement of the relevant skills, the growth of productivity, workers' participation, break periods and labour discipline. At the same time, the agreements embody pledges by the management or the state in regard to material incentives, labour safety measures, the improvement of working conditions, consumer supplies, recreation and other welfare measures. They are then registered with the arbitration tribunal which, in case of subsequent disputes hands out a ruling guided primarily by the 'social interest'.

Collective agreements are not negotiated in all workplaces, but rather in the more important enterprises or branches of the economy. The proportion of the working population (outside the military forces) covered by the agreements in the European socialist countries ranges from one-third to two-thirds. Thus in the USSR, the branches covered are industry, construction, trade, agriculture and forestry, transport, communications, public catering and some other services. In Poland collective agreements are concluded mostly at the branch-of-industry or economy levels, involving ministries or branch associations, on the one hand, and branch trade unions, on the other.

But in most other socialist countries, agreements at the enterprise level are also concluded. In the German Democratic Republic provisions are now specifically included to protect or enhance the position of women and young persons. Collective agreements are typically concluded for one year (usually in February), but in Hungary the periods may be longer – up to five years.[33] In Yugoslavia, there are no collective agreements either in the capitalist or the socialist sense. Under self-management, Workers' Councils settle controversial questions in each Basic Organization of Associated Labour within the framework of the guidelines laid down by the state.

Taking a broader view, we may conclude with the following generalizations on collective bargaining under the different social systems. It has helped remove some of the inherent weaknesses of capitalism. Collective bargaining can be looked upon as a form of workers' participation; it has tended to reduce strikes and the standards agreed upon in many cases are adopted as national norms. From the original defensive position, workers, through their increasingly powerful trade unions, have come to play an assertive part, especially in the industrialized Western countries.

An official of the ILO described collective bargaining 'as a flexible and dynamic instrument for reconciling the interest of capital and labour and promote . . . healthy industrial relations', and 'as an effective means of redistributing income'.[34] Another specialist in the field pointed out that 'Collective bargaining has created a system of constitutionalism or industrial jurisprudence . . . . Autocratic capitalism has been greatly modified by collective bargaining . . . which has thereby contributed to continued acceptance of private property and private enterprise'.[35]

However, in some respects, the process of collective bargaining has proved disappointing to the workers or the public. Some workers may not be organized in trade unions (for example, over 80 per cent in the USA). Although collective bargaining may take place with workers organized only on an *ad hoc* basis (as, for example, in Chile, Costa Rica, Ecuador, Peru, Uruguay, Venezuela), they are less capable of pursuing their demands on a systematic basis.[36] There are many small trade unions whose bargaining power may be weak in relation to their large or organized employers. This is particularly so in many less-developed countries, where unions and non-union labour are manipulated by employers, on the one hand, and by the state, on the other.

Conversely, in industries where unions are powerful, the conditions enjoyed by their members may be disproportionately better than in those of their less fortunate brethren elsewhere. Powerful unions (sometimes described as 'labour monopoly') may, by their excessive demands, cause unreasonable damage to employers, foment inflation, reduce the level of employment and may inconvenience and even exasperate the public.

The limitations of collective bargaining are particularly prevalent in the socialist centrally planned economies. With the qualified exceptions of Poland and Yugoslavia, the most critical terms and conditions of work and employment, such as standard wage scales, wage funds, standard hours of work, holidays, indicators regulating bonuses, are centrally determined, and thus are pre-empted from collective negotiations. Moreover, with the exception of Poland and Yugoslavia, trade unions are not in a position to go on strike, although this weapon has traditionally been considered, in the democratic capitalist world, to be indispensable.

Even in Hungary, where collective bargaining is supposed to play a prominent part under the New Economic Model, collective agreements are not what one would expect them to be. J. L. Porket appraised them as follows:

But in negotiating them, enterprise trade union committees showed inertia, incompetence and timidity. And the collective agreements themselves were often adopted without effective participation of the workers and suffered from the omission of significant issues and inclusion of excessive detail and trivia.[37]

F. INTERNATIONAL TRADE UNIONISM

The beginnings of the international trade union movement go back to 1864, when the International Workingmen's Association was created in

London (in which Marx was one of the most active leaders). It originally linked workers' organizations in England, France, Germany and Italy, but it soon extended to other European countries. It lasted up to 1876 and was followed by the Second International, 1889–1919 (while the IWA was referred to as the 'First International').

The first two Internationals combined industrial and political objectives, with an increasing emphasis on the latter. But after the First World War the two aspects of the international labour movement became clearly separated, with a proliferation of organizations in each stream reflecting ideological differences. On the political side, the following warrant mentioning. The Third International (better known as 'Comintern', with a revolutionary Marxist programme, in existence from 1919 to 1943), the Second-and-a-Half International (moderate socialist, 1921–23), the Labour and Socialist International (social-democratic, 1923–51), the Fourth International (Trotskyite, 1938–), Cominform (revolutionary Marxist, 1947–56) and the Socialist International (social-democratic, 1951–).

Similarly, the industrial side of the working class movement has suffered from ideological differences, with a consequent lack of unity on the world scale. Soon after the First World War the following organizations emerged.

(1) The International Federation of Trade Unions – moderate socialist and social-democratic, in existence from 1919 to 1945.
(2) The International Federation of Christian Trade Unions – dominated by Christian churches, 1920–68.
(3) The International Workers' Association – anarcho-syndicalist, 1922– .
(4) *Profintern* (abbreviated from the Russian *Profsoyuznyi Internatsional*, meaning the 'Trade Union International') – this organization, also known as the 'Red International of Labour Unions (or the 'Red Labour International'), was created in 1921 and was based in Moscow; it united revolutionary trade unions under the general auspices of Comintern and its purpose was to encourage and co-ordinate trade union activities in different countries, designed to lead to proletarian revolutions on the industrial front.

After the Second World War, most of the above union organizations were transformed into new ones, whilst the one which was not (the IWA) is now virtually inactive. The three world trade union organizations today, arranged in ascending order of left-wing radicalism, are as follows.

(a) The International Confederation of Free Trade Unions

It was founded in London in 1949 in protest against the communist domination of the World Federation of Trade Unions (created in 1945, see below). The ICFTU is an indirect successor to the International Federation of Trade Unions and it supports social-democratic principles of government and is opposed to revolutionary tactics and to totalitarian as well as to imperialist oppression.

Its activities are directed towards the promotion of such goals as the dignity of labour, higher levels of employment, the improvement of working conditions, the introduction and extension of social security and a worldwide system of collective security. The ICFTU's headquarters are in Brussels, with branch secretariats in Geneva and New York and regional offices in Mexico, Monrovia, New Delhi and Djakarta. It represents 126 national centres and unions in 90 non-socialist countries, with a total membership of 70m (in 1980).

Under its auspices are also the European Trade Union Confederation (founded in 1973 and embracing unions in the European Economic Community and the European Free Trade Association) and the following 'Associated International Trade Secretariats'.

(1) International Federation of Building and Wood Workers (founded in 1896 and based in Geneva).
(2) International Federation of Chemical and General Workers' Union (1904, Geneva).
(3) International Federation of Commercial, Clerical and Technical Employees (1904, Geneva).
(4) International Federation of Free Teachers' Unions (1951, Brussels).
(5) International Federation of Petroleum and Chemical Workers (1954, Denver, USA).
(6) International Federation of Plantation, Agriculture and Allied Workers (1959, Geneva).
(7) International Graphical Federation (1949, Zurich).
(8) International Metalworkers' Federation (1893, Geneva).
(9) International Secretariat of Entertainment Trade Unions (1965, Vienna).

(10) International Textile, Garment and Leather Workers' Federation (1970, Brussels).
(11) International Transport Workers' Federation (1896, London).
(12) International Union of Food and Allied Workers Association (1920, Petit-Lancy, Switzerland).
(13) Miners' International Federation (1890, London).
(14) Postal, Telegraph and Telephone International (1920, Geneva).
(15) Public Service International (1935, Feltham, England).
(16) Universal Alliance of Diamond Workers (1905, Antwerp).

(b) The World Confederation of Labour

This organization subscribes to religious ideals and is a broadened successor to the International Federation of Christian Trade Unions, having adopted its present name in 1968. The WCL's headquarters are also in Brussels, aided with regional offices in Geneva, Montreal, Caracas and Manila. It embraces affiliated national (con)federations and trade 'internationals' in 78 non-socialist countries (with the conspicuous exceptions of Sweden, the United Kingdom and the USA). Its total membership is about 15m.

The WCL's declared objectives are to defend workers' interests and to develop human society united in freedom, labour dignity, justice and fraternity, irrespective of creed, race, nationality and sex, and it is guided by the Universal Declaration of Human Rights and the United Nations Charter. In its activities, it attaches a good deal of importance to the training of labour leaders and technical specialists for the less-developed countries of Africa, Asia and Latin America.

In recent years the WCL has steered a course to the left, in some cases sympathetic to Marxism and the socialist countries, probably through its association with the World Council of Churches which is considered by many observers in the West to be an international communist front organization. In several respects the WCL has followed a middle course between the conservative or moderate and rather complacent ICFTU and the militant, communist-dominated WFTU. In his encyclical proclaimed in 1981, Pope John Paul II urged trade unions to press for radical changes in the Third World to improve the lot of agricultural workers and poor peasants.[38]

Affiliated to the WCL are the following international organizations.

(1) International Federation of Christian Miners' Union (founded in 1901, with its present secretariat in Brussels).

(2) International Federation of Christian Trade Unions of Graphical and Paper Industries (1925, Amsterdam).
(3) International Federation of Textile and Garment Workers (1901, Ghent, Belgium).
(4) International Federation of Trade Unions of Employees in Public Service (1922, Brussels).
(5) International Federation of Trade Unions of Transport Workers (WCL) (1921, Brussels).
(6) World Federation of Teachers (1963, Brussels).
(7) World Federation of the Metallurgic Industry (1920, Brussels).
(8) World Federation for Energy, Chemical and Miscellaneous Industries (1920, Brussels).
(9) World Federation of Agricultural Workers (1921, Brussels).
(10) World Federation of Building and Woodworkers Unions (1936, Utrecht, the Netherlands).
(11) World Federation of Trade Unions of Non-Manual Workers (1921, Antwerp).
(12) World Federation of Workers in the Food, Drink, Tobacco and Hotel Trades (1948, Brussels).

(c) The World Federation of Trade Unions

Founded in Paris in 1945 as the successor to the International Federation of Trade Unions, it soon became dominated by the state-controlled trade union establishments of the socialist countries and some communist-led Western unions (this fact led in 1949 to the withdrawal of most Western trade unions and the formation of the ICFTU). In 1951 the WFTU was expelled from France for subversive activities and its headquarters were transferred to Vienna, from where, after another expulsion in 1956, they were finally moved to Prague.

The WFTU's declared aims include: the exchange of information and experience in trade union work, the training of workers for trade union operation and international unity, the strengthening of the international solidarity of trade unions, the enhancement of the class-consciousness of the workers in different lands and the protection and advancement of workers' interests in international organizations. It also actively supports the peace movement, co-operating with the World Peace Council. The WFTU is ideologically contemptuous of the ICFTU and the WCL, which are sometimes described as 'Yellow Internationals'.[39]

In terms of membership, the WFTU is the largest of the three international organizations, viz. 190m (of which the Soviet share is

130m). All the official trade union establishments in the 23 socialist countries (China and Yugoslavia excepted) are affiliated to it. China was an active member up to 1966, but she has ceased her involvement since, due partly to Soviet opposition and partly to domestic problems.

Yugoslavia, although not a member of any international trade union organization, has been anxious to co-operate with national trade unions in any country. Thus in April 1980 the Yugoslav Trade Union Confederation organized a World Trade Union Conference on Development to speed up economic progress in the less-developed countries; 140 trade union organizations from 90 countries (including China) participated.

About 50 non-socialist countries are represented in the membership of the WFTU. Amongst them are mostly (but not exclusively) less-developed nations; included are such countries as Argentina, Austria, Bangladesh, Brazil, Finland, France, India, Indonesia, Pakistan and the Philippines. In addition, the following 'Trade Unions Internationals' are affiliated to the WFTU.

(1) Miners' Trade Unions International (founded in 1949 and based in Warsaw).
(2) Trade Unions International of Agricultural, Forestry and Plantation Workers (1949, Prague).
(3) Trade Unions International of Chemical, Oil and Allied Workers (1950, Budapest).
(4) Trade Unions International of Metal and Engineering Workers (1949, Prague).
(5) Trade Unions International of Public and Allied Employees (1949, East Berlin).
(6) Trade Unions International of the Textile, Clothing, Leather and Fur Workers (1949, Prague).
(7) Trade Unions International of Transport Workers (1949, Prague).
(8) Trade Unions International of Workers in Commerce (1959, Prague).
(9) Trade Unions International of Workers of the Building, Wood and Building Materials Industries (1949, Helsinki).
(10) Trade Unions International of Workers of the Food, Tobacco and Beverage Industries and Hotel, Cafe and Restaurant Workers (1949, Sofia).
(11) World Federation of Teachers' Unions (1946, East Berlin).

In addition to the three world trade union organizations, there is the International Workers' Association, a revolutionary anarcho-syndicalist organization, founded in Berlin in 1922 but virtually defunct today (its present office is in Clermont-Ferrand, in France). In its programme ('Principles of Revolutionary Syndicalism') it stands for 'libertarian syndicalism' advocating a gradual transition from capitalism to liberal communism by industrial action and the transfer of production and public functions in society to trade unions. It rejects the dictatorship of the proletariat, state coercion, nationalism, militarism and political tactics. In its heyday in the late 1920s, with a membership of 3m, the IWA was very active as a co-ordinating centre for anarcho-syndicalist groups in Argentina, Chile, Denmark, France, Germany, Mexico, the Netherlands, Portugal, Spain, Sweden, Switzerland and Uruguay. It suffered from fascist and Nazi persecutions between the two World Wars. Although it held a number of meetings after the Second World War, it has not succeeded in arousing wider interest and support.

In spite of the deep-rooted ideological differences, the relations amongst the international trade union organizations have occasionally been marked by direct contacts and dealings and offers of co-operation, mostly under their own respective conditions in the so-called 'spirit of the international solidarity of the working class'. Considerable trans-ideological trade union co-operation has been achieved under the auspices of the European Trade Union Confederation in Western Europe, in its efforts towards the 'Europeanization of labour ideologies'.[40]

It may be mentioned that the ICFTU and WCL have given support to the independent trade unions in Poland (Solidarity) and the USSR (The Free Inter-Professional Association of Workers in the USSR).[41] On the other hand, the WFTU has boycotted these unions and considers only the state-controlled union establishments as legitimate spokesmen for their respective countries (even though, for example Solidarity has 11m members and the remnants of the old establishment only 2m).

A few observations are warranted on trade unions' attitudes to East–West trade and industrial co-operation. One of the sensational features of East-West trade is the occasional socialist dumping of products in Western markets at prices up to 75 per cent below the local levels, leading to the disruption of local production and losses of jobs. The low prices may be due to lower labour costs in the socialist countries ('the exploitation of labour by the socialist state'), or the disregard of certain costs (such as rent, interest and normal profit), which may be legitimate in the context of Marxist theory but are unfair and irrational by the standards and realities in capitalist private enterprise economies.[42]

Of particular concern to the trade unions in the capitalist world are the dealings of the multinational corporations with the socialist countries. Under industrial co-operation agreements, Western companies often transfer the production of labour-intensive components or products to the socialist partners. This operation presents three advantages to the Western multinationals: lower labour costs in the East, the reliability of supplies (owing to the virtual illegality of strikes there), and it also strengthens their hand in dealing with western trade unions.

For example, it was conceded in a Polish source that Fiat – plagued by frequent strikes – was sub-contracting the production of certain components to Poland, the USSR and Yugoslavia.[43] Furthermore, many multinationals, such as Chemico (USA), Fiat (Italy), ICI (UK), Linde (Federal Republic of Germany), Technip (France), Teijin (Japan) and Voest–Alpine (Austria), have constructed complete industrial plants in the socialist countries with the most efficient technology available. This enables these countries to export to the capitalist world, leading to the loss of jobs and the weakening of the Western trade unions' bargaining power.[44]

The multinationals, including multinational banks, have extended large loans at very low interest rates to, and made direct investments in, the socialist countries. Transfers of capital of this nature generate employment in the East, whilst many badly needed projects in the capitalist world are neglected. One of the first Western trade union leaders to have recognized these problems is Charles Levinson, a Canadian and the Secretary-General of the International Federation of Chemical and General Workers Union (affiliated to the ICFTU).[45] What is further surprising is the fact that, as was pointed out in the organ of the ICFTU, Western governments actually encourage such deals.[46]

Bukovsky, the Soviet dissident referred to earlier, also agreed that Western industrial co-operation with the USSR was based on the exploitation of Soviet cheap labour and directly damaged the interests of the workers in the West. He proposed that, for example, US unions should 'have the right to examine all cases of investment of American capital in the USSR, the working conditions and pay where American capital is applied and to prevent money being made on the lack of rights of Soviet workers'.[47] Bukovsky also revealed that the KGB operated with US-made audio-visual surveillance devices, handcuffs and work equipment.[48]

These questions were raised at the Congress of the WCL in October 1977 and a resolution was passed condemning the socialist countries' co-operation and collusion with the multinational corporations.[49]

These problems have caused considerable concern in certain circles in the East. A Polish writer warned against antagonizing Western trade unions, whether they had legitimate reasons or not. He urged the authorities to cultivate the unions' goodwill by entering into closer contacts and exchanges of views. Indeed, the Central Council of Trade Unions in Poland (the central body of the old establishment) initiated round-table conferences with the Austrian, Finnish and West German trade unions in 1978 and 1979, and a more ambitious 'East–West European Trade Union Conference' was planned on the subject.[50]

Many Marxist ideologists have been critical of the penetration of the world economy by the multinationals. Thus B. Marković (Deputy Director of the Yugoslav Institute for International Politics and Economy) recently explained:

the growth and power of multinational corporations upset the balance of forces between employers and trade unions . . . The activity of multinational corporations is aimed directly at weakening the position of the working class. By taking advantage of their power and the favourable conditions on the international labour market, multinational corporations manage to raise the level of exploitation of the working masses on a worldwide scale. They employ cheap labour in developing countries and in this way depress the wages of people employed in the parent companies in developed countries.[51]

Marković called upon the labour movement to organize itself 'for the transnational class struggle against transnational capital' and for the creation of 'transnational collective bargaining' first on a regional, and in due course on a world, scale.[52]

RECOMMENDED FURTHER READING

1.* All-Union Central Council of Trade Unions, *Soviet Trade Unions: Their Role in Society, Functions and Rights* (Moscow: Profizdat, 1977).
2. F. Deppe, 'Trade Unions', in C. D. Kernig (ed.), *Marxism, Communism and Western Society. A Comparative Encyclopaedia* (New York: Herder & Herder, 1973) vol. 8, pp. 208–9.
3. M. Gamarnikow, 'New Tasks for Trade Unions', *East Europe* (New York) April 1967, pp. 18–26; and 'New Trends in East European Trade Unionism', *East Europe*, June 1969, pp. 13–19.
4. I. Greig, *The Ultra-Left Offensive Against Multinational Companies: Moscow's Call for World Trade Union Unity* (Richmond, Surrey, UK: Foreign Affairs Publishing, 1979).

5. June M. Hearn, 'W(h)ither the Trade Unions in China?,' *J. Industrial Relations* (Sydney) June 1977, pp. 158–72.
6.* L. Héthy, 'Trade Unions, Shop Stewards and Participation in Hungary', *Int. Lab. Rev.* (Geneva) July–Aug. 1981, pp. 491–503.
7. R. Hyman, *Marxism and the Sociology of Trade Unionism* (London: Pluto Press, 1971).
8. ILO, *Freedom of Association: Digest of Decisions of the Freedom of Association Committee of the Governing Body of the ILO*, (Geneva: ILO, 1976).
9. ILO, *Trade Union Rights in the USSR*, Documents Relating to the Case Concerning the USSR, dealt with by the Commission on Freedom of Association of the Governing Body of the ILO (Geneva: 1959).
10. V. Lichtenstein, 'The Communist Experience in American Trade Unions', *Industrial Relations* (Berkeley: Spring, 1980), pp. 119–30.
11.* K. Lipkovics and M. Novikov, 'On Behalf of the Working People: Trade Unions in the Political System of Socialism', *World Marxist Rev.* (London) July 1981, pp. 79–88.
12. B. Magnuson, 'Independence of Trade Unions from Whom?', *World Marxist Rev.*, March 1981, pp. 124–27.
13. D. Mandel, 'The Polish Workers and the Crisis of Bureaucratic Socialism', *Labour Capital and Society/Travail Capital et Societé* (Montreal) April 1981, pp. 74–86.
14. R. Martin, *Communism and the British Trade Unions 1924–1933: A Study of National Minority Movement* (Oxford: Clarendon Press, 1969).
15.* M. I. Mikhailov and K. L. Maidanik, 'International Working-Class Movement', in *Great Soviet Encyclopedia* (New York: Macmillan, 1977) pp. 76–86.
16. L. Molnar, 'Internationalism', in Kernig (ed.), *A Comparative Encyclopaedia*, vol. 4, pp. 329–42.
17. H. Momsen, 'Labour Movement', in Kernig (ed.), *A Comparative Encyclopaedia*, vol. 5, pp. 73–93.
18. G. Morris, 'How Independent Are U.S. Unions?' *Political Affairs* (New York) Feb. 1981, pp. 31–7.
19.* V. E. Mozhaev, 'Trade Unions', in *Great Soviet Encyclopedia*, vol. 21, pp. 696–700.
20.* Ni Chi-fu, 'Basic Principles for Trade Union Work in the New Period', *Peking Rev.*, 3 Nov., 1978, pp. 7–13.
21. A. Pankert, 'Some Legal Problems of the Workers' International Solidarity', *Int. Lab. Rev.*, July–Aug. 1977, pp. 67–74.
22. B. A. Ruble, 'Dual Functioning of Trade Unions in the USSR', *British J. Industrial Relations*, July 1979, pp. 235–41.
23.* Jadwiga Staniszkis, 'The Evolution of Working-Class Protest in Poland: Sociological Reflections on the Gdansk–Szczecin Case', *Soviet Studies* (Glasgow) April 1981, pp. 204–31.
24. H. Ticktin, 'The Victory and Tragedy of the Polish Working-Class', *Critique* (London) no. 13, 1981, pp. 69–77.
25. J. F. Triska (ed.), *Blue-Collar Workers in Eastern Europe* (London: George Allen & Unwin, 1981).

* *Indicates contributions by writers from the socialist countries.*

5 Industrial Democracy and Workers' Participation

A. INDUSTRIAL DEMOCRACY

Decision-making in the workplace was traditionally regarded in capitalist countries as a prerogative of the employers and little was done in practice to share it with the workers, in spite of the development of political and social democracy. That traditional view was later systematized and vested with scientific justification, as exemplified by such pioneering classics as *The Principles of Scientific Management* by F. W. Taylor (1911) and *General and Industrial Management* by H. Fayol (originally published in French in 1916).

But even under socialism the traditional Western practice became partly established, too. The initial enthusiasm in the USSR for the workers' management of factories led to widespread chaos, ineptitude, laxity and waste. By the early 1930s the rule of 'one-man management' had been firmly established in accordance with the principle of democratic centralism and in the prevailing atmosphere of Stalinist authoritarianism. Later other socialist countries adopted a similar system, although officially it was always stressed that 'one-man management under socialism has nothing in common with the despotic rule of enterprise owners and the capitalist production system'.[1]

The idea of industrial democracy[2] can be traced back to the social reformers of the era of the early Industrial Revolution (such as Ch. Fourier, R. Owen, P. J. Proudhon, S. H. Saint-Simon) and even before. The term 'industrial democracy' was first popularized by Sydney and Beatrice Webb in their book under that title (first published in 1897). Some practical attempts to introduce it were made between the two World Wars, especially in Germany in the 1920s and Spain and Sweden in the 1930s.

But in its modern sense, the development of industrial democracy dates only from the Second World War, first in Sweden (1948) and other

97

Scandinavian countries, then in the Federal Republic of Germany and later (especially after 1970) in many other Western European countries, such as Austria, Belgium, France, Ireland and the Netherlands. For a long time Britain was lagging behind and as late as 1968 the Donovan Report pronounced against workers' participation. But in 1976 the Bullock Committee reported in its favour and the government undertook some action in this direction in a White Paper issued in 1978. Industrial democracy has become the accepted policy of the European Economic Community and isolated schemes have been introduced in many other countries, such as Australia, Canada, Israel, Japan and New Zealand (and in some less-developed countries of the Third World).

In the socialist countries, workers' self-management (the term which is preferred there to industrial democracy) was first developed on a systematic basis in Yugoslavia after 1950. Similar attempts had been made once in the USSR in the 1920s and later in Poland (1956–8), Czechoslovakia (1968–9) and China (1966–76). More sustained schemes have been embarked upon in the German Democratic Republic since the mid-1960s, in Hungary since 1968, in Romania since 1973 and in Poland since 1981. There has also been indirect workers' participation in decision-making through trade unions, but its degree and extent have varied from one socialist country to another.

Socialist spokesmen often point out that whilst there may be political (parliamentary) democracy under capitalism, the socialist countries excel in economic democracy by virtue of the social ownership of the means of production, the absence of capitalist employers and the ideological commitment to equality.

However an examination of socialist industrial relations indicates that workers do not necessarily see it in that light and they have been increasingly demonstrating their concern and even assertiveness on the matter.

The concept of industrial democracy is now used in a general sense and it covers several different forms of workers' involvement.

(1) Joint consultation with management.
(2) Participation in administration.
(3) Indirect participation in management through trade union officials.
(4) Direct participation by workers or their elected representatives.
(5) Workers' control.
(6) Workers' self-management.
(7) Workers' participation in, or complete, ownership.

Theoretically, the highest form of industrial democracy could be reached under anarcho-syndicalism, where owners, decision-makers and workers would be the same people in a particular co-operative workshop, without a formal employer and state authority. Each workplace would not be too large, there would be no distinct employer, there would be no coercive powers of the state, and instead the independent work entities would be linked into loose co-operative federations. Schemes along these or similar lines were attempted or experimented with in the past, especially in the nineteenth century (mostly motivated by religious or other idealistic considerations), but hardly any of them have survived in the industrial sphere.

A number of circumstances have favoured or demanded a revived and sustained interest in industrial democracy since the Second World War – in both capitalist and the socialist countries. There has been a growing reaction against authoritarianism and elitism and instead a persistent predisposition to democratization in the political and social sphere. This has been paralleled by the declining power of capital and the state and the increasing power of organized labour.

The high level of affluence and social security in developed countries have been impelling workers to shift their focus of attention away from purely material conditions to wider objectives involving the distribution of power in the workplace and the 'quality of life' in general. Owing to the extension of education, better access to information made possible by modern mass media and the decreasing hours of work, workers are more and more capable of perceiving unnecessary authoritarianism and of making contributions to decisions which affect them.

At the same time, employers have been finding it expedient to respond positively in order to counteract workers' alienation and militancy, and in particular the loss of efficiency caused by go-slow tactics, strikes and sabotage.

B. WORKERS' PARTICIPATION AND OWNERSHIP

Marxists have traditionally attributed all social evils to the institution of private property.[3] In their view, the private ownership of the means of production has led to greed, exploitation, social classes, crime and wars – and the associated domination of the powerless workers by the propertied employers.

One of the first acts of the communist regimes after their accession to power was the socialization of land and capital and the transformation of private firms and farms into state or co-operative entities. However, historical experience since the First World War has demonstrated that ownership itself is not as relevant to industrial democracy as Marxists had originally claimed – whether under capitalism or socialism. Private ownership neither precludes workers' participation in capitalist countries, nor does socialized ownership in the socialist centrally planned economies automatically give the workers the power of direct decision-making or even a share in it.

Owing to technological progress and the consequent changing patterns of the division of labour, the real controllers of workplaces are not so much the owners as the managers. Managers are highly trained professionals and they are typically salaried employees, not owners nor even shareholders. These processes under capitalism can be traced back to the inter-war period and even earlier,[4] but they have been accentuated by the technical and scientific revolution since the mid-1950s.

Under these conditions as far as labour is concerned even nationalization does not change the actual control much. Referring to the developments in workers' participation in the Federal Republic of Germany, J. Schregle aptly summed it up:

> The labour movement, in its desire to have a greater say in industry, has attempted to achieve this objective not by changing the system of ownership, but by introducing workers' representation into the management structure. The trade unions have said, time and again, that co-determination works irrespective of whether industry is under private or public ownership.[5]

But it may be mentioned that the ownership of workplaces in the capitalist world is no longer limited to capitalists or even public authorities. In most Western countries workers now own shares in companies, especially in those in which they are employed. Their shareholding may be acquired either by ordinary purchase in the market or through allocation by the employing company at concessional prices.[6] There are also cases of trade unions owning shares. This practice is quite common in North America; but not in other parts of the capitalist world, either on ideological grounds (as in Western Europe) or simply because the unions are too poor (as in less-developed countries).

There are also cases of companies which are owned by the personnel working in them and which are usually operated as workers' co-operatives, as exemplified by the British firms Scott Bader Commonwealth, Upper Clyde Shipbuilders, and Kirby Manufacturing

Enterprises. [7] In some countries, trade unions own and operate business ventures, such as Bank für Gemeinwirtschaft (a commercial bank) in the Federal Republic of Germany, Koor Industrial and Trading Concern in Israel and Solo Service Stations in Australia.

A different kind of co-operative ownership and management is being developed in many less-developed countries, where collective (communal) ownership is combined with commercial pursuits. Western management methods are blended with local traditional practices in a spirit of egalitarianism. Among the most interesting schemes along these lines are the Tanzanian 'communal village enterprises', noted for their extended family participation (*ujama*). They have been promoted by President Nyerere since the nationalization of major industries, banks, insurance companies and wholesale and foreign trade after the Arusha Declaration in 1967.

Before we examine the situation under socialism, it must be emphasized that the mere ownership of shares by workers or even trade unions in capitalist countries does not necessarily give them the control of the companies concerned. Their ownership is likely to be in the minority, but even in the case of majority shareholding the real control is still likely to be in the hands of the management. Similarly, experience in the past has shown quite clearly that public ownership does not guarantee workers' participation or control. As Tom Clarke, the British radical thinker, pointed out:

> No attempt was made to shift power towards the workers in the nationalized industries . . . Future nationalization could only be successful as part of a democratic socialist society if the workers themselves take control of their industries. [8]

Contrary to the idealists' as well as workers' expectations, the socialization of the means of production in the socialist countries has not overcome the employee–employer conflict or workers' alienation either. The socialized workplaces are owned either by the state or by the collectives of workers, the latter being of little consequence outside agriculture. Although the workers are told that they are the owners, this is only a fiction and no worker can exercise any property rights. As far as the individual worker is concerned, he has merely exchanged the private capitalist employer for the state capitalist employer.

In fact, in several respects the worker is more dominated by the owner under socialism than is his counterpart in a capitalist economy. The socialist state is not only the owner and employer, but also the manager (through its appointee the 'director'), the central planner, the legislator and the enforcer of its own laws and regulations. The same state also rules under the mono-party system of government and it does not have to respond to popular pressure to stay in power after the next election.

Certainly in the past, there was little industrial democracy in socialist enterprises. But in the more liberal countries this fact has come to be recognized by many. Two Hungarian economists described the situation in the following words:

> In Hungary today our most urgent task is to create a favourable climate among individuals and their groups, and to adapt the structure and functioning of organisations in a manner favourable to participation. The fact that the means of production are owned by the State and that political power is in the hands of the working class and its party certainly makes it easier to adopt the necessary measures but it does not bring them about automatically. As the Eleventh Congress of the Hungarian Socialist Workers' Party pointed out, the development of shopfloor and factory democracy and that of socialist democracy need systematic and purposeful efforts now and in the future.[9]

We shall now examine the nature and content of workers' participation in management, as distinct from ownership, under the two systems.

C. WORKERS' PARTICIPATION IN MANAGEMENT

The most developed forms of workers' participation in decision-making in the capitalist world have so far been achieved in the EEC and the Scandinavian countries. The Federal Republic of Germany has been the leader both in the comprehensiveness of legislation (especially the Acts of 1951, 1952 and 1976) and its practical implementation. The system is known as 'co-determination' (*Mitbestimmung*), that is, joint decision-making by negotiation and agreement.

There are three levels at which the West German workers can play their part, represented by the Works Councils, Supervisory Boards, and Management Boards. At the lowest, operational, level, in every workplace with five or more employees the entire workforce elects a *Works Council*, consisting of the workers' representatives only. In addition to its advisory and consultative function, it has the power of co-decision (approval or disapproval) on such matters as the organization of work time, holidays, vocational training, job evaluation and pay structure, the alleviation of hardship in case of redundancies, health and safety amenities and work discipline in general.

In the case of a company (not being family-owned) employing more than 500 persons, representatives elected by the workers sit on the *Supervisory Board* where they constitute from one-third to (with more than 1000–2000 employees) one-half of that policy-making body. The Supervisory Board which meets four times a year, also appoints members of the *Management Board*, a full-time executive body which oversees the former's operations and approves (or rejects) its decisions of major consequence. Amongst the appointees to the Management Board is a *Labour Director*.[10]

Workers' Councils also exist in Belgium, France, Italy, Luxemburg and the Netherlands. But the range of decisions submitted for the workers' approval is smaller. Workers' representation on Supervisory Boards also exists in most other Western (but not Southern) European countries, where they constitute about one-third of board membership.

In its policy of the harmonization of industrial legislation and practices, the EEC has been promoting workers' participation to near West German levels, especially since the mid-1970s. For example, in its 'Green Paper on Employee Participation and Company Structure of 1975', the EEC Commission recommended that any company employing more than 500 persons should have a Supervisory Board with representatives of the shareholders, employees and outside interests, each constituting one-third of the membership. Works Councils and Labour Directors are also recommended.[11] It is interesting to note that the European Trade Union Confederation, although in favour of the extension of industrial democracy, has not devised its own model for workers' participation, but is rather satisfied with that put forward by the EEC Commission.[12]

In some respects, Sweden is more advanced in industrial democracy than any other capitalist country. Since 1948 workers have had representation on the National Labour Market Board, a tripartite body representing labour, employers and the government, which participates in economic planning (it is assisted by some 25 Local Labour Market Boards). By the legislation of 1972 and 1977 workers' representation has been extended even to fairly small firms (employing more than 25 persons) and it provides for full consultation with employees and full participation by their representatives in decision-making from the shop floor to the top management level.

Some Swedish firms have embarked upon far-reaching innovative schemes of worker participation by transferring decision-making and responsibilities to the shop floor level. Thus Volvo has reorganized its production into fairly independent departments, in which groups or teams of workers (for example, about 20) largely decide amongst themselves how to organize their work. There are periodical (weekly or monthly) meetings of workers with management at different levels to consider work tasks and problems, and innovations are encouraged to come from the workers rather than be imposed from above. Workers' self-discipline, responsibility and co-operation are emphasized.[13]

The cause of workers' participation is in many cases effectively served by collective bargaining. This avenue is particularly important in the countries where formal legislation on industrial democracy is poorly developed or non-existent, as in Italy, Japan, Spain and the USA, not to mention the Third World. Workers' participation has aroused considerable interest in a number of less-developed countries and some practical steps have been taken in this direction. But the initiative in some of them has come not so much from the workers or trade unions, as from the governments as, for example, in Bangladesh, India, Jamaica, Pakistan, Peru and Tanzania. The authorities are aware of the class conflict that capitalist economic development (especially industrialization) brings in train, and workers' participation is seen as a way of avoiding the social problems that emerged in the Western countries.[14] There is also a determination to enlist the support of labour for accelerated economic development and restraint in wage claims in the interest of high levels of investment.

Although officially the socialist countries describe themselves as 'workers' states' with virtually no private capitalist employers, the extent and degree of workers' participation in management there are surprisingly small. The directive and centralized system of planning and management at the national level, the principle of one-man management in enterprises and the economic and political authoritarianism prevailing in most of these countries in general are not conducive to workers' participation in crucial decision-making. But there are some conspicuous exceptions.

Of the socialist countries Yugoslavia has been in the forefront of workers' participation. It emerged as a reaction against the Soviet-style 'state capitalism' noted for the separation of the elitist managers and technocrats from the shop floor workers, where trade unions are largely a tool of the party and state establishment. In the Yugoslav view, that system merely replaces private capitalism and it still leads to exploitation (not by private capitalists, but by the omnipotent state) and alienation.

The Yugoslav set-up, known as *Workers' Self-Management*, can be traced back to 1949 when first *Workers' Councils* were created, but it was formally introduced in 1950 and further developed by legislative Acts of 1952, 1965, 1971, 1974 and 1978. Workers' self-management exists in production and service enterprises and other work entities outside agriculture, and in private firms employing more than five persons. In all, it involves nearly 4m persons, or 40 per cent of the working population.

Although the means of production are formally owned by the state, they are placed at the disposal of the workers, economically grouped in the *Basic Organizations of Associated Labour*.[15] Each BOAL elects a Workers' Council, typically of 20–30 representatives for two years, which if large may create an inner body known as the *Management Board* (usually from 3 to 11 members). Care is taken to ensure that manual workers and technical and professional personnel have proportional representation. Members are elected by secret ballot for two years, one-half being replaced every year. In the case of larger enterprises, there may be more than one Workers' Council (one-fifth of the 7800 Yugoslav enterprises are in this category), whilst in a small BOAL all members may constitute the Workers' Council.

Within the rules laid down by the state, each Workers' Council adopts a Constitution, which provides a basis for the operation of the entity to suit local conditions. The Workers' Council or the Management Board appoints the *director* (general manager) in accordance with the regulations laid down by the state. The Workers' Council also determines the local *Labour Code*, the composition of production and/or services, the size and direction of investment, borrowing and lending operations, prices, working conditions, employment, current income payments, the distribution of residual profits and the provision of socio-cultural amenities.

But it must be pointed out that the enterprise 'director' still commands a good deal of influence and effective power. He can suspend the decisions of the Workers' Council if they are inconsistent with the state interest. The new emphasis on socio-economic plans contained in the Constitution of 1974 has further enhanced the role of the director. According to a Canadian specialist, A. Whitehorn, the influence ranking in a Yugoslav factory looks like this: the director, the Workers' Council, the Management Board (if there is one), the League of Communists (the

Yugoslav communist party), technical staff, supervisors, the trade union, skilled workers, unskilled workers.[16]

There were attempts to establish workers' participation in management in some other socialist countries, viz.: in the USSR (in the late 1920s), Poland (1956–8), Czechoslovakia (1968–9) and China (1966–76). But in each case the powers of the workers' representative bodies were soon restricted and followed by a reversion to traditional authoritarian management.

Nevertheless the desire for workers' participation has always been present and there has been a revival of interest in it since about 1970. Of special relevance are some recent developments in several East European countries and the USSR. Since the late 1960s Production (or Plant or Factory) Committees have been created or given power in Bulgaria, the German Democratic Republic, Hungary and the USSR to advise on and supervise the operation of enterprises.

These committees usually include elected workers' representatives, the chairmen of the party and trade union committees, some senior executives, a few specialists from outside and the enterprise director. But the Production Committees have no power of decision-making. In the German Democratic Republic their purpose is to enlist popular support for innovations and efficiency, whilst in Hungary it is 'to mediate between differing and often conflicting needs and interests of workers and other social groups (including managers) and to reconcile their respective aspirations and possibilities . . . under the changing conditions of our working class, society and economy'.[17] In the USSR it is claimed that 40m workers now participate in the management of production, with over 140 000 Production Consultation Committees or Production Councils in existence.[18]

A more ambitious system has been introduced in Romania under the name of 'collective management' by the legislation of 1968, 1971, 1973 and 1978 and the Polish industrial upheavals of 1980–81 have further spurred progress in this direction. It exists at three levels of the hierarchical economic management – the enterprise (Workers' Council), the industrial central (Administrative Council) and the economic ministry (Ministerial College) levels.

Each body includes elected representatives from the lower echelon. The most relevant here is the Workers' Council (*Consiliior Oamenilor Municii*, or *COM*) which consists of (1) workers' representatives elected from the General Assembly (of the workers in the enterprise, which meets twice a year); (2) managerial, technical and engineering staff sitting *ex officio*; (3) representatives of the party, trade union, the Union of Communist Youth and some outside specialists.

Although the Workers' Council has the power of decision-making, binding on the enterprise director, the range of matters over which it makes decisions is narrowly limited. The Workers' Council is now headed by the local party secretary and its basic functions is to prepare the production plan and devise the most effective ways of its fulfilment within the framework of the national economic plan. More importantly (as in the case of the Production Committees elsewhere, referred to before), workers' representatives are in the minority. Thus of the membership of 15 to 35 (depending on the size of the enterprise) workers' representatives chosen in uncontested elections number from 7 to 17.[19] In the Administrative Council, whose total membership ranges from 35 to 53, the workers' elected component is only 5–15.

The national system of planning and management in Romania is still highly centralized, so that workers' power along the Yugoslav lines would be completely incompatible with it. A Romanian economist concluded:

> it stands to reason that workers' participation in management must be developed and operate within the framework of the national economic plan, whilst the management of the whole economy is strengthened in the spirit of democratic centralism.[20]

D. WORKERS' PARTICIPATION AND TRADE UNIONS

Workers' participation in management is a sensitive area in relation to organized labour, both in capitalist and (less so) in the socialist countries. Views on the role of trade unions differ not only amongst trade unions but also amongst workers themselves, employers and even governments. In some countries, the majority of trade unions have adopted a positive attitude and have co-operated in the development of workers' participation directly or indirectly. This has been so particularly in the Scandinavian countries, the Federal Republic of Germany and the Netherlands.

Thus in the Federal Republic of Germany, many workers' representatives on the different bodies are selected by trade unions. Amongst such representatives there may be experts not necessarily employed in the enterprise in question, and these specialists in fact may dominate the workers' side. The Supervisory Board in a medium or large West German enterprise also includes a representative of the managerial staff. This fact has been of long-standing concern to the West German unions, as in their view such a person, although an employee, is predisposed to support the shareholders against the workers' representatives, which violates the principle of employer–employee parity. In Britain, although trade unions are increasingly inclined to participate in management, they see the labour directors as their representatives in an adversary role to management. Trade unions are not enthusiastic about Works Councils, as they might undermine shop stewards representing unions.

In most other developed capitalist countries, such as Australia, Belgium, Canada, Italy, Japan and the USA, trade unions have tended to keep aloof, preferring not to share responsibilities for unpopular decisions and instead continue to rely primarily on collective bargaining.

Traditionally, trade unions in the industrialized capitalist countries regarded themselves as the only legitimate champions of workers' interests in the industrial scene. The more radical ones also rejected the existing social system and worked towards its replacement by a socialist or syndicalist society. Indeed it may be argued that in order to defend the workers and to keep on improving their economic and social position, trade unions must continue operating in an adversary position, that is, refrain from participating in management, as it may involve collaboration with the employers.

A union representative participating in management may find himself in an embarrassing situation. Sound management and economic rationality may dictate large-scale automation and sustained retrenchments of labour, which militates against the conscience of a genuine workers' representative. To many ideologically-conscious union leaders, workers' participation represents a threat to the traditional function of the union as the sole representative of the workers. It also blunts the revolutionary spirit of the class struggle, thereby only delaying the overthrow of capitalism. According to Tom Clarke:

> Democracy may be introduced in industry only *in opposition* to capitalist control, not as part of it, which entails a heightening not diminution of industrial militancy. To achieve this, the maintenance of independent workers' organisations is necessary.[21]

Another question that arises is whether trade unions alone should select workers' representatives to the different co-management bodies.

In Britain and France trade unions have the sole or priority right to do it. But in most other capitalist countries, directly elected non-union representatives are also admissible and in some cases even preferred. Some workers do not belong to any union and they may not want to be dominated by extremist militant union leaders.

It may be argued that trade unions should continue their efforts to improve the conditions of the working class on their front, whilst workers' participation represents a different front and it should be pursued by other *ad hoc* representatives. In some companies, there may be more than one union, which may create inter-union conflicts on workers' representation. Furthermore, many employers prefer to deal with *ad hoc* representatives who are genuinely interested in reasonable co-operation and not with union leaders used to adversary posture and bound by the union straitjacket. Largely for these reasons the EEC authorities have been in favour of *ad hoc* workers' representatives rather than trade union nominees. Some radicals, such as Tom Clarke, see it as an attempt to split the working class.[22]

The situation is different in less-developed countries where workers are, on the whole, less educated and less assertive. It is widely held that workers' participation under such conditions can function effectively only with the support of strong trade unions, as otherwise workers' representatives would merely become 'captives of management'.[23]

In the socialist countries, trade unions represent the traditional form of 'indirect' workers' participation. Trade unions at different levels of their hierarchical structure participate in the preparation of economic plans and then co-operate with management in devising the most appropriate methods of implementing the targets and other planned tasks. Trade unions have to be consulted by management before a worker can be dismissed and the unions also see to it that safety and health standards are observed as prescribed by the Labour Code and other regulations. They also act as watchdogs over management's compliance with 'collective agreements'. Thus according to the leader of the official trade union establishment in the USSR, A. Shibayev, Soviet trade unions:

have the right to take part in more than 70 managerial functions, and another 20 such functions come wholly within their competence. All matters pertaining to sackings, rate-fixing and adjustment and output quotas are determined by the unions exclusively. The unions can have managerial staff demoted or sacked if they fail to observe collective agreements, are bureaucratic or inefficient or violate labour legislation. A union technical inspector can stop production in a shop or sector of industry if health or safety regulation is not complied with.[24]

According to another Soviet source, in 1978 (as in 1977), 10 000 managers of various categories were dismissed from their posts in the USSR at the demand of trade unions.[25]

It must be realized, however, that workers' participation through the official socialist trade union establishments is not genuine as understood in the West. The unions are, in fact, an instrumentality of the socialist state, however much it is officially denied. There are no free union elections and the union establishment is dominated by the party-nominated officials, who in crucial matters typically take the side of the state and management, rather than of the workers. The principle of one-man management still prevails with some qualified exceptions in China, Romania and Yugoslavia.

It is largely the preceding state of affairs which led in Poland in 1980–81 to the emergence of free trade unionism Solidarity, independent of the party and the state. From the very outset, Solidarity advocated genuine workers' self-management. But the government stubbornly opposed it. In September–October 1981 a compromise was reached, whereby the choice in the appointment of managerial personnel was to be shared by the government and workers with a conditional power of veto by either side. Solidarity announced at its first Congress in October 1981 that it would conduct a referendum on workers' self-management. However, the imposition of Martial Law on 13 December, 1981 has placed the matter of workers' participation in management under a question mark.

E. CONCLUSIONS AND LIMITATIONS

Workers' participation in ownership and particularly in management has come to command increasing interest in both capitalist and socialist countries, especially since about 1970. Contrary to historical experience and classical Marxist assertions, the ownership of workplaces – whether by private capitalists or by public authorities under capitalism, or by the socialist state – neither precludes nor automatically enables workers' participation in decision-making.

The role of the state in the development of industrial democracy has differed from one country to another. In most Western countries where it exists, it has originated 'from below', that is, amongst workers themselves or trade unions. This is still largely the case in such countries as Britain, Canada, Japan and the USA, where workers' participation is pursued mainly by collective bargaining at the enterprise level. But in most other capitalist countries the state becomes involved either by passing and enforcing appropriate legislation and perhaps (especially in less-developed countries) initiating and even imposing participatory schemes of one sort or another 'from above'.

Imposition by the state from above is almost the exclusive rule in the socialist centrally planned economies. The two Hungarian economists mentioned before frankly conceded that 'the initiative in introducing shopfloor democracy in Hungary is taken primarily at the political level' (even where management is against it).[26] But even in the countries where workers' participation has been advanced most, viz. in Romania ('collective management') and Yugoslavia ('workers' self-management'), the schemes have been initiated and prescribed in detail by the party and the state. In fact, since the mid-1970s the role of the party in the operation has been strengthened in both countries.

But there are some exceptions now, viz. Solidarity in Poland and illicit dissident unions elsewhere (such as the 'Free Inter-Professional Association of Workers in the USSR'), whose programmes postulate meaningful workers' participation. In contrast to the EEC, the CMEA authorities[27] have not taken any steps to promote industrial democracy and the harmonization of national policies and practices.

A close examination of the experience of workers' participation in capitalist as well as socialist countries in the last decade or two indicates that it has resulted in neither the spectacular gains to the workers hoped for by some, nor in disastrous effects on production and social organization forewarned by others. On the positive side, it has produced better attitudes amongst workers, reduced their predisposition (or ability) to resort to industrial disputes and enhanced efficiency and economic development.[28]

However, the limitations of workers' participation must be recognized. To most employers it represents an unwelcome burden involving time-consuming arguments with workers' representatives, the provision of information, and interference with efficient management, and it may also weaken work discipline. This state of affairs has occurred not only in capitalist firms, but also in socialist enterprises as reported by the Hungarian economists.[29] In fact nowhere does workers' participation extend to the day-to-day management of enterprises.

A factor that militates against industrial democracy is modern technology. Many thinkers both in the West and in the East agree that the scientific and technical revolution that the world has been experiencing since the mid-1950s inevitably leads to the diminution of human participation in production processes. This is mainly due to ever-widening mechanization and automation and to enterprises increasing their size in order to utilize economies of scale. Furthermore, the complexity of technologies, organization and marketing, irrespective of the social system, demand that in the interest of efficiency decision-making be limited to the professional managerial and technocratic elite.[30]

Both Western left-wing radicals and the leaders in the socialist countries are critical of the workers' participation schemes in the capitalist world. E. J. Vaughan regards workers' participation 'as a useful means of increasing control over subordinates . . . a technique to persuade employees to accept decisions that have already been made by management'.[31] Tom Clarke maintains that industrial democracy will lead to the:

> likely absorption of workers' representatives into capitalist forms of control, not a transcending of these. . . collective bargaining and worker participation are means by which employers may preserve and consolidate their existing partial degree of control.[32]

Clarke believes that the real answer to the problem is social ownership.[33]

A Hungarian economist sees workers' participation in the capitalist world as a desperate 'trouble-shooting' stratagem calculated to rescue ailing capitalism from its inherent contradictions. In his view the working masses themselves do not participate, only their nominated or elected representatives do. He further points out that, with some exceptions in the Federal Republic of Germany, workers' representatives on the supervisory or management boards are in the minority and this minority is developing into 'representative oligarchies'.[34] He describes the developments as:

> rather careful not to upset socio-economic relations taken in the wider sense . . . While having created a more or less successful mechanism for settling conflicts within enterprises, they conjured up a dangerous professionalization of those called upon to represent the workers and through this, the selection of a narrow elite within the working class.[35]

There are inexorable limitations to workers' participation in the socialist countries under the existing system of central economic planning (Yugoslavia excepted). The real dilemma for communist leaders is how to reconcile the conflicting interests implied in the accepted principle of 'democratic centralism'. How to preserve the party supremacy and its image as the sole legitimate spokesman for workers' interests, and at the same time to create industrial democracy with genuine workers' participation in decision-making, given the mono-party system of government, central economic planning and ambitious developmental objectives. The Romanian Party leader, N. Ceausescu, has made well-meaning efforts along these lines, with a good deal of propaganda effect, but with little substantive power accorded to the workers.

Unreserved workers' participation in management under a socialist centralized, directive system of planning and management is not feasible, however desirable it may be on ideological and propaganda grounds. Crucial decision-making is in the hands of the party elite (Politburo), the government and the State Planning Commission (in that order of precedence), and the targets, the allocation of resources, the distribution of output and wage funds are pre-determined at the central level. Circumscribed decision-making is then allowed down the hierar-chical ladder – to the ministries, industrial branch associations, regional authorities, enterprise directors, departmental managers and foremen. Within that framework, it is simply impracticable to allow workers to make decisions that suit them, but not necessarily the plan, as they may only lead to a whole chain of disruption, unfulfilment and bottlenecks. However, the workers are encouraged to participate in devising the most suitable and effective ways of implementing the predetermined plan (in addition to various social, recreational and welfare activities in their workplace).

In those cases where special bodies have been created for management–worker consultation, workers' representatives are in the minority (as in capitalist countries, with some exceptions), while managerial, technical and party nominees predominate.

To create a viable basis for genuine workers' participation, the whole system of planning and management would have to be liberalized and decentralized, in particular the hierarchical structure would have to be dismantled and tight planning abandoned. So far only Yugoslavia has done it, which has created a viable basis for workers' self-management. Hungarian reforms have not gone far enough, whilst the situation in Poland is too uncertain at present. In other socialist countries, including Romania, in spite of several attempts at economic reforms little substantive progress has been made on this front.

Referring to the experience in Hungary, L. Héthy and Cs. Makó pointed out:

> the development of factory democracy cannot be promoted in the long run by isolated changes in the organisational structure but needs a whole series of changes . . . including the introduction of participation bodies, the selection of decisions suitable for participation, a decentralised decision-making system, training to develop the workers' knowledge of their environment, the establishment of channels of information and a system of motivation supporting the whole programme by increasing the workers' willingness and ability to participate.[36]

Evaluating the experience of 'collective management' in Romania, the two Romanian specialists referred to before found the following shortcomings.

(1) The meagre, if any at all, information available to the workers' representatives (not to mention the workers themselves).
(2) The incompetence and inexperience of the workers' representatives.
(3) The persistence of the traditional gap between the exalted management and the workers and their representatives.
(4) Personal incompatibilities.
(5) Poor motivation and interest on the part of the workers and their representatives.[37]

Although Yugoslavia, with her 'workers' self-management' has made the greatest progress in the socialist bloc – and in principle her system is often regarded as the highest form of industrial democracy anywhere – in practice workers do not do as much decision-making as it may appear at first. Workers' Councils are dominated by professional managers together with engineering, economic and other specialists. The enterprise director in fact becomes the state's watchdog – he can suspend the decisions of the Workers' Council if he thinks that they are inconsistent with the regulations laid down by the government and incompatible with the interests of the socialist state.

These developments and realities were first brought to light by M. Djilas (former Vice-President of Yugoslavia, turned dissident) in his well-known books.[38] A critical Western thinker, V. Holesovsky, appraised the facts of industrial life in Yugoslavia thus:

workers do not really manage the enterprises . . . Workers' Councils
. . . serve mainly to legitimize the exercise of real executive power
which is in the hands of professional managers . . . the upstart heir to
private capitalist entrepreneurs.[39]

RECOMMENDED FURTHER READING

1. V. Andrle, *Managerial Power in the Soviet Union* (London: Teakefield, 1977).
2. Ellen T. Comisso, 'Yugoslavia in the 1970's: Self-Management and Bargaining', *J. Comparative Economics*, New Haven, 4/1980, pp. 192–208.
3. P. T. D. Drent *et al.*, 'Participative Decision Making: A Comparative Study', *Industrial Relations* (Berkeley) Fall 1979, pp. 295–309.
4. B. Horvat, *The Yugoslav Economic System: The First Labor-Managed Economy in the Making* (New York: M. E. Sharpe, 1980).
5. ILO, *Workers' Participation in Decisions within Undertakings* (Geneva: ILO, 1981).
6. D. N. Nelson, 'Workers in a Workers' State: Participation in Romania', *Soviet Studies* (Glasgow) Oct. 1980, pp. 542–60.
7. W. L. Parish, 'Egalitarianism in Chinese Society', *Problems of Communism* (Washington) Jan.–Feb. 1981, pp. 37–53.
8. J. L. Porket, 'Participation in Management in Communist Systems in the 1970s', *British J. of Industrial Relations*, Nov. 1975, pp. 371–87.
9. J. Ramondt, 'Workers' Self-Management and Its Constraints: The Yugoslav Experience', *British J. of Industrial Relations*, March 1979, pp. 83–94.
10. L. Sirc, *The Yugoslav Economy Under Self-Management* (London: Macmillan, 1979).
11. A. Steinherr, 'The Labor-Managed Economy: A Survey of the Economics Literature', *Annals of Public and Co-operative Economy* (Liège) April–June 1978, pp. 129–48.
12. J. Svejnar, 'Workers' Participation in Czechoslovakia', *Annals of Public and Co-operative Economy*, April–June 1978, pp. 177–201.
13. J. Vanek, *The General Theory of Labor-Managed Market Economies* (Ithaca, NY: Cornell University Press, 1970).
14. B. Ward, 'The Firm in Illyria: Market Syndicalism', *Amer. Econ. Rev.*, Sept. 1958, pp. 566–89.
15. M. Yanovitch (ed.), *Soviet Work Attitudes – The Issue of Participation in Management* (Oxford: Martin Robertson, 1979).

6 Technology and Labour

A. TECHNOLOGICAL CHANGE AND LABOUR

Technological change has been a labour issue ever since the Industrial Revolution. It has also come to command the attention of Marxists who have added their own ideological interpretation to it. Marx and Engels (in *German Ideology*, written in 1845–46) stressed that the different stages in the development of societies were essentially determined by the techniques of production, that is, what really matters historically is not so much *what* output is produced but *how* it is produced. Insisting on this interpretation, they distinguished six 'socio-economic formations'– primitive communism, slavery, feudalism, capitalism, socialism and (full) communism.

Marx saw technological change in two different lights – negative under capitalism and rather favourable in the future communist society. He argued that under capitalism technological change exacerbated class conflicts by favouring propertied classes and damaging workers. In his view, the mechanization and reorganization of production led to an increasing intensity of work and larger profits. He blamed the 'fetishism of technology' (continuous innovations) for steadily raising the 'organic structure of capital' (capital–labour ratio) and the consequent expansion of the 'industrial reserve army' (unemployment).[1]

Ever since Rosa Luxemburg highlighted the role of military production in capitalist accumulation and imperialism (in *The Accumulation of Capital*, 1913), many Marxist writers have linked technological change under capitalism with militarism and, more recently, with 'military-industrial complexes'.[2]

Most Western thinkers disagree with this disparaging Marxist interpretation of technological change under capitalism. One school of thought, which can be described as 'technocratism', maintains that technological change in its broadest sense is capable of solving not only the problem of scarcity (poverty) but also all the basic social conflicts. It is also held that the ills of society are often caused by ideologists and

116

politicians, who make biased and distorted partisan decisions. Further, it is postulated that a modern society should be increasingly run by 'technocrats' on a scientific basis in accordance with technical and economic rationality, irrespective of the social system.[3]

Some Western thinkers believe that modern technology is creating an equitable industrial (or post-industrial) society – not unlike the Marxist 'classless' society – eliminating the traditional class conflicts and the need for a proletarian revolution (see Chapter 1B). Technological progress has raised the level of personal income of the masses, at least in the industrialized countries. Workers are no longer dominated by capital as propertied classes have lost much of their power to professional managers and specialists who themselves are employees.

On the whole, technological change has been producing beneficial effects on the conditions of work in both capitalist and socialist countries. The mechanization of work has tended to eliminate or at least lighten the burden of heavy manual labour. But it appears that the socialist state is more genuinely interested and active in this respect than either the governments or private employers in the capitalist countries. The improvements in the conditions of work in the latter countries are rather a product of profitability considerations (especially in the long run) and the pressure of organized labour and perhaps the electorate.

Marx argued (in *Manuscripts of 1844*) that historically specialization led to the impoverishment of the worker 'reducing him to a machine'. A century later (in 1944) Mao Tse-tung pointed out that, 'Any specialized skill may be capitalized and so may lead to arrogance and contempt of others'.[4]

Whilst conceding the benefits of the industrial and territorial division of labour in terms of efficiency, Marxists stress the disadvantages of occupational specialization. In their view, under capitalism the most interesting and remunerative occupations are reserved for the ruling classes, whilst the working classes are usually reduced to the most arduous, manual and routinized occupations noted for low pay, monotony and boredom, leading to alienation. Marx and Engels (in *German Ideology*) envisaged that in an ideal society there would be typically a 'universal man' of many skills and occupations. Such a model man would engage in different types of work – manual, mental and creative – and under full communism the occupational division of labour would virtually disappear.

In actual practice in the socialist countries today, the division of labour is pursued to a similar extent and degree as in the capitalist world, which indicates that technological change has its own logic transcending social systems. In fact, in most of them the division of labour was pushed to extremes in the form of narrow occupational specialization. In the earlier stages of their economic development, these countries had large supplies of unskilled labour and to adapt it to the radical and rapid structural changes in the economy, vocational training in many cases was shortened with a concentration on specific tasks. In the circumstances, it was probably a sensible practice, which may provide a useful lesson to less-developed countries.

Western economists, following Adam Smith's pioneering ideas, have traditionally extolled the benefits of specialization which is inseparable from technological progress. But to the classical Marxists the division of labour was inextricably linked with private property, and in fact they often used the two interchangeably as the basic faults of capitalism.

Under both systems, there is a continuous process of substitution of capital for labour (increasing capital–labour ratio). But this process is conditioned by different forces. In developed capitalist economies, it is stimulated by rising labour costs, whilst in the socialist economies it is shortages of labour and the underestimation of the cost of capital that are responsible. Where the labour-saving process does take place in the less-developed countries of the Third World, it is in many cases impelled by the equipment and technologies available from the industrialized (capitalist or socialist) economies. This sometimes produces an irrational utilization of resources, substituting the already scarce capital for cheap, abundant and under-employed labour (see section C of this chapter).

One of Marx's assumptions for an ideal society was that the distinction between mental and manual and between urban and rural workers should be eliminated, as a condition of the 'classless society'. Although at the time the idea appeared almost utopian, technological change (which Marx largely despised) has in fact been obliterating former sharp distinctions not only under socialism but also in capitalist societies. As Charles Dufour concluded:

> the increase in the number of skilled jobs (particularly in the tertiary sector) has in the long run entailed an overall improvement in working conditions. In addition, the distinction between manual and non-manual work is gradually giving way to a more fundamental division of workers into the skilled and the unskilled.[5]

Table 6.1 demonstrates the effect of technological progress on the distribution of working population amongst the main branches of the

TABLE 6.1 Redistribution of the working population in selected capitalist and socialist countries, 1960–79 between the major branches of the economy

Country	Year	Agriculture and forestry (%)	Industry and construction* (%)	Services† (%)
Australia	1960	9	37	54
	1970	8	36	56
	1979	7	31	62
Canada	1960	13	34	53
	1970	8	32	60
	1979	6	29	65
Japan	1960	9	42	49
	1970	5	34	61
	1979	4	30	66
Philippines	1960	61	15	24
	1970	54	17	29
	1979	50	16	34
United Kingdom	1960	4	49	47
	1970	3	45	52
	1979	3	39	58
USA	1960	9	37	54
	1970	8	36	56
	1979	7	31	62
Bulgaria	1960	56	27	17
	1970	36	39	25
	1979	25	43	32
Czechoslovakia	1960	26	46	28
	1970	19	47	34
	1979	14	48	38
German Democratic Republic	1960	17	48	35
	1970	13	50	37
	1979	11	51	38
Hungary	1960	39	34	27
	1970	26	43	31
	1979	22	42	36
Mongolia	1960	61	19	20
	1970	47	21	32
	1979	40	22	38
Poland	1960	44	32	24
	1970	35	38	27
	1979	27	41	32

(*continued*)

TABLE 6.1 (*Contd.*)

Country	Year	Agriculture and forestry (%)	Industry and construction* (%)	Services† (%)
Romania	1960	66	20	14
	1970	49	31	20
	1979	31	44	25
USSR	1960	39	32	29
	1970	25	38	37
	1979	21	39	40
Yugoslavia	1960	26	46	28
	1970	19	47	34
	1979	14	48	38

* Including mining, electricity and gas.
† Including pursuits not adequately described.
Sources. Based on: *Year Book of Labour Statistics 1964* (Geneva: ILO, 1964) pp. 119–37, and *1980*, pp. 160–95; *Statistical Abstract of the United States 1980* (Washington: US Dept. of Commerce, 1980) p. 406; *Statisticheskii ezhegodnik stran-chlenov SEV 1980* [Statistical Yearbook of the CMEA Countries 1980] (Moscow: Statistika, 1980) pp. 403–5.

economy in selected capitalist and socialist countries. It confirms the well-known fact that the higher the stage of economic development, the higher the proportion of the working population engaged in industry and services. This broad redistribution of the labour force takes place irrespective of the social system.

But three qualifications must be added in the application of this generalization to the socialist planned economies. At a given stage of economic development, the proportion found in agriculture is higher, and in the services, lower, than would normally be the case in a capitalist market economy. This is due to the planned neglect of agriculture in respect of investment and innovations (so that a larger labour force is needed there than would otherwise be the case) and various restrictions on the 'drift to the cities'. There are also restrictions on the growth of services, as most of them (that is, other than transport, communications and trade) are considered by Marxists to be 'non-productive'. On the other hand, the proportion in industry rises faster owing to the policy of accelerated industrialization.

Technological change produces more disruptive effects on labour in capitalist market economies than under socialist central economic planning. The urge and freedom to innovate are greater in the former and the processes are spontaneous and sensitive to cyclical fluctuations. But under socialism, innovations are pursued on a centrally planned basis, whereby disruptions can be avoided or minimized by appropriate planned measures in advance.

B. THE GROWTH OF LABOUR PRODUCTIVITY

The tendency for output per man-hour to grow is a well-known consequence of economic development in capitalist as well as in socialist countries. Thus in spite of the reduction of working hours since the Industrial Revolution from over 60 to about 40 per week (in addition to the increasing annual and public holidays), production per worker has risen about tenfold, at least in the industrialized countries. This fact carries important implications for industrial relations, wages and social welfare in general.

Although Marxists have been critical of capitalism as a social system, they have acknowledged its great capacity for technological progress and the consequent rapid growth of labour productivity. The classical Marxist thinkers recognized the critical importance of the growth of efficiency as the indispensable means of ensuring high levels of affluence and an ideal working environment, the necessary conditions to full communism. Addressing *subbotniki* (see p. 53) in June 1919 Lenin emphasized:

> Communism begins when the *rank-and-file workers* display an enthusiastic concern that is undaunted by arduous toil to increase the productivity of labour, husband *every pood of grain, coal, iron* and other products, which do not accrue to the workers personally or to their 'close' kith and kin, but to their distant kith and kin, i.e. to society as a whole, to tens and hundreds of millions of people united first in one socialist state.[6]

More recently a Polish economist pointed out that 'socialism can defeat capitalism . . . only when the level of the productivity of labour it achieves is higher than in capitalist countries'.[7] As a matter of ideological curiosity rather than of practical importance, it may be mentioned here that syndicalism implicitly rejects radical technological change merely for the sake of increasing the productivity of labour and efficiency in general.

Economic growth can be achieved from the physical extension of the resources employed (that is, labour, capital and land) or from productivity increases. These two different sources of growth are sometimes described as 'extensive' and 'intensive', respectively. Normally both sources contribute to growth, but at a particular time one usually predominates. On the whole, in the earlier stages of economic development extensive factors predominate contributing two-thirds or more of economic growth, whilst intensive factors contribute one third or less. In the more advanced economies these relative shares are usually reversed.

Up to about the early 1960s the socialist countries overwhelmingly emphasized the extensive growth strategy. But since that time, owing to the virtual exhaustion of underutilized resources, economic setbacks and a better understanding of growth processes, they have been increasingly turning to the intensive growth factors, that is, the growth of productivity deriving from technological progress – greater specialization, scientific management, the economies of scale, the improvement in the quality of resources and a greater participation in the international division of labour.[8]

The measurement of the growth of productivity is a complex task and historical figures are rather fragmentary. In the countries for which statistics are available over long periods (mostly highly and medium developed capitalist countries), annual increases over the last century have mostly been within the range of 1.5–2.5 per cent. The official rates in the socialist countries since the Second World War have been about twice as high. But their figures are not reliable, or at least not necessarily comparable with the capitalist rates, owing to the distorted price structure and partly unintended bias conditioned by the peculiarities of the socialist national income accounting.

According to the data given in United Nations sources, labour productivity in industry over the period 1955–70 increased in capitalist and socialist countries as shown in Table 6.2 (indexes, with 1970 as the base year).

TABLE 6.2

	1955	*1970*	*1975*	*1977*
Capitalist countries	62	100	109	119
Socialist countries	44	100	137	152

Source. Based on: *Statistical Yearbook 1971* (New York: United Nations, 1972) p. 38, *1978*, p. 42 and *1979–80*, p. 36.

From these figures, over the quarter-century, productivity in the capitalist world doubled, whilst in the socialist world it more than trebled.

It must be noted here, however, that the socialist growth of labour productivity in industry as officially given conveys an exaggerated impression of overall productivity. The rates are much lower in agriculture and services – roughly only one-third of those in industry – owing to the traditional neglect of these branches of the economy, whilst industry has enjoyed top priority.

Factors which are peculiar to socialism and contribute to low labour productivity are frequent political meetings, sport, music and social activities in working hours, the unnecessary hoarding of labour and stoppages due to internal mismanagement and external bottlenecks in deliveries of materials and equipment. Many socialist specialists frankly concede the low labour productivity performance, especially in recent years. A Soviet labour economist pointed out: 'In spite of the steps resorted to to accelerate technological advance and to increase labour productivity in the economy, progress is in fact slowing down and it is necessary to reverse the process.'[9] He also concluded that the official indicators of labour productivity in the USSR were unsatisfactory.[10]

As explained by Czechoslovak and Hungarian economists, the common sources of inefficiency in the socialist countries are an obsession with the retention of obsolete equipment and even complete plants and a reluctance to transfer labour to more modern workplaces, where there are often acute shortages of labour.[11] In Hungary, one of the most dynamic and progressive socialist countries, it was conceded that labour productivity was only one-third to one-half of the Western level.[12] J. Balint also believes that the relative position of Hungary in the world scene has not changed significantly since the early 1950s.[13]

A brief note is warranted on the attitudes of organized labour to innovations under the two social systems. Ideally, any technological change that increases productivity or makes work easier should be positively accepted and facilitated, irrespective of the immediate microeconomic dislocation and other disadvantages to individual workers or enterprises, provided the adverse effects are mitigated or corrected, so that on balance society as a whole benefits.

In capitalist countries trade unions' attitudes to innovations range from limited co-operation to extreme hostility. Some unions may at one stage or another collaborate with their employers as the new methods and equipment clearly provide a better basis for higher wages and improved working conditions. Thus some American unions employ efficiency experts to advise their employers on how to increase profits, provided that the union members also benefit in one way or another. In Sweden, unions go even further by participating in manpower planning and in many cases initiate innovations of direct interest to them. In several less-developed countries trade unions actively participate in the modernization of their economies.

But these attitudes and practices are rather exceptional under capitalism. Unions are conscious of the private ownership of the firms, further reinforced by the traditional division of functions between those of ownership and management (making decisions), on the one hand, and of workers (more or less passively carrying out the decisions), on the other. By and large innovations are seen to be primarily contributing to private profits and/or capital appreciation, and furthermore reducing the worker to positions subservient to machines.

In the socialist countries, the role of trade unions in technological change is, of course, more positive and participatory. If it is accepted that workers collectively own their workplaces, innovations are seen to be of direct or indirect benefit to them. Technological improvements create a better capacity for wage increases (private consumption), social services (collective consumption), shorter hours and better working conditions. Trade unions are neither interested in opposing technological change, nor in fact are they in a position to obstruct or prevent it.

First of all, they acknowledge the primacy of the party and the right of the state and central planners to the choice, initiation and the general framework of innovations. Trade unions have been assigned an active part in the intensive growth strategy embarked upon by the European socialist countries since the mid-1960s and in China some ten years later. On the whole, the unions have readily accepted their enhanced responsibilities. Unions are the chief promoters of what is known as 'socialist emulation', a form of labour competition, designed to increase output and efficiency by applying better methods demonstrated by outstanding workers (see Chapter 3A).

But more specifically, trade unions periodically stage rationalization promotion campaigns and the promotion of inventions by its members. The state now offers generous incentives for such improvements. In China, since the death of Mao Tse-tung in 1976, the role of trade unions has been strengthened and a prominent union leader, Ni Chi-fu, has described them as 'carriers of technological change'.[14]

However, the role of trade unions in technological progress in the socialist planned economies can be easily exaggerated. The main directions of technological change are predetermined by the party, then laid down by central planners in technical plans, further spelled out in detail by the relevant ministries and industrial associations and finally worked out by management in individual enterprises. Major innovations are introduced mostly in newly created plants before trade unions have a chance to participate. The unions' role is rather limited to the most effective implementation of the plans laid down or worked out by some other authority.

C. TECHNOLOGICAL UNEMPLOYMENT

Technological unemployment is caused by the replacement of labour by capital and improvements in the methods of production, work organization or management, leading to the elimination of certain jobs, occupations, workplaces and even industries. Under technological unemployment we may also include those redundant workers who obtain part-time jobs or have to work in jobs below their qualifications – a phenomenon which has come to be known as 'de-skilling', 'downward occupational drift' or (in the USA) 'skidding'. Technological unemployment is distinct from seasonal and cyclical unemployment and that caused by the perennial deficiency of demand. It is narrower in scope than structural unemployment, as the latter may also be caused by changes in the structure of population, consumer tastes and government policies.

The share of technological unemployment in total unemployment where it exists is open to controversy and in the past little attention has been given to its precise measurement. Official statistical returns give overall figures without specifying causes. As of 1981 the total number of unemployed (not including the under-employed) in the capitalist world added up to at least 78m, which on the average represented 6 per cent of the total workforce (see Chapter 2C). Rough estimates suggest that on the whole in recent years technological unemployment has constituted from one-tenth to one-third of total unemployment (the main component being cyclical unemployment, or insufficiency of demand).

Western establishment economics traditionally assumed that although technological change leads to some job abolition, it eventually creates new jobs through a more or less automatic, self-balancing mechanism. It was postulated that higher productivity tends to reduce prices, increase real income and consequently demand for the product in question and/or other items; the expanded output in the existing and new industries, it was claimed, raises employment to higher levels, so that, given time, near-equilibrium employment is restored.

Practical experience has demonstrated beyond any doubt that that mechanism has hardly ever worked either smoothly or consistently.

(1) Prices may not fall in line with productivity increases, owing to monopolistic, oligopolistic or official practices.
(2) The price and even income elasticity of demand for products may be low, so that even where there are price reductions or income increases, demand does not necessarily rise *pari passu.*
(3) Even if demand does rise, output can be increased by utilizing idle capacity or by turning to labour-saving methods (including the substitution of capital for labour).
(4) But even if new job positions are created, it does not necessarily mean that the released workers are fully absorbed, owing to the difficulties of re-training at short notice and the geographical immobility of labour.

Modern technological progress tends to lead to what is now known as 'productivity overhang', resulting in an excess of job abolition over job creation. In the past, the releases of labour from agriculture, forestry and some manufacturing industries and construction were to a considerable extent absorbed by the service sector whose many branches until recently were labour-intensive. But this is now changing. Computers and particularly minicomputers and microprocessors have been playing havoc with employment, especially in banking, communications, retailing and typing.

In less-developed countries, technological unemployment is aggravated by the use of labour-saving equipment originally designed for high-wage countries, by the generous minimum-wage legislation (making unskilled labour too costly in relation to capital) and by the official over-valuation of the currency (making imports of capital unduly cheap in relation to local labour). Furthermore, these countries suffer from under-employment, much more so than the industrialized capitalist economies.[15]

As has been pointed out in Chapter 2C, unemployment is detrimental not only to the individual person concerned, but also to society. The problems produced by technological unemployment are in a sense more serious than ordinary unemployment caused merely by the insufficiency of demand. As J. de Givry put it: 'Too often a worker feels diminished rather than dignified by labour . . . he is a victim . . . of the ravages of progress'.[16] A British Marxist, Ken Gill, noted that whilst the first Industrial Revolution mostly brought about a quantitative replacement of manual labour by machines, the scientific and technical revolution since the mid-1950s has been having a more radical impact on social relations, as now robots are taking over not only operational but also command and creative functions.[17] It may be contended that under capitalism labour has in fact been the ultimate risk bearer of technological change.[18]

Up to the early 1970s there was, on the whole, little concern in the capitalist world about technological redundancy, as the dislocating effects on workers were offset by good alternative employment opportunities, the shortening of the hours of work and rising affluence. But since that time the problem has been aggravated by the high level of unemployment caused by the overall deficiency of demand.

In the socialist centrally planned economies, although the problem of technological redundancy does appear, it does not result in serious open unemployment (Yugoslavia excepted, see Chapter 2C). The socialist state has the necessary powers and determination on the macroeconomic scale to ensure continuous full employment (discussed in the following section) and, in fact, there are prevalent shortages of labour. This is remarkable, considering the rapid economic development of these countries, especially accelerated industrialization and the consequent potential for large technological redundancies (see Table 6.1). In a discussion of technological change and unemployment, a Soviet writer summed up the situation under socialism:

> Technological progress under socialism is not an evil depriving people of jobs, but a boon, making it possible to increase leisure time and release people for the sphere of non-material production – education, the health service, science, culture, and so on. Only socialism is really and fully capable of ensuring the working people's right to work.[19]

Nevertheless, there are several forms of disguised unemployment in the socialist countries. There are various factors impeding the dismissal of redundant workers and favouring the hoarding of labour. Management, as a rule, has to first find alternative employment for such workers elsewhere, which may be difficult. Moreover, owing to the communal spirit and mutal loyalty prevailing in socialist work entities, management often hesitates to discharge a worker (very likely an older person) with a satisfactory past record. A redundant worker may also be retained in the expectation that work will be available later and the prevalent shortages of labour further act as a restraint.

The planned depressed level of wages makes the hoarding of labour less costly to socialist enterprises than would be to private firms in capitalist market economies. The hoarding of labour is further encouraged, as a Soviet economist observed, by the system of material incentives to workers and management, the amount allowed for bonuses depending on the size of the enterprise wage fund (that is, employment).[20]

The phenomenon of the 'downward occupational drift' has also spread to the socialist countries. For example, in Czechoslovakia about one-third of the workforce is not employed in jobs commensurate with its training. Every eighth person with higher education and one-in-five with secondary education work in capacities below their qualifications.[21]

Estimates by socialist economists indicate that disguised unemployment in the form of hoarded labour in the CMEA countries ranges from 5 to 20 per cent of total employment[22] (or 8–30 m in absolute numbers). As there is virtually no unemployment caused by the deficiency of demand, most of the under-employed are technologically redundant. M. Bornstein concluded that, although open unemployment in socialist countries is lower than in capitalist market economies, disguised unemployment is rather higher.[23]

Thus we may conclude that under socialist central economic planning there is a sort of a systemic contradiction; while there are shortages of labour at the macroeconomic level there are hidden surpluses of labour in the microeconomic sense.

D. TACKLING TECHNOLOGICAL REDUNDANCY

It is widely recognized in both capitalist and the socialist countries nowadays that technological unemployment, in whatever form, has become a major problem not only to the individual workers affected but also to society in general. The ILO has been prompting the member countries for years to introduce protective and compensatory schemes, and most countries have responded (to varying degrees). The measures adopted can be divided into defensive and positive, the former predominating in capitalist, and the latter in the socialist, countries.

Traditionally in capitalist market economies employers enjoyed the prerogative of hiring and firing. Although this state of affairs still predominates, in many developed countries dismissals of workers are now regulated in one way or another. This is particularly the case where workers' participation has been firmly established, viz. in Western Europe. In the EEC, according to the legislation passed in February 1975, employers planning collective dismissals must first consult with workers' representatives, and also public authorities must be informed. At least a month's warning must be given of the contemplated retrenchment during which alternative solutions are to be considered. Another piece of legislation, adopted in February 1977, regulates possible dismissals in the case of mergers of firms. Before the firms amalgamate, workers' representatives must be informed of the reasons and of the possible consequences for the workers; if the employer and the workers disagree on the solution or compensation, the dispute may be referred to arbitration.[24] Similarly in Sweden employers are now required to negotiate co-determination with the workers on employment and dismissals.

In the countries where there is no explicit legislation, these matters are often negotiated in collective agreements. Specific solutions to the problem that may be agreed may include the following.

(1) The elimination of overtime.
(2) The reduction of working hours.
(3) Limitations on sub-contracting.
(4) Work-sharing.
(5) Re-training.
(6) Transfers to other plants.
(7) Early retirements.

Otherwise, the measures resorted to by the parties involved and by the government are the same as in tackling ordinary unemployment (the details of which can be found in Chapter 2C). However, taking the capitalist world as a whole, the measures resorted to to tackle technological unemployment have obviously not proved successful, judging by the persistence of high levels of unemployment averaging at least 6 per cent in recent years.

In a special category is Japan, where mutual loyalty between employers and employees is quite extraordinary by any standards. Companies usually provide lifetime employment. When some jobs disappear, the workers are usually retained and retrained at the employer's expense and transferred to some other section or plant of the company. Japanese companies, in fact, treat their wage costs as part of fixed costs (rather than the variable cost). The Japanese procedure is exceptional and it is somewhat akin (unintentionally) to the socialist practice.

In the socialist centrally planned economies, the approach to the problem of technological redundancy is much more systematic, comprehensive and unfailing. First of all, economic planning ensures that there is no overall unemployment, rather an excess of vacancies over possible redundancies. This is achieved by setting appropriate production targets (including the expansion of the existing, and the creation of new, workplaces), on the one hand, and ensuring a sufficiency of effective demand (by the appropriate manipulation of the wage funds and prices), on the other.

The general *economic plan* is supplemented with two other plans bearing on the problem of possible redundancies. The *technical plan* (usually covering long periods of 15-20 years) embodies anticipated or desirable technological developments and the necessary means of adjustment or implementation. But of greater practical relevance is the *manpower plan*. In addition to the 'static' distribution of the labour force, it encompasses school enrolments, vocational training and retraining schemes, in which attention is given to the phasing out and in of certain skills or occupations, together with such related matters as working hours, the extent of shiftwork, recreation leave, wage funds, incentives and labour productivity. Manpower plans are dovetailed into investment plans to accommodate the planned employment and training targets, in which provision is made for the absorption of labour in existing or new workplaces.

Thus in the USSR, the 1971–5 plan provided for the release, retraining and relocation of 20m workers and the 1976–80 plan for 25m.[25] The Soviet experience of the 1970s showed that from two-thirds to three-quarters of the redundant persons had to change their occupation or be transferred to other enterprises.[26]

It must also be realized that in most socialist countries (Yugoslavia being a conspicuous exception) the state guarantees employment to its citizens, and management cannot dismiss redundant workers unless the local trade union agrees to it and an alternative job is found for the person affected.

The problem of the hoarding of labour in enterprises is well recognized by the authorities and some specific measures have been introduced to minimize it.

(1) *The penalization of excessive employment.* Some socialist countries have introduced labour taxes and/or increased social insurance

contributions payable by enterprises. Thus, in Hungary in the mid-1960s, a wage tax was introduced – 8 per cent of the enterprise's wage fund in addition to the 17 per cent of the wage fund for social insurance; as from 1976, the former has been raised to 13 per cent and the latter to 22 per cent (thus now totalling 35 per cent of the enterprise's wage fund).[27]

(2) *The stimulation of the release of hoarded labour.* Several incentive schemes have been introduced, or at least experimented with, to encourage enterprises to release unnecessary workers. The best known is the Shchekino Scheme pioneered in the USSR. It was initiated at the Shchekino Chemical Combine in 1967, to spur enterprises to greater efficiency by minimizing their employment. Up to 70 per cent of the wage bill saved by the reduction of employment, whilst maintaining or increasing production, can be shared by the remaining personnel. The scheme has also spread to several Eastern European countries.[28]

From the above discussion we may conclude that socialist central economic planning has a better system than the capitalist market economies for preventing or re-absorbing technological redundancy. But if the reader is inclined to believe that socialism has all the answers to the problem, his enthusiasm must be moderated somewhat.

Ex-ante economic plans, including their technical and manpower components, may look consistent and neat on paper. But they do not turn out so ideally *ex-post*. Technological change by its very nature embodies uncertainty and unpredictable developments. The planners make errors and even if the plans are sound at the time of their construction, unexpected subsequent developments may render the plans erroneous. Furthermore, the microeconomic logic in the workplaces – either on the part of management or of the workers – does not necessarily correspond to the planners' objectives or society's best interest.

The repetition of public exhortations, experiments, directives and regulations in this sphere in virtually all the socialist countries over the past two decades indicates that the problem is complex and not easily overcome. Yugoslavia has had a good deal of experience in this respect and one of her economists pointed out a few years ago that although full employment can be easily attained under socialist economic planning, its achievement is usually 'economically irrational resulting in lower labour productivity'.[29]

RECOMMENDED FURTHER READING

1. R. Baum, 'Diabolus ex Machina: Technological Development and Social Change in Chinese Industry', in F. J. Flerons (ed.), *Technology and Communist Culture* (New York: Praeger, 1977) pp. 315–56.
2. B. J. L. Berry (ed.), *Urbanization and Counterurbanization* (London: Sage, 1977).
3. R. Callus and M. Quinlan, 'The New Unskilled Worker', *J. Australian Political Economy* (Sydney) Nov. 1979, pp. 74–84.
4. A. B. Cherns, 'Speculations on the Social Effects of New Microelectronics Technology', *Int. Lab. Rev.* (Geneva) Nov.–Dec. 1980, pp. 705–21.
5.* B. Dolejsc, 'Labour Productivity, Wages and the Satisfaction of the Needs of the Population', *Eastern European Economics* (White Plains, NY) Fall 1980, pp. 77–100.
6.* J. Drecin, 'Technological Progress and Economic Growth', *Acta oeconomica* [Economic Papers] (Budapest) vol. 17, 2/1976, pp. 111–22.
7. G. R. Feiwel, 'Causes and Consequences of Disguised Industrial Unemployment in a Socialist Economy', *Soviet Studies* (Glasgow) July 1974, pp. 344–62.
8. A. H. John and A. Zauberman, 'Industrialization', in C. D. Kernıg (ed.), *Marxism, Communism and Western Society: A Comparative Encyclopedia* (New York: Herder and Herder, 1972) vol. 4, pp. 244–60.
9.* S. V. Kazantsev, 'The Relationship between the Social Productivity of Labour and Capital per Worker', *Problems of Economics* (New York) Oct. 1979, pp. 59–72.
10.* L. A. Kostin, 'Problems of Labour Productivity in Soviet Industry', *Int. Lab. Rev.*, Sept.–Oct. 1980, pp. 595–608.
11. N. Lampert, *The Technical Intelligentsia and the Soviet State: A Study of Soviet Managers and Technicians 1928–1935* (London: Macmillan, 1979).
12. J. Musil, *Urbanization in Socialist Countries* (Armonk, NY: M. E. Sharpe, 1980).
13.* M. Nasilowski, 'Types and Trends of Intensive Growth', *Oeconomica polona* [Polish Economics] (Warsaw) 1/1980, pp. 1–25.
14. J. Sigurdson, *Technology and Science in the People's Republic of China: An Introduction* (Oxford: Pergamon, 1980).
15. P. J. D. Wiles, 'Technical Progress and Productive Efficiency', *Economic Institutions Compared* (Oxford: Blackwell, 1977) pp. 385–416.

* *Indicates contributions by writers from the socialist countries.*

7 Wages, Incentives and Living Standards

A. WAGE THEORIES, POLICIES AND PRACTICES

Wages, much more so than other prices, are central to industrial relations, and in fact go to the very foundations of social relationships. In pre-industrial societies wages were basically an outcome of custom, in many cases moderated by social morality, and that system remained basically unquestioned for a long time. But the Industrial Revolution upset that apparent inertness and passivity and wages have become an object of ideological controversy.

In capitalist countries, four major theories of wage formation emerged in the wake of the industrial upheavals. The first of these was the *subsistence theory*, according to which wages tend to settle at the level just sufficient to maintain a worker and his family, including its necessary education and job training. The theory can be traced back to F. Quesnay (1694–1774) and A. R. J. Turgot (1727–81) of France, but was formulated most clearly by the early British classical economists, viz. A. Smith (1723–90), T. R. Malthus (1761–1834), D. Ricardo (1772–1823), R. Torrens (1780–1864) and J. S. Mill (1806–73), whilst F. Lassalle (1825–64) of Germany gave it the widely known name, 'the iron law of wages' and elaborated on its economic, social and political implications. It was maintained that at the subsistence level the supply of and demand for labour could be equated, whilst wages above that level would only lead to an excessive supply of workers (through higher birth rate and lower death rate), thereby depressing wages back to the subsistence level. Consequently, any efforts by trade unions or the political labour movement to raise wages above the subsistence equilibrium were pointless.

The proponents of the *wages fund theory* contended that at any time there is a fixed volume of resources available to the working class for consumption, corresponding to the wages paid out under normal

133

competitive conditions. Wages raised by organized labour above this 'natural' level inevitably lead to either higher prices of consumer goods (as demand exceeds the available supply) or to unemployment (as the available wage fund is insufficient to pay all workers). This theory was first indicated by A. Smith, but was more fully formulated by J. Bentham (1748–1832), J. R. McCulloch (1789–1864) and J. S. Mill. A variant of this theory was the *residual claimant theory*, put forward by W. S. Jevons (1835–82), according to which labour can be paid only after all other claims are met, viz. rent, interest rates and taxes.

Next in the historical sequence is the *marginal productivity theory*, according to which wages are basically determined by the marginal productivity of labour in the context of other factors of production. It is argued that an employer continues to employ labour until the marginal product of labour is equal to the cost of additional workers employed. An upward departure from this wage level in the case of a particular worker would mean losses to the employer whilst a downward attempt could lead to missed profit opportunities.

The marginal productivity theory, which is in fact more appropriately described as a principle, has been applied to the remuneration of all the factors of production. Amongst its many contributors and exponents, the most prominent were L. Walras (1834–1910) in France, E. Barone (1859–1924) in Italy, A. Marshall (1842–1924) in England, K. J. Wicksell (1851–1926) in Sweden and J. B. Clark (1847–1938) in the USA. In a sense, this principle can be considered to be the most general of all the other theories and its *economic* rationality in the long run cannot be denied.

A more practical explanation of wage determination, in developed capitalist market economies of the twentieth century, is provided in the *bargaining power thesis*. This tenet emphasizes the relative strength of labour and employers in respect of organization, size and other associated realities which determine power relations. It was put forward in its different variants by such writers as J. Davidson (in 1898), J. Pen (1952) and A. M. Cartter (1959) in the USA, G. L. S. Shackle (1957) in Britain and F. Zeuthen (1930) in Denmark. M. Dobb, a British Marxist, also subscribed to this explanation.[1]

In a sense, the social theory of wages, formulated by a Russian (non-Marxist) economist, M. I. Tugan-Baranovsky (1865–1910) in the early years of this century, can be considered as a forerunner of the marginal productivity theory and the bargaining power thesis. He thought that wages basically depended on two factors: the social productivity of labour (determining total production available to society) and the social strength of the working class (determining the share which labour can extract from the social cake).

Marxists have two theories of wages – one for each social system. In application to capitalism, Marx (in 'Wage Labour and Capital' and in *Capital*, vol. I) subscribed to the subsistence theory, that is, that workers are remunerated to the minimum level of the reproduction cost of labour, even though they create value in excess of that cost, viz. the *surplus value*. In the Marxian formula of value $(c + v + s)$, these two elements are designated v and s, respectively.[2]

Marx also maintained that the exploitation of labour was increasing, which was reflected in the disappearance of the yeomen and independent craftsmen together with the growing 'industrial reserve army', paralleled by the rapid accumulation of capital. Marxists stressed that the only hope for the working class to escape the doom of the subsistence and wage fund theories was to overthrow capitalism and establish communism.

As a matter of historical fact, Marx's prediction of the 'increasing immiseration of the proletariat' has not eventuated. On the contrary, workers (at least in the industrialized capitalist countries) have enjoyed substantial increases in real wages, paralleled by improving conditions of work. Although conceding this fact, Marx and other Marxist thinkers pointed out that the subsistence level still applied, as the cost of the reproduction of labour increased substantially with technological change (higher cost of raising children, of education and of vocational training – greater stresses to which the worker is subjected).[3]

The idealistic Marxian principle governing work and the distribution of income under full communism is 'from each according to his ability, to each according to his needs.' Although the idea was first put forward by a French utopian socialist, C. H. Saint-Simon, it was Marx who elaborated upon it, popularized it and vested it with ideological significance.[4] The principle means that in an ideal society, each person able to work should contribute as much labour to society as he is capable by virtue of his physical and mental capacity. At the same time, his income should not be proportional to his work but according to what he legitimately needs. Under this system a perfectly fit person with outstanding work performance would receive less income from society than a non-working handicapped person.

However, Marx conceded that during the transitional period which he called the 'lower phase of communism', or 'socialism', the principle of 'from each according to his ability, to each according to his work' was to apply. This principle was officially adopted in Soviet Russia in 1921 and, in spite of changes in emphasis at different times, it has been accepted by other socialist countries, too. Its application has been further strengthened since the economic reforms – in Yugoslavia after 1950 and in the USSR and Eastern Europen after the early 1960s. China, for a long time emphasizing distribution 'according to needs' (especially during the Cultural Revolution, 1966–9), has gradually abandoned that ambition since the death of Mao Tse-tung (1976). In China's new Constitution of 1978, Article 10 reads: 'The state applies the socialist principle: "He who does not work, neither shall he eat" and "from each according to his ability, to each according to his work".'

The practical application of the principle 'according to work' is reflected in the following assumptions, policies and practices.

(1) Labour is the only socially legitimate source of personal income (except social security).
(2) Standard wage scales are differentiated according to the quality and intensity of work or occupation and the social importance of the branch of the economy.
(3) Bonuses payable to workers by enterprises are based on their performance, and similarly overtime work is remunerated accordingly.

Wage determination in capitalist market economies has traditionally been shaped in the labour markets on a decentralized basis between the parties involved. Wages are now typically negotiated in collective agreements, in which labour productivity, the cost of living, the capacity of the employer to pay and relativities to other wages are taken into account. Owing to the 'multiple labour market segmentation' and 'non-competing labour groups', there may be little consistency and justice in the structure of wages. The market mechanism operated in its extreme unrestricted manner under laissez-faire capitalism, roughly up to the First World War (up to the early 1930s in the USA).

Under socialist central economic planning, wage determination (like other economic processes) is centrally shaped. In this task the socialist state is guided by a variety of considerations, most of which are in conflict with each other, viz.

(1) Plan consistency and its orderly implementation.
(2) Economic development.
(3) Efficiency.
(4) Economic welfare.

(5) Social justice.
(6) The advancement of society to full communism.

In the promotion of these objectives, wages have been employed, especially since the economic reforms, as a flexible instrument of economic policy. As a Soviet economist put it:

> Wages are a real economic lever in the hands of the socialist state, by means of which workers and production collectives are motivated to increase production, raise its quality, and heighten labour productivity and the effectiveness of socialist production.[5]

The planning process embraces the total wage fund in the economy, the wage funds of the employment entities and the structure of wage earnings.

Marx condemned capitalism for the exploitation of labour by not paying the full equivalent of the value created by the workers. But at the same time he attacked F. Lassalle's idea that under socialism the worker would receive the 'undiminished' or 'whole proceeds of his labour'. Marx pointed out that a portion of the value created in material production must be retained by the state for replacement and new investment and for the upkeep of the non-productive sphere (wages and investment). Referring to the actual practice under modern socialism a Polish economist admitted frankly:

> It is clear that a worker has never received, nor can he receive, a full equivalent of his work in wages. The essence of the problem consists not in equivalence, but in a sensible wage policy, embracing not only a fair distribution of the wage fund, but also the implementation of the principle of material motivation, i.e. the stimulation of the attitude to work and its quality.[6]

In determining the total wage fund, central planners start from the material production sphere of the economy.[7] Only about one-half of the net value (that is, depreciation deducted) so created is allowed for the total wage fund, the rest being reserved for investment, wages in the non-productive sphere and social consumption. This share in fact tends to decline, owing to the rising 'organic structure of capital' (capital–labour ratio) and the ideologically-promoted social consumption.[8]

On the whole, total wage payments are restricted below the level that would prevail in a capitalist market economy in order to reserve

sufficient resources for rapid economic development (via high investment) and defence (especially in the case of the USSR, China and
Vietnam). Wage funds are also set at the microeconomic level for
individual employment entities, either in the form of absolute maximum
amounts (commonly practised before the economic reforms) or allowing branch associations or enterprises to work them out in conformity
with centrally laid down guidelines, wage scales and various conditions.
In addition, there are material incentive funds, which are formed
separately and in accordance with centrally imposed indicators.

There is, naturally, constant pressure on the part of the employees and
enterprises to maximize wage earnings, and central planners have to
guard against it. The total wage bill in the economy (including the non-
productive sphere), less net personal saving, but plus social consumption, must be roughly equal to the goods and services allowed for the
consumer market. Otherwise, either shortages or accumulating stocks
appear. In their efforts to avoid them, central planners devise ways of
linking wage payments (in the productive sphere at least) to the value (or
sometime volume) of production. In this intricate process various
incentives play an important part (see the following section).

From the above discussion, the reader will appreciate the fact that the
socialist state is naturally placed to pursue an 'incomes policy' on a
comprehensive and systematic basis, and it has been pursued in the
socialist countries ever since the adoption of central economic planning
(long before the familiar term was introduced in Western Europe in the
1960s).

Thus, to generalize, the determination of wages in the past was
decentralized and free in capitalist market economies, and centralized
and directive under socialist central economic planning. However, there
have been substantial departures from the original extreme models on
both sides which, no doubt, must be gratifying to the supporters of the
convergence thesis.

In many developed as well as less-developed capitalist countries,
industrial legislation (setting minimum standards for juveniles and
women, minimum wage laws, standard working hours and the consequent overtime payments, the arbitration of labour disputes) has
brought the state to the industrial scene. The enforcement of the uniform
laws throughout the country has enhanced the role of the government
and the work of the ILO has further favoured state intervention and
departures from laissez-faire practices. The administration of protective
import duties on labour-intensive products (as in Australia and New
Zealand) represents another form of state intervention.

A number of Western countries (such as Australia, Britain, Denmark, France, the Netherlands, Norway and Sweden) have also introduced or experimented with 'incomes policies', designed to link changes in wages to productivity. The extension of the public sector has also involved the state in wage formation in one way or another. These measures, sometimes described as 'national wage policies' have been prompted by the working class through the ballot box.

On the other hand, in the socialist countries there have been some departures from the centralized directive system of wage determination, especially since the economic reforms. The central fixing of wage funds for enterprises is now rather an exception. Enterprises have gained some freedom in how to arrive at and distribute their wage funds, provided they conform to certain norms.

Incentives and disincentives (including labour taxes) are increasingly relied upon in preference to imposed directives. The flow of wages is shaped more and more by labour productivity in the interest of greater efficiency. Moreover, in many cases, owing to the shortages of labour, there is informal bargaining between management and the individual worker – even the foreman has some power to fix the actual wage. The 'wage drift' (the payment of above-award wages) is no longer limited to certain Western countries, it also occurs in the socialist planned economies, as is indicated by periodical revisions of norms by the authorities.

Liberalization and decentralization have gone furthest in Yugoslavia, where state ownership and control have been largely replaced by workers' self-management (see Chapter 5B, C). The wage system was abolished in 1958 and the workers in the self-managed entities share in the net disposable value added (roughly corresponding to wages and dividends). The rates of pay are determined by the Workers' Council, within the limits set by the law, differentiated according to seniority, skill and effort. Owing to the varying degrees of success in different enterprises, workers' earnings differ considerably from one enterprise to another, even for the same job classification. However, workers are guaranteed a minimum income.

B. INCENTIVES

Although the existence of incentives to workers can be traced back to ancient times, they have reached the most elaborate and sophisticated forms under capitalism. First of all differentiated rewards or compensation are built into the standard wage (including salary) scales, reflecting skills, responsibility, experience and perhaps historical antecedents (as in the case of some professions).

Flexible incentives may be paid for non-standard hours (overtime, night-shift, holidays and the like) or for extra output (piecework). About one-third of the workers in the capitalist world are paid by piece-rates, the proportion being smaller in the USA (about one-quarter) and higher in Western Europe (about two-fifths, and up to three-quarters in Scandinavia). In addition, there are the so-called 'fringe benefits', which may include the use of employer's car, accommodation, medical cover, life insurance, pensions, retirement gratuities, and so on. These benefits have become the most dynamic element of total earnings since about 1960. In the 1960s, the percentage represented by supplementary benefits in total earnings in manufacturing was: Britain – 14, Sweden and Switzerland – 15, the USA – 18, the Netherlands – 30, Belgium – 31, the Federal Republic of Germany – 35, France – 51 and Italy – 74.[9]

In some countries, such as the USA, the introduction and extension of fringe benefits are a product of collective bargaining, but in others, especially in continental Western Europe, they are largely a product of industrial legislation (even though the benefits are provided by private employers). These differences can be partly explained by the weakness of the ideological orientation of the working class movement and by the tradition of minimum state intervention in the USA in contrast to Western Europe. In some firms, especially in the USA and Western Europe, there are profit-sharing schemes, which in some cases may assume the issue of shares to workers (see Chapter 5B). There is also a number of systematic and sophisticated schemes emphasizing some particular achievement or procedure, such as Beddaux, Emerson, Halsey, Rowan–Scanlan, and Taylor plans.

Marxists have, generally speaking, been critical of incentives in capitalist society. Marx condemned capitalism for forcing the workers to greater effort by the constant threat of poverty and starvation (the 'industrial reserve army'; that is unemployment) and by enlarging or creating materialistic wants amongst workers.[10] A modern Chinese writer represented the situation under capitalism as follows:

Employing both stick and carrot, the bosses in capitalist society use bonuses and piece-work to induce workers to create more profits for them, and then give them out a few crumbs to split the ranks of the workers or to corrupt them. This practice no longer exists in Socialist China. Workers are the masters of the country.[11]

Fringe benefits are regarded as devices to tie the worker to a particular employer, and it is held that most of them (such as medical cover, pensions) should not be treated as special favours, but as social entitlments to be provided by the state.

The possible use of incentives under socialism or communism has always been a controversial issue in Marxist ideology. In socialist theory and practice, a good deal of significance is attached to the distinction between two different types of incentives.

(1) *Material and moral incentives.* Material incentives are the conventionally understood rewards in money or kind and they appeal to the material cravings of the worker. Moral incentives (also known as 'non-material' or 'idealistic') are meant to appeal to the worker's ideological convictions, social consciousness, patriotism, occupational pride, comradeship and reputation, and they may assume the form of certificates, entries on boards of honour in factories, badges, medals, orders, appearances on the public media, an invitation to join the communist party, and the like.

(2) *Individual and collective incentives.* Whilst the former are awarded to individual workers, the latter involve a group of workers, such as a team, brigade, plant, enterprise or industry. These incentives can be either material (for example, a cash bonus) or moral (for example, the title of the Exemplary Enterprise, or the industry banner awarded to a factory.[12]

Ideologically, moral motivation ranks ahead of material incentives and collective awards are superior to individual incentives. It is assumed that under full communism, when distribution will be governed by the principle 'according to needs', moral incentives will prevail with an emphasis on collective motivation.

Practical policies on the desirability, content and extent of incentives under socialism have fluctuated from one extreme to another ever since the establishment of the first socialist state in 1917. But since the economic reforms (in Yugoslavia after 1950, in Eastern Europe and the USSR after 1962 and in China after 1978) the role of material incentives has been strengthened, owing to the decline in the effectiveness of moral motivation and the adoption of profit as the main criterion of enterprise performance. According to an investigation carried out in the Polish textile industry on whether it was worthwhile to be a 'good worker', 57 per cent of the workers said that they were clearly motivated by material incentives – more than by all other forms of motivation combined.[13]

Furthermore, to enhance the effectiveness of individual material incentives, the authorities have tended to de-emphasize social consumption in favour of private consumption. The former is financed by society and is received in the form of cash social benefits, or in kind, or in services, free of charge; it is considered ideologically to be superior as it represents distribution 'according to needs'. In the past, social consumption tended to grow faster than private consumption and by the mid-1960s it had reached 20–35 per cent of total consumption (compared with 5–20 per cent typically under capitalism).

On the other hand, private consumption is paid for out of the household's own earnings and is not determined by the authorities, but is based on the freedom of choice and is conducive to greater satisfaction and personal pride. But it is not enough to merely pay workers more money. For incentives to be really effective, they must be backed up by more goods, especially luxuries, available in shops which can be easily bought by private consumers in accordance with their individual preferences.

Material incentives have become an important sphere of interest to the Council for Mutual Economic Assistance (CMEA) since the early 1970s, as reflected in the *Report on Wage Methods in Industry in CMEA Member Countries*, prepared by the Working Group of the Conference of Heads of State Labour Organs.[14]

As in capitalist countries, the incentive element is partly built into the standard wage scales, taking account of the worker's qualifications, experience, responsibility and state priorities. It is partly built into the flexible supplement, depending on the worker's effort, certain job disadvantages and the employing enterprise's success. In the absence of the direction of labour, the differentiation of standard wages and incentives performs important allocative functions. The scale differentials and guidelines for flexible supplements are naturally fixed by the state on the advice of the appropriate 'commissions of experts'. There has, however, been a tendency to give greater freedom to enterprises in administering the flexible element of incentives according to local circumstances.

The incentive differential in the standard time wage scale typically ranges from the lowest to the highest in the ratio of 1:3, which is comparable to most capitalist countries, except that the upper extremes are much higher in the latter countries. It is worth mentioning here that up to the late 1950s, most socialist countries had emphasized 'payment by results', and about two-thirds of the workforce was remunerated by piece-work. But since then, time wages have become the rule and now only about one-third of the workers are paid by piece rates (roughly the same proportion as in most Western countries). Time wages are supplemented with compensatory margins (for example, for overtime, unpleasant work, danger) and bonuses.

The flexible incentive payments are financed in each enterprise out of a special Material Incentives Fund. In addition, there is a Socio-Cultural and Housing Fund, serving obvious purposes. In most socialist countries, these funds are now linked to enterprise profit or profitability. Poland represents a significant exception as she dropped it in 1973; incentive payments are made out of ordinary wage funds and are treated as part of the prime cost. It may be further added that in the USSR incentives paid for the saving of materials are treated as ordinary costs (and thus do not depend on enterprise profit). In Romania export incentives are financed directly from the state budget or a special fund determined by the Council of Ministers.

Where there is a profit-incentive link, deductions from enterprise profits for the incentive funds are dependent on the fulfilment of certain 'norms', with an increasing emphasis on efficiency and quality (as distinct from the sheer volume of output). In the USSR, there are now three such norms: the fulfilment of planned profitability, the planned volume of output actually sold (not merely produced) and above-plan labour productivity. In China (where incentives are paid out of the enterprises' wage funds), there are six norms (their relative weight is indicated by percentages in brackets): acceptable quality (30 per cent), exceeded output (20 per cent), the saving of materials and components (20 per cent), a satisfactory industrial safety record (10 per cent), good work attendance (10 per cent) and shop tidiness and sanitation (10 per cent); about 10 per cent of the wage fund can be used for incentives.[15]

The share of incentives in total wage earnings is considerable, and in fact surprising, considering the ideological commitment to egalitarianism. Even in China, with a long tradition of 'anti-economism', bonuses in agriculture may constitute 10 per cent of the basic wage and may amount to one-sixth of annual earnings; further extensions were reported to be on the way.[16] In Czechoslovak industry in 1977, flexible incentives represented from 10 to 18 per cent of the base pay.[17] On Polish state farms material incentives in 1969 constituted 23 per cent of the wage earnings (compared with 0·2 per cent before).[18] In the USSR in the enterprises which have adopted the Shchekino Scheme, up to 70 per cent of the wages saved from reduced employment (whilst maintaining or increasing output) can be placed in the incentive fund and the individual worker can get incentive payments of up to 60 per cent of his basic time or piecework wage.[19]

In general, the incentive differentiation is greater in the case of managerial and specialist personnel. Thus, in Bulgaria, incentives received by such employees represent up to 50 per cent, and in Czechoslovakia up to 60 per cent, of their base pay.[20] In 1969–70 it was reported that in Hungary material incentives could constitute up to 80 per cent of the base salary in the case of managerial personnel, up to 50 per cent in the case of middle-ranking employees, but only about 25 per cent in the case of ordinary workers.[21] In Poland, as reported in 1978, the managerial loading ranged from 300 to 5000 zlotys a year and in Romania, from 128 to 1353 lei a year.[22]

Experience shows that the flexible incentive element in earnings, depending as it mostly does on enterprise profit, fluctuates widely, thereby accentuating the extremes.[23] This means that, in a sense, the worker is in fact the ultimate risk bearer, which contrasts with capitalism where risk is essentially borne by the owner–employer. In the latter case, the recipients of distributed profits (dividends) are usually in the upper income groups and probably earning high salaries elsewhere (not necessarily in the companies they own), and so are more able to face such fluctuations. But not so under socialism, where income from work in the given enterprise is for all practical purposes the only source of income.

C. THE DIFFERENTIATION OF EARNINGS

Income disparities have always existed at least in historical times, although their full extent has never been known precisely, and is not even today. This applies to both capitalist and socialist countries, where upper extremes – for a variety of reasons – are usually hidden from popular scrutiny.

As is well known, of all the social systems that have ever existed, income differences are greatest under capitalism. This is due to the wide disparities in the ownership of property, so that the usual differences in wages and salaries are further accentuated by property income in the form of rents, interests and profits. In fact the upper extremes of income are due to property income and in many cases the richest persons (millionaires, multi-millionaires, billionaires) do not work for wages or even salaries (except perhaps nominally).

According to the limited information available, in Britain in 1973 a quarter of the adult working population earned less than £625 gross (in the whole year), but 10 per cent of non-manual employees earned well over £2000 gross and it is known that the managing director of a trading stamp company scored £260 000.[24] Although in most Western countries there are laws on 'equal pay for equal work', women's earnings from work in reality are still one-fifth to one-quarter lower than men's. The lower extremes are further accentuated by various forms of widespread discrimination against certain races, ethnic groups and immigrants.

According to two Chinese writers, there are three strata of workers in rich capitalist countries: the upper 10 per cent whose life has been 'bourgeoisified', the middle 70–80 per cent who find it difficult to make ends meet, and the lower 10 per cent living well below the poverty line.[25] The well-known British Marxist R. Hyman, believes that the inequalities are resignedly accepted by workers as inevitable, and trade unions as well as the capitalist state perpetuate the existing disparities:

> The apparently 'spontaneous' acceptance by most employees that large inequalities are 'natural' and inevitable is moreover reinforced by the tendency for trade unionism to contain and institutionalize industrial conflict through the established procedures of collective bargaining . . . The state plays an important role in preserving the structure of class inequality by giving powerful institutional and legal backing to the rules and procedures which decide the distribution of advantages and the process of recruitment to different positions . . . By giving legal and institutional backing to the 'laws' of supply and demand the state effectively buttresses existing inequalities of reward in favour of the non-manual or dominant class . . . [and] state power is used to support the prestige and privileges of an elite occupational group.[26]

Income disparities under socialism have been even more controversial than incentives and the controversy has a long history. A number of idealist socialist thinkers, such as T. More (1478–1535), T. Campanella (1568–1639), F. N. Baboeuf (1760–97), E. Cabet (1788–1856), and W. Weitling (1808–71), advocated absolute equality and believed that it was feasible at any stage of economic development. That view was to some extent supported by Mao Tse-tung (1893–1976), especially during the Cultural Revolution (1966–9), to the extent even of idealizing egalitarian poverty.

Marxism is partly opposed to the above view, maintaining that income distribution is a function of the stage of economic development and it is only under full communism that society can afford reasonable equality. Marx envisaged that only then would there be no distinction in remuneration between the skilled and unskilled, between mental and manual, between urban and rural and between managerial and non-managerial employees. In fact the Marxian principle to govern work and personal income 'from each according to his ability, to each according to his needs' postulates not only reasonable income equality, but also implies that the handicapped and unproductive should receive more than the able-bodied and efficient ones should.[27]

Compared with capitalism, personal income disparities under socialism are, naturally, smaller as the spread in wage scales is generally narrower, especially between mental and manual workers. Thus in Poland, judging by the wage and salary structure in 1960, the earnings of the white-collar employees were *25 per cent lower,* and of the blue-collar workers *45 per cent higher* than in capitalist times (in 1937).[28] If we accept the assertion by a Soviet writer, A. Guber, the urban worker in the USSR is 10 times and the peasant 13 times, better off today than before the Bolshevik Revolution in 1917.[29] Of all the socialist countries, Cuba is noted for the smallest income differentiation (as she still largely relies on moral motivation), followed by China. It must also be realized that under socialism labour is virtually the only source of personal income, to the almost complete exclusion of property income.[30]

But in the traditional conflict between idealistic egalitarianism and practical productivity considerations, the latter have firmly reasserted themselves and *even the known income differences* today are embarrassingly wide. Although most socialist countries now occasionally publish figures on the distribution of income,[31] they are given in broad averages concealing lower and upper extremes.

First of all, there are differences in earnings between different branches of the economy, as is illustrated in Table 7.1 by reference to Romania. For various reasons (skills, difficult working conditions, shiftwork) construction, science and scientific work and transport are usually at the higher extreme of the scale, whilst telecommunication, forestry and trade are at the lower end. As of March 1979, 4.0 per cent of the Romanian working population received monthly earnings of less than 1300 lei and 18.4 per cent earned over 2500 lei per month.[32]

In a comparative study of income differentiation, based on published figures, P. Wiles concluded that, compared with the United Kingdom and most capitalist countries (including Australia), income inequalities were smaller in Eastern Europe but greater in the USSR.[33] A similar conclusion was reached by J. Cromwell with regard to some East European countries.[34]

TABLE 7.1   *Average net earnings per person employed in Romania according to the branch of the economy in 1960 and 1979*

Branch of the economy	Per month (in lei)	Percentage of the national average	Per month (in lei)	Percentage of the national average
Construction	821	102	2 346	111
Science and scientific work	935	117	2 316	110
Transport	876	109	2 205	105
Industry	829	103	2 118	100
Education, culture, arts	819	102	2 084	99
Agriculture	703	88	2 008	95
Public health and fitness	760	95	1 958	93
Local government	742	93	1 867	89
Trade	697	87	1 835	87
Forestry	601	75	1 822	86
Telecommunication	752	94	1 820	86
National average	802	100	2 108	100

Source. Based on: *Annuraul statistic al Republicii Socialiste România 1980* [Statistical Yearbook of the Socialist Republic of Romania 1980] (Bucharest: Central Directorate of Statistics, 1980) p. 123.

The distribution of earnings under socialism is illustrated in Table 7.2 using Czechoslovakia as an example – a country which, on the whole, appears to be less secretive than other socialist countries. The ratio of the lowest to the highest income brackets is 1 : 6 at least, but in fact it must be greater because the lower and upper extremes are concealed in the open ranges.

In China, according to the new personal income tax schedule adopted in 1980, annual incomes range from less than 800 yuan (on which no tax is payable) to over 12 000 yuan (subject to a 45 per cent tax rate).[35] In 1979 it was reported that there were still over 800 former capitalists receiving incomes of more than 300 yuan per month.[36] It may be mentioned that the communist regime in many cases co-opted former capitalists in mixed state–private enterprises, especially if they supported the regime and had some valuable expertise (such as managers and specialists). Such persons, in addition to their usual salary received a certain amount of profit or interest on their former productive assets. Those property payments were discontinued with the onset of the Cultural Revolution in 1966, but have been resumed since late 1978.

TABLE 7.2   Levels of gross earnings in Czechoslovakia in the socialized sector, 1970, 1975 and 1979

Range (Korunas per month)	Percentage of earners in each range		
	1970	1975	1979
below 800	0.65	0.24	0.05
801–1 000	2.64	0.73	0.36
1 001–1 200	6.55	2.41	1.01
1 201–1 400	10.45	5.16	2.57
1 401–1 600	11.95	8.29	4.71
1 601–1 800	11.74	9.52	6.97
1 801–2 000	11.88	10.10	8.33
2 001–2 200	10.76	10.16	8.57
2 201–2 400	8.80	10.21	8.73
2 401–2 600	6.86	9.19	8.67
2 601–2 800	4.94	7.76	8.47
2 801–3 000	3.66	6.21	7.79
3 001–3 200	2.60	4.84	6.72
3 201–3 400	1.83	3.66	5.68
3 401–3 600	1.29	2.82	4.69
3 601–3 800	0.90	2.08	3.71
3 801–4 000	0.66	1.54	2.92
4 001–4 500	0.90	2.23	4.69
4 501–5 000	0.43	1.11	2.39
5 001 and above	0.54	1.34	2.97
National average (Korunas)	1 937	2 304	2 579

Source: Statistička ročenka Československé Socialistické Republiky 1980 [Statistical Yearbook of the Czechoslovak Socialist Republic 1980] (Prague: SNTL, 1980) p. 209.

There were 760 000 former capitalists in this position in 1956, but by 1980 their number had dropped to about one-third of the previous figure.

In Poland in 1967, when the minimum monthly wage was 850 zlotys (and the average in the socialized sector stood at 2195), there were 5000 persons who earned 10 000 zlotys or more per month.[37] In 1981, it was reported that the monthly salary (without other pickings) of the First Secretary of the Polish United Workers' Party (the ruling communist Party) was 28 100 zlotys and of other Secretaries of the Central Committee was 25 900 zlotys.[38] In Hungary in 1975, when the *average* annual earnings in the economy were 33 852 forints, there were 130 000 persons whose reported incomes ranged from 100 000 to 200 000 forints in that year.[39] In the USSR, a worker may receive income of up to 8.48 times his basic rate.[40] In Yugoslavia in 1976 the *average* monthly earnings of persons in electric power generation with a doctorate were 11 110 dinars, but of unskilled labourers in education they were only 2099 dinars.[41]

In the highest income group are top party dignitaries, state bureaucrats, technocrats, inventors, professionals (writers, actors, architects, scientists, engineers, designers), especially if they have the opportunity of operating freelance, together with artisans, traders, market gardeners and personal plot holders.[42]

On the whole, there has been a tendency in capitalist countries for the disparities in earnings to be reduced, owing to minimum wage legislation, the pressure of trade unions, the diffusion of skills and the declining share of margins for skill in relation to base pay. Progressive taxation (of personal and company income, consumer goods and services, especially luxuries, and of inheritable wealth) and the provision of social welfare (mostly available to the lower income groups) have further reduced inequalities in disposable income.

The tendency is less discernible in the socialist countries. On the one hand, in the past (especially over the period 1956–65), minimum wages were raised much more than total earnings; in fact up to the mid-1950s the socialist countries seemed to have no explicit minimum wage legislation. On the other hand, the increasing role of skills and material incentives, a better capacity of some workplaces to make higher profits than others and some liberalization and revival of private enterprise have tended to raise the upper levels of earnings. But all in all, it may be generalized that since the economic reforms the disparities have tended rather to increase in most socialist countries, which contrasts with the capitalist tendency for the differences rather to decrease.

D. STANDARDS OF LIVING

In simplest terms, the standard of living can be defined as the consumption level of goods and services and the conditions of work and life in general. Although the concept is well established, the measurement of the standard of living is a complicated task. The problem is compounded if comparisons are made between different countries, especially if they are operating under different social systems noted for different objectives, definitions, valuations and interpretations. Conscious of these difficulties, we shall make international comparisons of living standards, highlighting the factors which entail different effects under each system.

The most basic, or rather the starting, indicator of the standard of living is the amount of goods and services produced per head of population in a year. As capitalist and socialist figures are not directly comparable, complex adjustments have to be made to bring them to the same basis. Figure 7.1 represents adjusted figures of national income per head in US dollars in 1979.

It will be noted that the greatest potential for high living standards has been attained in industrialized and resource-rich countries, and the lowest in undeveloped agricultural nations. Of the socialist countries only the European (except Albania) are above the world average (of $1900 in 1979). Even the German Democratic Republic and Czechoslovakia, the most affluent socialist countries, are less than half the Swiss income level. The lower figures of the socialist countries,

FIGURE 7.1   *Per capita national income in selected capitalist and socialist countries in 1979* (in US dollars)*

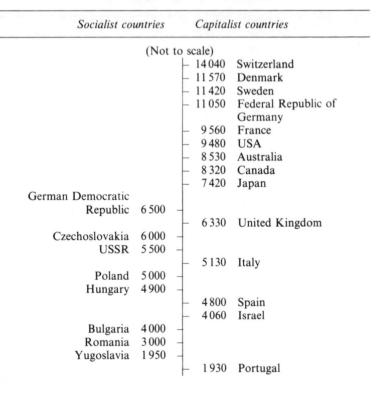

Socialist countries		Capitalist countries
	(Not to scale)	
	14 040	Switzerland
	11 570	Denmark
	11 420	Sweden
	11 050	Federal Republic of Germany
	9 560	France
	9 480	USA
	8 530	Australia
	8 320	Canada
	7 420	Japan
German Democratic Republic 6 500		
	6 330	United Kingdom
Czechoslovakia 6 000		
USSR 5 500		
	5 130	Italy
Poland 5 000		
Hungary 4 900		
	4 800	Spain
	4 060	Israel
Bulgaria 4 000		
Romania 3 000		
Yugoslavia 1 950		
	1 930	Portugal

FIGURE 7.1 (*Contd.*)

World average	1 900	World average
	– 1 670	Brazil
Mongolia 1 600 –		
	– 1 540	Mexico
	– 1 480	Korea (South)
Cuba 1 400 –		
	– 1 330	Panama
Albania 1 300 –		
Korea (North) 1 200 –		
	– 1 060	Tunisia
	– 950	Colombia
China 600 –		
	– 580	Philippines
	– 540	Thailand
Angola 300 –		
	– 290	Indonesia
	– 240	Tanzania
	– 190	India
Vietnam 180 –		
	– 100	Bangladesh
Kampuchea 80 –		

* The Western concept of the National Income at Market Prices applies throughout. The figures are rounded, to avoid a misleading impression of the possibility of precise measurement.
Sources. Based on United Nations, Western and socialist statistics and the author's estimates.

compared with the developed West, are at least partly due to their later start in industrialization.

A *per capita* income (that is, in fact, production) figure does not provide a measure of the standard of living. It is only an initial magnitude of which only a portion is actually used for current consumption. The processes governing this portion are different under each system. Thus, when comparing capitalist and socialist figures, we must take into account the following policies and practices which affect the actual standard of living.

(1) *The proportion of national income devoted to consumption.* In a capitalist market economy the division of national income between current consumption and saving (that is, indirectly, investment) is essentially left to individual persons and the free market forces, and even where the government intervenes its role is rather marginal and

it does not interfere with the market mechanism as a system. Under socialism the relative proportions of consumption and saving are predetermined at the top political level. Furthermore, even proportions of private and social consumption, and necessities and luxuries, are centrally shaped. On the whole, the socialist countries devote smaller proportions of their national income to current consumption than is usually the case in capitalist market economies – roughly 65–75 per cent against 70–85 per cent, the difference typically being 10 per cent *at the same level of economic development.* This policy is aimed at maintaining high levels of investment in the interest of accelerated economic development (especially industrialization).

(2) *Defence expenditure.* This represents a diversion of production to defence, in a sense at the expense of current consumption. On the whole, the socialist countries sacrifice relatively more for defence than capitalist countries do (see Table 7.3). Furthermore, owing to the lower stage of economic development attained in the socialist countries, the burden of the same percentage of the GNP and of per capita GNP is greater in comparison with the rich capitalist countries.

TABLE 7.3 *Defence expenditure in selected capitalist and socialist countries in 1980, as a percentage of the GNP and in US dollars per head of population**

Capitalist countries		Socialist countries	
Australia	3.0 % ($272)	Bulgaria	3.4 % ($128)
Brazil	0.7 % ($ 13)	China	10.0 % ($ 56)
Britain	5.4 % ($437)	Cuba	8.5 % ($111)
Canada	1.7 % ($177)	Czechoslovakia	4.0 % ($229)
Denmark	2.4 % ($274)	Germany (East)	6.1 % ($285)
France	3.9 % ($374)	Hungary	2.3 % ($101)
Germany (West)	3.2 % ($410)	Korea (North)	8.0 % ($ 74)
India	3.8 % ($ 7)	Poland	3.2 % ($131)
Italy	2.4 % ($155)†	Romania	1.3 % ($ 66)
Sweden	3.2 % ($432)	USSR	12–14 % ($700)
USA	5.5 % ($644)	Yugoslavia	5.6 % ($164)†

* The Western concept of the Gross National Product at Market Prices applies to both capitalist and socialist countries.
† In 1981.
Source. Based on: *The Military Balance 1981–1982* (London: International Institute for Strategic Studies, 1981) pp. 112–13, and the author's estimates.

(3) *Working time.* Compared with the West, the socialist countries have 3 – 6 hours per week longer working hours and also shorter annual holidays (see Chapter 3B).

(4) *Taxes.* The level of personal income taxation is lower in the socialist countries than in the capitalist economies, the respective taxes typically administered being 10–20 per cent as against 20–50 per cent or more. The communist regimes are committed to the abolition of the personal income tax in the long run altogether.

(5) *Savings.* Not all disposable income is immediately spent on consumption, but partly saved, mostly in the form of savings bank deposits. There has been a tendency for these deposits to rise in both the developed capitalist world and in the socialist bloc. The growth in the former has been due to inflation, uncertainty (especially as to employment) and high levels of income. In the socialist bloc, the growth has been quite remarkable. Thus in the European socialist countries in the early 1960s savings represented 1–4 per cent of personal consumption, but over the period 1971–75 the percentage rose to 3.4 in Hungary, 4.2 in the USSR, 5.4 in Czechoslovakia, 7.3 in Bulgaria and 8.1 in Poland.[43] Over the two decades 1960–79 personal savings increased as follows.

German Democratic Republic – by 5.4 times, to 5795 marks;
Czechoslovakia – by 6.8 times, to 9692 korunas;
Bulgaria – by 10.5 times, to 1073 lev
USSR – by 10.9 times, to 556 roubles
Mongolia – by 11.1 times, to 256 tugriks
Hungary – by 23.0 times, to 12 691 forints
Poland – by 23.6 times, to 12 446 zlotys

Source. Based on: *Statisticheskii ezhegodnik stran-chlenov Soveta Ekonomicheskoi Vzaimpomoshchi 1980* [Statistical Yearbook of the CMEA Countries 1980] (Moscow: Statistika, 1980) p. 62.

This tendency may be interpreted in two different ways in its effect on the standard of living. On the one hand, the increasing savings may be indicative of the rising incomes and well-being of the population. On the other, the scope for spending one's income may be restricted due to one reason or another, such as a narrow range of goods and services available, shortages, poor quality, severely limited consumer credit (necessitating own cash for the purchase of consumer durables) and the expectation of better supplies in the future. All these developments, realities and hopes have in fact played their part in the socialist countries. But the rising savings at least prove one thing: people must be reasonably well off, as paupers have no option of being Hobson choosers.

(6) *The distribution of personal income.* Excessive income differentiation reduces overall social welfare, as a rich person's satisfaction from spending marginal units of his income is smaller than in the case of a poor individual. On the whole, income inequalities under capitalism are far greater than in the socialist countries. On this score, it may be said that the total amount of social welfare from a given total personal income and consequently the average standard of living are greater in the socialist countries, where income disparities are smaller.

(7) *Social consumption.* Social welfare benefits (in cash, kind and professional services and recreation) are much more developed and more generous under socialism than in the capitalist world (provided the countries compared are at the same stage of economic development). The share represented by social consumption in total consumption in the socialist bloc ranges from 15 per cent (in the poorer countries) to 35 per cent (in the USSR), whilst in the capitalist world the range is typically 5–20 per cent.[44] According to a Soviet writer, A. Guber, the average Soviet household has four-fifths of its cash income left for spending, compared with only two-fifths in the USA (after taxes, social insurance, medical treatment, educational expenses and rent are deducted).[45]

(8) *Other comparative conditions affecting living standards.* On the one hand, in contrast to the capitalist world, the socialist countries (except Yugoslavia) are noted for continuous full employment and a reasonable stability of prices (see Chapters 2C and 8A,D). In addition, the dignity of labour and the feeling that the workers are not dominated and exploited by capitalists but are (at least in theory) masters in their own workers' state, in a sense enhances workers' well-being. But on the other hand, there are several conditions in the socialist countries – again in comparison with the capitalist world – which detract from the people's well-being. There is a high proportion of married women at work, to the obvious detriment of family life and child care. Their outside work is not a matter of restless comfort and boredom, typical of female labour in the affluent Western countries, but is rather a matter of economic necessity and deliberate state policies. As an expression of sex 'equality', women are found in heavy manual occupations, such as builders' labourers and farm workers (see Chapter 2A, B). There are

inadequate supplies of many consumer goods, such as tea, coffee, meat, fancy foods, modern household gadgets and various luxuries. Queues in shops and long waiting lists for housing, cars and some other consumer durables are familiar features, as are black markets. There is formal rationing of some food and even some items of clothing in at least China, Cuba, Poland, Romania and Vietnam. The quality of industrial products is usually below the levels in the industrialized capitalist countries. Housing is not only scarce, but the dwellings also have small living space and are poorly equipped with modern conveniences. The range of entertainments is small and foreign travel is restricted, especially to capitalist countries. Owing to the prevalent sellers' markets, the quality of service in shops is deplorably poor. To the above, we must add the violations of human rights by the state. The mono-party system of government, the over-developed police system (including the powerful secret police), censorship, labour camps, psychiatric asylums and political imprisonment are the facts of life.

When all factors are considered, the rank order in Figure 7.1 still reflects *relative* standards of living with one major qualification. Owing mainly to very heavy defence spending, the positions of China and the USSR are in fact lower – the former is probably below Thailand and the latter below Hungary and perhaps Spain.

RECOMMENDED FURTHER READING

1. J. Adam, 'System of Wage Regulation in the Soviet Bloc', *Soviet Studies* (Glasgow) Jan. 1976, pp. 91–109; 'The Present Soviet Incentive System', *Soviet Studies*, July 1980, pp. 349–65.
2.* S. Balazsy, 'The "Unsolvable" Dilemma of Regulating Earnings in Hungary', *Acta oeconomica* [Economic Papers] (Budapest) 3/1978, pp. 247–67.
3. R. Bernardo, *The Theory of Moral Incentives in Cuba* (Alabama: University of Alabama Press, 1971).
4.* P. G. Bunich, 'Wages as an Economic Incentive', *Problems of Economics* (New York) May 1981, pp. 3–18.
5. Janet Chapman, 'Wages', in C. D. Kernig (ed.), *Marxism, Communism and Western Society* (New York: Herder and Herder, 1973) vol. 8, pp. 293–98.
6.* Cheng K'ang-ning and Hsia Wu, 'Labor and Wage Planning Tables', *Chinese Economic Studies* (Armonk, NY) Winter–Spring, 1977–8, pp. 108–22.
7. A. Chilosi, 'Income Distribution under Soviet-Type Socialism: An Interpretative Framework', *J. Comparative Economics* (New Haven) 4/1980, pp. 1–18.

8. D. Conn, 'Comparison of Alternative Incentive Structures for Centrally Planned Systems', *J. Comparative Economics*, Sept. 1979, pp. 261–76.

9. H. Flakierski, 'Economic Reform and Income Distribution in Poland: The Negative Evidence', *Cambridge J. Economics*, June 1981, pp. 137–58.

10. C. Howe, 'Wages, Prices and Standard of Living of Urban Workers in the PRC', *The China Business Rev.*, Jul.–Aug. 1978, pp. 10–16.

11. L. Hurwicz, 'Socialism and Incentives: Developing a Framework', *J. Comparative Economics*, 3/1979, pp. 207–16.

12.* Ji Zhe, 'China's National Capitalists: Past and Present', *Beijing Rev.*, 28 April 1980, pp. 18–24.

13.* M. Kabaj, 'Productivity, Wages and Motivation at the Enterprise Level (Recent Experience in Methodology and Application), *Oeconomica polona* [Polish Economics] (Warsaw) 1/1981, pp. 59–73.

14.* L. Kheifets, 'Material Rewards for the Work Force and the Improvement of the Economic Mechanism', *Problems of Economics*, June 1981, pp. 32–45.

15. D. Laibman, 'The "State Capitalist" and "Bureaucratic–Exploitive" Interpretations of the Soviet Social Formation: A Critique', *Rev. Radical Political Economics* (New York) Winter 1978, pp. 24–34.

16. A. McAuley, 'The Distribution of Earnings and Incomes in the Soviet Union', *Soviet Studies*, April 1977, pp. 214–37; and *Economic Welfare in the Soviet Union: Poverty, Living Standards and Inequality* (London: George Allen and Unwin, 1980).

17.* Zofia Morecka, 'Evolution of Distribution Relations in Socialist Economy', *Oeconomica polona*, 1/1980, pp. 47–60.

18. J. E. Roemer, 'Differentially Exploited Labor: A Marxian Theory of Discrimination', *Rev. Radical Political Economics*, Summer 1978, pp. 43–54.

19. Ch. A. Schwartz, 'Economic Crime in the USSR: A Comparison of the Khrushchev and Brezhnev Eras', *International and Comparative Law Q.* (London) April 1981, pp. 281–96.

20.* S. Shatalin, 'Methodological Problems in the Analysis of the People's Well-Being', *Problems of Economics*, Aug. 1981, pp. 20–38.

21.* V. Voronin, 'Personal Household Plots and Trade', *Problems of Economics*, March 1981, pp. 3–15.

22.* Wu Ching-ch'ao, 'Wage Planning', *Chinese Economic Studies*, Spring 1977, pp. 81–92.

23. M. Yanovitch, *Social and Economic Inequality in the Soviet Union* (London: Martin Robertson, 1977).

24.* A. Zaitsev, 'The Personal Savings of the Working People under Developed Socialism', *Problems of Economics*, Feb. 1981, pp. 64–77.

25.* Zhou Shulian, Wu Jinglian and Wang Haibo, 'The Profit Category and Socialist Business Management: Retaining a Percentage of the Profit as Bonus Funds', *Chinese Economic Studies*, Winter–Spring 1980–1, pp. 63–88.

* *Indicates contributions by writers from the socialist countries.*

8 Inflation and Labour

A. THE EVIDENCE AND SOURCES OF INFLATION

Inflation can be defined as a situation in the economy where the volume of money purchasing power persistently exceeds the supply of goods and services, inducing a continuous rise in the price level and a consequent decline in the value of money. In the context of different economic systems, it is useful to make distinctions between different types of inflation.

Open inflation occurs when prices are free to rise without any government intervention, whilst *repressed* (or *suppressed* or *hidden*) inflation exists where there are governmental controls of one sort or another, whereby prices are officially laid down at lower than free market levels. *Demand-pull inflation* is prompted by excessive demand (that is, relatively high incomes and money supply) for goods and services, whilst *cost-push inflation* is caused by increases in the costs of materials and labour. *Structural inflation* appears when prices of particular goods or services rise substantially in relation to others.

In capitalist market economies, inflation is usually of the open type, which is consistent with the freedom of enterprise. On the other hand under socialist central economic planning repressed inflation prevails, which is in line with the directive system of planning and management.

Normally both demand-pull and cost-push processes operate with mutual cause and effect. But a generalization may be ventured that, up to about 1970 in capitalist countries demand-pull was dominant, whilst in the socialist bloc cost-push played a greater role, at least in the official periodic (upward) price revisions and reforms. But since that time, the role of these inflationary pressures appears to have been reversed. In the capitalist world the steeply increased prices of fuels and other raw materials, industrial disputes and wage increases have exerted strong inflationary pressures on the cost side. On the other hand, in the (European) socialist countries the substantial increases in minimum wages, the strengthened role of material incentives, the large accumulated savings, the liberalization of consumer credit and the contagious effect of Western consumption patterns, all have intensified pressure on the demand side.

Both types of economy have experienced structural inflation in the last decade or two. In the capitalist world fuels (especially oil), mineral raw materials and food have risen faster since the early 1970s than manufactures. In the socialist countries, the steeply rising costs in mining and agricultural production (especially meats), together with the infectious influence of the world (capitalist) market have accelerated price increases of these products.

In this study we are primarily interested in retail prices, that is, those affecting consumers (as distinct from wholesale prices which are of greater concern to producers). As is well known, inflationary pressure has accelerated in the capitalist world since the early 1970s. But the rates of inflation have differed widely from one country to another. This is indicated in Table 8.1 by the consumer price index in certain representative countries in ascending order of inflation, 1970 being the base year (the food component is shown in brackets). It can be concluded that the highest rates of inflation have been reached in some of the less-developed countries. Chile, formerly under a democratic Marxist regime but since 1973 under a military reactionary rule, has led the way where prices rose more than 4000 times over the decade.

TABLE 8.1

	1975		1980	
Switzerland	149	(141)	163	(163)
Austria	142	(136)	184	(170)
Netherlands	151	(139)	203	(124)
USA	139	(153)	212	(217)
India	175	(179)	212	(203)
Canada	143	(164)	217	(264)
Egypt	134	(152)	245	(297)
France	153	(158)	251	(254)
Australia	163	(142)	269	(271)
United Kingdom	184	(206)	361	(396)
Mexico	160	(169)	419	(423)
Brazil	188	(199)	1 321	(1 503)
Turkey	218	(235)	1 639	(1 638)
Argentina	1 202	(1 187)	259 090	(62 163)
Chile	27 752	(35 821)	419 601	(500 946)

Source. Based on: United Nations *Monthly Bulletin of Statistics*, (New York), Oct. 1981, pp. 186–95.

A Polish Marxist, M. Mieszczankowski, sees the basic root of capitalist inflation in the structural transformation of capitalism and its entry into the stage of 'state monopoly capitalism'.[1] The socialist view of capitalist inflation is coloured by ideological considerations and is regarded as an inherent feature of capitalism. It is attributed to eight sources. First, there is conflict between capital and labour regarding the division of national income between capitalists and workers, resulting in industrial disputes and losses of production.

Second, the unscrupulous monopolies in their quest for profit maximization restrict output and force their prices up. Third, the governments, in their efforts to maintain higher levels of economic activity, promote the excessive expansion of money and credit, as otherwise capitalism is incapable of ensuring continuous full employment. Fourth, governments also incur budgetary deficits caused by financial mismanagement and the reluctance to increase taxation, owing to the fear of possible adverse electoral reaction.

Fifth, there is the continued over-development of the non-productive sphere (sales promotion, public administration, banking and finance, entertainment, and so on) as a cure for unemployment. Sixth, the governments, prodded by the military–industrial complexes, maintain high levels of military spending. Seventh, the operations of the greedy multinational corporations and international cartels induce higher prices and transmit inflation from one country to another. Finally, there has been the over-expansion of international liquidity through the irresponsible US balance-of-payments deficits calculated to finance the American economic and military domination of the world (foreign investment, the Eurodollar market, wars and 'neo-colonialism' in general).

For a long time, the socialist leaders denied the existence of inflation under socialist central economic planning. As late as 1976, a Soviet weekly published in English in London assured Western readers (quoting an assertion by Y. Chaplygin, a Soviet economist):

> In the socialist economy there are no objective conditions for inflation . . . The stability of money is ensured by the planned and proportionate development of the national economy and complete state control of currency and foreign trade, and also by a healthy state budget and by a planned price policy.[2]

The above assertion was later reiterated by N. Glushkov, Chairman of the USSR State Price Commission, maintaining that the Soviet economy could be shielded from capitalist inflation: 'Soviet economic advances provide a reliable barrier against the inflationary pressures which rage in the economies of the capitalist countries.'[3]

Indeed, by official statistics the rates of inflation in the socialist countries appear to be negligible. In fact according to classical Marxist thinking, in the long run prices should fall, owing to the increasing 'organic structure of capital' (capital–labour ratio) and technical progress in general, so that increases in living standards should be achieved by falling prices, rather than by rising nominal incomes. That belief has found its practical expression in the German Democratic Republic, where over the period 1950–70 retail prices were gradually reduced by one-half and over the period 1970–79 by 2 per cent.[4]

The consumer price indexes in the socialist countries (which supply such information to the United Nations) over the period 1970–80 are shown in Table 8.2 (1970 is again the base year, food in brackets).

TABLE 8.2

	1975		1980	
German DR	98	n.a.	98	n.a.*
USSR	100	(101)	101	(102)
Czechoslovakia	101	(101)	112	(106)
Hungary	115	(110)	155	(165)
Poland	110	(114)	137	(155)†
Yugoslavia	243	(244)	559	(592)

n.a. not available.
* In 1979.
† In 1978.
Sources. Based on: *Statistisches Jahrbuch der Deutschen Demokratischen Republic 1980*, (East Berlin; Staatsverlag der DDR, 1980) p. 265; UN *Monthly Bulletin of Statistics* (New York) Oct. 1981, pp. 186–95.

The degree of inflationary suppression is smaller in Yugoslavia than in other socialist countries. As the above figures indicate, the Yugoslav rate of inflation is quite high – much higher in fact than in most capitalist countries (certainly, the developed ones). Other evidence of inflationary price increases officially conceded may be given. In the USSR over the first five-year-plan period (1928–32), retail prices rose 2.5 times.[5] In Hungary the official retail price index over the period 1950–74 rose by 96 per cent.[6] Even in China, the country noted for strict anti-inflationary policies, over the period 1952–57 retail prices officially rose by 18 per cent.[7] In 1980 the Chinese authorities conceded that in 1979 the rate of inflation had been 5.8 per cent.[8]

The official prices are, of course, below free market prices, if they are tolerated and known. Thus in China, according to Katharine Hsiao, in the overall annual rate of inflation of 3.5 in the 1950s, the officially conceded element was 1.7 and concealed inflation constituted 1.8.[9] In Poland in 1974, the official contract (procurement) prices and the prices allowed in free markets, in that order, per 100 kg of the main agricultural products were as follows.

rye	–	296 and 366 zlotys,
wheat	–	395 and 480 zlotys,
potatoes	–	142 and 177 zlotys,
oats	–	289 and 377 zlotys,

which revealed the following degrees of inflation: 17, 22, 25 and 30 per cent, respectively.[10] It may be mentioned here that there were some spectacular increases in the official prices of food in July 1980, ranging from 20 to 100 per cent, and in February 1982 up to 400 per cent.

Another indicator of inflationary pressure is provided by the black market exchange rates of the socialist currencies. The official tourist rates and black market rates, together with the degree of inflation so measured, of selected socialist currencies in late 1981 were as shown in Table 8.3 (units of national currency per US dollar).

The causes of what has come to be known as 'socialist inflation' are complex – partly inherent in the system and partly imposed by unexpected circumstances and developments. It is possible to distinguish nine different causes.

(1) *Social ownership.* As the means of production are almost wholly owned by society, the purchasing power of money in terms of land and capital is virtually nil. This applies not only to private persons, but also to socialized entities which cannot acquire the means of production even if they have money unless the acquisition of such assets is sanctioned by the plan and allocated by the state.

(2) *High planned accumulation.* The proportion of national income reserved for investment is usually higher, by roughly 10 per cent, than in capitalist market economies at the same stage of economic development. This is further accentuated by a heavy military commitment of resources and economic aid to less-developed countries. The consequent restriction of current consumption

TABLE 8.3

	Official tourist rate	Black market rate (percentage above the official rate in brackets)	
China	1.73 renminbi	1.97 renminbi	*(14%)*
Yugoslavia	39.13 dinars	45.50 dinars	*(16%)*
Hungary	29.54 forints	38.35 forints	*(30%)*
Czechoslovakia	11.94 korunas	26.90 korunas	*(125%)*
Bulgaria	0.85 lev	2.80 lev	*(229%)*
German Democratic Republic	2.44 DD marks	9.35 DD marks	*(283%)*
Laos	10.00 new kips	41.50 new kips	*(315%)*
Kampuchea	4.00 riels*	18.00 riels	*(350%)*
USSR	0.75 rouble*	3.62 roubles	*(382%)*
Romania	4.47 lei*	43.80 lei	*(880%)*
Poland	33.20 zlotys	507.00 zlotys	*(1,427%)*
Cuba	0.78 pesos	22.00 pesos	*(2,721%)*

* Commercial rate in visible trade.
Sources. Based on: UN *Monthly Bulletin of Statistics* (New York) Nov. 1981, p. 201; *World Currency Report* (New York: Pick) 11 Dec., 1981, pp. 10–11.

creates tension on the consumer goods market. Thus, in the mid-1970s, the estimated percentage of the GNP devoted to capital formation was 31, 32, 35, 40 and 42 in the USSR, Bulgaria, Hungary, Romania and Poland (respectively), compared with 19, 20, 21 and 28 in the USA, Britain, Sweden and the Federal Republic of Germany; furthermore, the proportion in the socialist countries has tended to rise.[11]

(3) *Tight planning.* In their determination to accelerate economic development, planners tend to overcommit the available resources and allow relatively small or no reserves. Errors in planning or unexpected developments lead to unfulfilled targets, bottlenecks and shortages. In such contingencies, priority is usually given to safeguarding the output of military equipment and producer goods, rather than of consumer goods. A Polish monetary expert, Z. Fedorowicz, frankly admitted:

> So far no socialist country has succeeded in the preparation and implementation of such a system of economic planning which would eliminate all conflicts amongst the economic entities involved and excessively tight targets making them unrealistic.

This may lead to an inflationary situation as a consequence of *ex post* unbalanced plans.[12]

(4) *Liberal credits in the production sector.* Virtually automatic credits are usually available at low interest rates for the implementation of the targets specified in the economic plan. It is generally assumed that if resources are available, economic development should not be hampered by a lack of finance. The common delays in the completion of investment projects, the extra credits often demanded owing to the revisions of original plans and the laxity in the repayment of credits often lead to the expansion and extension of credits beyond the planned levels and periods.

(5) *The neglect of agriculture.* Inflation has been particularly pronounced in respect of primary products. Initially the prices of food, fuels and raw materials were fixed at very low levels in relation to manufactures, as a method of state absorption of differential rent and of taxing the peasant to finance industrialization. But this proved wasteful and socially grossly unjust and, furthermore, costs in primary industries have been rising very steeply. In the interest of economy and greater efficiency the prices of primary products have been allowed to rise faster than other prices. The rate of growth of agricultural output in the past was only about one-third or less of that of industrial output.

(6) *Weak or faulty motivation.* The bureaucratic central economic planning and management, the virtual absence of private enterprise, the weakness of material incentives, the weakness or non-existence of competition and the persistence and subsidization of loss-incurring enterprises are not conducive to maximum economies in the use of resources, but tolerate and even encourage waste at the microeconomic level.

(7) *Rising indebtedness to capitalist countries.* The socialist bloc's gross indebtedness to the capitalist world rose from $11 000m in 1970 to $45 000m in 1975 and further to $95 000m in 1980, involving a rapidly increasing burden of interest payments (about $8000m in 1980) and the repayment of the principal. The burden is particularly heavy in the case of Poland, whose total foreign debts amounted to $27 000m – about four times the country's exports, and virtually all exports are now needed for debt servicing (interest plus current repayments falling due).[13]

(8) *The impact of capitalist inflation.* Since the early 1970s the socialist countries have found it most difficult to shield themselves from the

rapidly rising prices in world (capitalist) markets. In intra-CMEA trade, the member countries use average world (capitalist) prices with certain adjustments. Previously, these prices were lagged at least five years behind world prices, but since 1975 upward revisions have been made every year. Trade with capitalist countries, in respect of both exports and imports, takes place at world market prices. Since the mid-1970s, the socialist countries have found it virtually impossible to insulate their domestic prices from foreign markets. The impact has been accentuated by the growing share of the capitalist world in socialist foreign trade – from 20 per cent in 1953 to 37 per cent in 1970, which further rose to 50 per cent in 1980.[14] It is known that in Hungary over the period 1968–73 the rising costs of imports accounted for 8 per cent of price increases in consumer goods, 18 per cent in agricultural products and as much as 45 per cent in industrial producer goods.[15] In Yugoslavia, a 1.0 per cent increase in import prices raises domestic prices by 0.3 per cent.[16]

(9) *Wages and incentive payments* have also played a part in socialist inflation, but their role will be examined separately in the next section.

There is no agreement in the socialist countries as to whether they have inflation or not. Most of the socialist economists now concede the fact and acknowledge the inability of socialist economic planning to prevent price increases, whether controlled or free. In the view of Z. Fedorowicz:

the mechanism of inflationary pressure in the socialist economy is fundamentally caused by the contradiction between the microeconomic conflict and macrosocial interests, generated mainly by the faulty system of incentives which after all, is one of the basic elements of the system of the management of the economy.[17]

But officially, the traditional denial is still adhered to. The well-known Hungarian administrator (heading Hungary's Materials and Prices Commission) and theoretician, B. Csikós-Nagy, pointed out a few years ago:

The socialist countries do not regard a rise in the price level as representing inflation. The elimination or narrowing of the gap between agricultural and industrial prices has relaxed increasingly acute social tensions and has contributed in no small measure to enhancing general social stability and to equilibrium. Similarly, if a rise in industrial production costs due to acceleration of the rates of technological development, of environmental protection and of increasingly demanding social requirements and other similar factors were to be described as inflation, this would imply an identification of economic stability with the preservation of historically evolved conditions of production.[18]

B. WAGES AND INFLATION

Wages are also a price (of labour), and as such become a central feature in the inflationary process. We shall examine how real wages are affected by inflation and how wages may contribute to inflation under each social system.

In a capitalist free market economy, price increases – including the cost of living – tend to precede increases in nominal wages. Employers, naturally, prefer to delay wage increases, and in addition there may be formalized procedures for wage adjustments, whereby wages may be raised periodically whilst prices have already increased. In effect, this delay in wages catching up with prices amounts to losses in the purchasing power of wages in the intervening periods. Even if nominal wage increases, when they do occur, are proportionate to price increases, the real loss is not necessarily revealed in published statistics covering fairly long periods (for example, a year).

This traditional laissez-faire pattern has been modified to varying degrees in different countries. The so-called cost-of-living adjustments are now made at shorter intervals – quarterly or more frequently where the inflation rate is high (as in some less-developed countries). Wage increases may also be back-dated or even anticipate price increases.

The situation has changed in some countries in the last two decades or so with the growing strength and militancy of trade unions. In some industries, wage increases in many cases have spearheaded inflation through cost-push. The cost burden has been further accentuated by pressure for shorter working hours, longer holidays and the high incidence of industrial disputes.

Table 8.4 shows movements in real wages in certain developed capitalist and socialist countries over the two decades 1960–79. According to the official statistics, the increases were in the order of one-third to one-half and they were comparable in both types of economies.

TABLE 8.4   *Movements in real wages in selected capitalist and socialist countries, 1960–1979: official indexes of monthly real wages (1970 = 100)*

Country	1960	1975	1979
Austria	60	130	139*
Canada†	79	112	116*
France‡	66	133	149*
Germany, FR of‡	57	120	130*
Great Britain‡	74	121	114*
Italy‡	60	135	157*
Japan	56	136	147*
USA‡	85	101	102
Bulgaria	70	116	119
Czechoslovakia	79	118	124
Hungary	77	118	125
Poland	84	142	149
Romania	68	120	149
USSR	74	119	131
Yugoslavia	61§	105	121*

* In 1978.
† Per week.
‡ Per hour.
§ In 1963.
Sources. Based on: *Rocznik statystyczny 1980*, p. 513; *Statisticheskii ezhegodnik stranchlenov Soveta Ekonomicheskoi Vzaimpomoshchi 1980* [Statistical Yearbook of the CMEA Countries 1980] (Moscow: Statistika, 1980) p. 51.

But, on the whole whilst the capitalist countries experienced larger increases in the 1960s, in the 1970s the socialist countries led the way.

The Marxist view of the relation between wages and inflation under capitalism is, of course, highly critical. It is emphasized that wage increases lag behind price increases and it is denied that wages are the cause of inflation. It is further stressed that in this process, the capitalist state supports the employers against the workers. These views are most often expressed by Soviet writers, as exemplified below:

The boards of major companies have devised an ingenious secret mechanism to prevent nominal and hence real wage rises that would bring down profits . . . Yet the growth of nominal wages does not cause either price increases by big monopolies or inflation. To begin with, wage rises are brought about by mounting prices of necessities. In other words, the workers' demand for higher wages is a protective reaction to attack on their standards of living. Secondly, anyone who assesses the ratio between wage and price increases should remember that since wages are only part of production costs and goods prices, a wage rise cannot cause an equal price increase.[19]

The same writers also stated that in US industry over the period 1967–73, although real wages increased by 9.7 per cent monopoly profits climbed by 60 per cent (from $46 400m to $74 200m).[20]

Two other Soviet economists further pointed out: 'Inflation acts as a factor in the state monopoly redistribution of national income at the expense of the working people in favour of the monopolies'.[21] In the same article it is indicated, by quoting an American source, that in the USA over the period January 1973–July 1978 the average real income per industrial worker privately employed fell by 2 per cent and the purchasing power of US pensioners declined by 25 per cent between January 1973 and September 1978.[22]

An American left-wing radical, Brian Burkitt, put forward a thesis that the capitalist employers and the state strive to raise the real value of profits. But, as he argues, under modern conditions with strong trade unions these attempts are restrained by the threat of inflationary consequences, as organized labour presses for wage increases setting off a wage-price inflationary spiral. His main point is that nowadays it is not the Marxian subsistence wage that constitutes the lower limit to fluctuations in the level of real wages, but the 'inflationary barrier'.[23]

In the socialist centrally planned economies real wages are less likely to be affected owing to smaller rates of inflation and the ideological commitment of the socialist state to the protection and improvement of workers' living standards, especially of the lower paid groups. The official statistics show a fairly steady growth of real wages, that is, even when there are price increases, they are usually more than compensated by increases in nominal wages, as is suggested in Table 8.4.

However, official statistics and pronouncements in the socialist countries must be treated with caution. First of all, the official indexes of wages and prices are not necessarily reliable. It must also be borne in mind that the socialist state is in a much better position than a capitalist government to manipulate definitions and bases of compilation to produce the best popular effect. These facts were in fact conceded by a Yugoslav economist, in the country which is more liberal than other socialist countries.[24] There were many instances in the past of unexpected price increases not necessarily matched by wage increases, some of which led to serious workers' riots – as in China, Czechoslovakia, the German Democratic Republic, Poland, Romania, the USSR and Yugoslavia (see Chapter 9B).

Considering that the socialist countries also have inflation, a question arises as to whether wages are responsible for it. There is no simple answer to this problem. On the one hand, the pressure for higher wages amongst workers and the inclination of the socialist state to give in are much smaller than under capitalism. The scope for spending by workers is limited, as money cannot buy the means of production (including shares), precious stones and metals, and there is usually a small variety of goods and plenty of empty shelves in shops. Luxuries are available, if at all, not so much for money but rather as 'fringe benefits' attached to positions of power or distinction, whilst social prestige associated with conspicuous consumption is minimal (and in fact can be negative). The overwhelming power of the state and directive planning apply systematic brakes on wage increases, which is further facilitated by the weakness or conformity of trade unions (with a qualified exception of Poland).

On the other hand, in practice there have been forces pushing wages and incentive payments up, with direct or (mostly) indirect inflationary effects. Owing to the shortages of labour, enterprises strive to attract workers or hold them by offering higher classifications than their productivity would warrant which, together with the consequent slack discipline often results in poor performance. Reaching and exceeding quantitative targets often involves a wasteful use of materials and a low quality of production. Z. Fedorowicz recently drew attention to the adverse effects of the system of incentives on productivity:

> It must be pointed out that the existing methods of regulating increases in wages in different enterprises and branches of production produce disproportions in wage earnings of workers within the same occupation with the same qualifications and with similar labour productivity. These disproportions lead to higher labour turnover and also greater pressure for raising wages in less privileged cases irrespective of efficiency.[25]

A similar conclusion was reached by M. Korosić who, discussing income inequalities in Yugoslavia, stated bluntly: 'The present system of distribution is a source of inflation, it is contributing to higher costs and is only promoting an inefficient economic structure'.[26] Of all the socialist countries, the most inflationary wage increases occurred in Poland in 1980–1. Average nominal net monthly earnings rose in 1980 from 5150 zlotys to 6350 zlotys, that is, by 23 per cent, whilst national income declined by 4 per cent; this development continued in 1981 when wages also rose by about 25 per cent whilst national income dropped further by 13 per cent. During the same period in black markets, the Polish currency depreciated in relation to the US dollar from 120 to over 500 zlotys (that is, by over 400 per cent).[27]

C. BROADER SOCIAL AND ECONOMIC EFFECTS

Inflation affects different social groups in different ways, and it may also lead to the distortion of economic processes. Persons on fixed incomes, or on only periodically adjusted incomes, lose in relation to incomes which grow at the same rate or faster than inflation. Similarly, holders of monetary assets lose compared with owners of other forms of property. This loss–gain differentiation occurs most strikingly in capitalist market economies. Thus purchasing power tends to decline in the case of pensioners, rentiers (mostly retired people receiving interest from their invested savings), students (on scholarships or other fixed allowances), as well as wage earners not embraced by strong and militant unions. On the other hand, employers and owners of land, buildings, shares, precious metals and stones and objects of art are protected or benefit from the rising values, often at faster rates than inflation.

These effects are further accentuated by unemployment – a twin accessory of the modern phenomenon of stagflation (especially since the early 1970s), and the consequent spread of poverty. There is an ideological difference in the interpretation of the cause of unemployment. The right-wing explanation dwells on rising wages, whereby labour (especially the less-skilled and less-adaptable) prices itself out of the market. On the other hand, Marxists maintain that unemployment is caused by monopolies, as profits can be maximized by restricting output and employment to the level where marginal cost is equal to marginal revenue – the level below that applicable to perfect competition. Although some (mostly small and medium) firms may suffer from profit squeeze, it is caused not so much by rising wages, but by increasing costs of materials, on the one hand, and restricted demand caused by the poverty of the masses, especially the unemployed, on the other.

Thus it can be concluded that, in a capitalist society, inflation leads to the redistribution of income, and to some exent of ownership, from the lower to the higher social classes. Marxists see these processes as being peculiar to capitalism and an expression of exploitation, further accentuating the class struggle. According to a Polish monetary ideologist: 'Inflation exacerbates class contradictions . . . as it usually transforms the struggle for economic interests into political struggle between the bourgeoisie, supported by the state, and the working class.'[28]

Other social and economic effects of ideological relevance may be briefly mentioned. Inflation under capitalism is usually accompanied by speculation, in which the wealthy and unscrupulous engage at the expense of others. Inflation discourages thrift and may further create balance of payments difficulties, as exports tend to decline in relation to imports, thereby aggravating the problem of unemployment. It also leads to distortions in the pattern of production, as the allocation of resources in a capitalist economy is essentially shaped by market prices; this contrasts with the socialist economy, where the allocation of resources is basically determined by planning, irrespective of inflationary price distortions. On the other hand, inflation may benefit debtors (mostly lower income groups) at the expense of creditors (usually propertied classes).

Most of the problems highlighted above do not appear in the socialist countries. Some do, although not to the same extent, and then there are others which are peculiar to their social and economic system. Suppressed inflation is largely responsible for the prevalent sellers' markets, noted for shortages, queues, long waiting lists (for housing and certain consumer durables), low quality, sales under the counter – and the consequent bribery, poor service in shops and demoralized consumers hopelessly subordinated to sellers, producers and the inexorable powerful state. Illegal additions to official prices, in fact, take place in one form or another.

Although the growth of savings in the socialist countries is sometimes claimed to be evidence of rising incomes and living standards (see Chapter 7D), in reality their size is rather a manifestation of economic disequilibrium and suppressed inflation. Rising nominal incomes, even with relatively stable prices, are of little consolation to consumers in the face of prevalent shortages and a limited range of goods and services. The accumulating savings are in fact largely forced savings.

Various estimates indicate that only one-fifth of the savings in the European socialist countries are genuine savings, and four-fifths are 'hot-savings' which are available for spending as soon as suitable products appear on the market. Hot savings represent a potentially destabilizing factor in a planned economy and they are of grave concern to the authorities. These savings are also potentially available for use in black market operations, thereby accentuating inflationary price increases.

The desperate socialist efforts to insulate domestic from foreign prices have not eliminated inflationary pressure, but have only divorced the internal price structure from world (scarcity) prices. In effect, consumers are confronted with some prices which are relatively too low and others too high, which does not promote the socially most rational structure of consumption and production in accordance with the actual patterns of the scarcity of resources.

In view of the price controls, socialist enterprises can secure higher prices primarily by the introduction of improved products. What happens in practice, however, is that low-priced necessities – however essential to consumers – tend to be phased out in favour of 'new' products, which in many cases are no improvements but merely alterations in some respect, of little value to consumers. [29]

D. ANTI-INFLATIONARY AND COMPENSATORY MEASURES

The disadvantages of inflation, in whatever form, are widely recognized and the authorities under each system make more or less concerted efforts to minimize or at least mitigate its adverse effects. In capitalist market economies, such efforts assume a diversity of forms with varying degrees of determination and success. In addition to the usual monetary and fiscal anti-inflationary measures, there may be more specific schemes, arrangements and procedures.

First of all, in order to restrain wage increases, governments in capitalist countries may tolerate or even create high levels of unemployment (especially if right-wing political parties are in power) in order to apply brakes on costs and consumer spending. A number of countries, such as those in Western Europe, have experimented with incomes policies, whereby the growth of wages is linked to productivity increases. These measures may also involve mild price restraints or controls. Some of the most successful countries in tackling inflation (and unemployment) have evolved highly sophisticated forms of negotiations between organized labour and employers either on a centralized (Austria, Norway, Sweden) or a decentralized (Japan) basis. In some cases (as in the Federal Republic of Germany), unions press for import liberalization to restrain domestic price increases (especially in the cost of living).

Anti-monopoly legislation, and its enforcement (which is a different thing), may also be regarded as anti-inflationary devices. There is also increasing pressure in many countries to exercise closer scrutiny of the output and pricing (including 'transfer pricing') policies and practices of the multinational corporations. Another counter-inflationary effect is produced by progressive taxation, especially the retention of the pre-inflationary scales; as income recipients enter higher brackets by sheer inflationary growth they have to pay increasing proportions of their income in tax.

Where the different measures are not very successful (which is usually the case), the governments may allow periodical cost-of-living adjustments. This may be done annually, quarterly or even more frequently, as a conciliatory or compensatory gesture to labour to minimize industrial disputes. This approach has been adopted in its extreme form in some less-developed countries which are unable to cope with inflationary pressures (such as Argentina, Brazil and Chile) and whose policies are more compensatory than anti-inflationary. Various charities, a time-honoured capitalist institution, to some extent alleviate the worst effects of inflation on some individuals.

Under socialist central economic planning the state is, of course, in a much better position to counteract inflation and we shall next highlight the policies and methods pursued to this effect.

(1) *The general framework.* The social ownership and control of the means of production, central economic planning and strict discipline over the budget and the balance of payments theoretically enable the state to achieve equilibrium in the allocation of resources in relation to demand. The socialist state is in a position to pursue an incomes policy on a planned basis, much more systematically and tightly than a capitalist government can ever do. Inflationary pressure is regularly analyzed in annual plans and appropriate measures can be taken if necessary. The absence of democratic elections and the control of the media protect the government while pursuing austere and unpopular policies. There is virtually no private enterprise to undermine government policies.

(2) *The maximum release of resources for production.* There are no monopolistic restrictions on output and virtually no unemployment (except in Yugoslavia) and it is in the interest of the socialist state to speed up the growth of production. Various incentives and penalties (including capital charges) have been introduced to discourage the hoarding of materials and equipment and to promote shorter periods of construction of investment projects (so that resources are immobilized for shorter periods). Most socialist

countries have also been borrowing heavily from the capitalist world for the development of technologically most advanced production (as distinct from consumption).

(3) *The diversion of more resources for the production of consumer goods.* Responding to popular pressure, many socialist governments are increasingly inclined to step up the production of consumer goods and the provision of various services to consumers – in contrast to the austere policies in the past.

(4) *Consumption steering.* Employing the state-owned media, the socialist state wages periodical campaigns to adapt consumption patterns in socially-desired directions, thereby counteracting structural inflationary pressures by discouraging the consumption or use of scarcer materials in favour of the more abundant ones.

(5) *The control of wage funds and incentive payments.* The wage funds are centrally planned – for the whole economy and for individual workplaces – to correspond to the planned amount of consumer goods allowed for the market (with given savings habits). Efforts are made to develop closer links between wage scales and incentives, on the one hand, and labour productivity, on the other.

(6) *Price controls and subsidies.* The socialist state in one way or another controls wholesale (including agricultural procurement) and retail prices. In particular, the prices of items entering the cost of living are treated very seriously, so much so that their determination (or approval) is usually reserved for the Council of Ministers. Whilst the prices of necessities are maintained at relatively low levels, usually by subsidization, those of luxuries are set at high levels to absorb large proportions of consumers' spending power.[30] Some efforts are made, especially in the German Democratic Republic and the USSR, to reduce prices of some items where it is possible (or expedient). In the German Democratic Republic special regional Price Advisory Boards have been established to press for price reductions and the improvement of the quality of consumer goods. These organs are composed of representatives of wholesale and retail trade, the State Price Office, the Ministry of Finance and of interested mass organizations (such as the Democratic Women's League).[31] In other socialist countries, on occasions when some prices are increased consumers are compensated by reduced prices of other items.

(7) *Labour discipline.* With the qualified exception of Poland, trade unions are not in a position to press for unplanned wage increases or shortened working hours. There have been attempts to

strengthen work discipline by stricter Labour Codes and by incentives, disincentives and organized campaigns and appeals.

(8) *Banking controls.* Banks in the socialist countries are essentially agencies of the Ministry of Finance. Their responsibilities include the supervision of wage payments in accordance with the planned wage funds. Each socialized enterprise and institution has to have a bank account with a designated branch and carry out virtually all its transactions by the so-called 'cashless settlements', thereby minimizing the use of cash (and the possibility of embezzlement). There are strict restrictions on consumer credit and, apart from banks and credit co-operatives, there are virtually no other sources of finance available in the economy.

(9) *Savings campaigns.* These are periodical drives accompanied by a good deal of publicity and pressure to encourage people to deposit parts of their income in savings banks or savings co-operatives, and at the same time to dissuade them from withdrawals. The aim is to reduce the amount of currency in circulation and the predisposition to immediate spending. The operation of state lotteries is also guided by similar objectives.

(10) *Protection from capitalist inflation.* In most socialist countries the insulation of domestic from foreign prices is still maintained, at least periodically. This is administered by budgetary equalization payments, whereby domestic importers are compensated by subsidies whilst exporters are subject to appropriate export taxes. To further neutralize the inroads of capitalist inflation over longer periods, the socialist countries revalue their currencies periodically, thereby making their import prices lower and export prices higher.[32]

However, the effectiveness of the measures outlined above has proved limited in both capitalist and socialist countries, as was evident in Section A. The continuing inflationary pressures have been a consequence of either inexorable forces beyond the power of the authorities, or in some cases (especially in the socialist countries) by reluctant planned choice. Before we conclude this chapter, a generalization may be made on the systemic resolution of the conflict between inflation and unemployment. Under the impact of Keynesian ideas in the capitalist world, it was widely believed up to the late 1960s that wages and prices were steady up to full employment. This was further symbolized by the popularity of the 'Phillips curve'.[33]

The persistence of stagflation since about 1970, however, has rendered those claims futile, as capitalist countries have suffered from both substantial inflation *and* unemployment for more than a decade now. But where conflict appears between these twin evils, capitalist market economics tend to give preference to fighting inflation rather than unemployment, whilst in the socialist centrally planned economies full employment takes precedence over inflation.

RECOMMENDED FURTHER READING

1. J. Adam, *Wage Control and Inflation in the Soviet Bloc Countries* (London: Macmillan, 1979).
2.* O. Bogdanov and S. Gorbunov, 'Sources and Consequences of Inflation', *Political Affairs* (New York) March 1980, pp. 29–35.
3. A. Brown, Z. M. Fallenbuchl, J. A. Licari and E. Neuberger, 'The Impact of International Stagflation on Systemic and Policy Changes in East Europe: Theoretical Reflections', in S. McInnes *et al.*, (eds), *The Soviet Union and East Europe in the 1980s: Multidisciplinary Perspectives* (Oakville, Ontario: Mosaic Press, 1978) pp. 309–23.
4. A. Gamble and P. Walton, *Capitalism in Crisis: Inflation and the State* (London: Macmillan, 1976).
5.* T. Gozhansky, 'Halt the Inflation Gallop', *World Marxist Review* (London) Sept. 1979, pp. 41–3.
6. Sylvia A. Hewlett, 'Inflation and Inequality', *J. Economic Issues* (East Lansing, MI) June 1977, pp. 353–68.
7. D. Laibman, 'Seven Ways to Find Inflation in the Soviet Union', *New World Review* (New York) July–Aug. 1975, pp. 12–19.
8.* E. Huszti, 'Social and Economic Impact of Inflation in Hungary', *Acta oeconomica* [Economic Papers] (Budapest) 1/1977, pp. 69–80.
9.* L. Miastkowski, 'Retail Price Movements in the Socialist Economy', *Oeconomica polona* [Polish Economics] (Warsaw) 2/1981, pp. 231–51.
10.* Peng Kuang-hsi, *Why China Has No Inflation* (Peking: Foreign Languages Press, 1976).
11. M. J. Piore (ed.), *Unemployment and Inflation: Institutionalist and Structuralist Views. A Reader in Labor Economics* (White Plains, NY: M. E. Sharpe, 1979).
12. R. Portes, 'The Control of Inflation: Lessons from East European Experience', *Economica*, May 1977, pp. 109–29.
13. P. Schram, 'China's Price Stability: Its Meaning and Distributive Consequences', *J. Comparative Economics*, Dec. 1977, pp. 367–88.
14. H. Sherman, *Stagflation: A Radical Theory of Unemployment and Inflation* (New York: Harper and Row, 1976).
15. Laura D. A. Tyson, 'The Yugoslav Inflation: Some Competing Hypotheses', *J. Comparative Economics*, June 1977, pp. 113–46.

* *Indicates contributions by writers from the socialist countries.*

9 Industrial Disputes

A. FREEDOM TO STRIKE

Strike consists in the stoppage of work by organized labour in support of economic or sometimes political demands. The official attitude to strikes differs in detail from one country to another, particularly where different social systems are involved. In spite of the lack of uniformity, certain generalizations can be formulated, and then the inevitable contradictory exceptions can be highlighted.

In the early stages of capitalism, strikes were legally considered a crime with subversive implications. However, beginning in 1825 (in England), strikes were gradually legitimized as an element of liberalization in the democratic countries. The right to strike has come to be accepted as one of the basic democratic freedoms and a logical concomitant of collective bargaining. This right may be spelled out in the country's Constitution (as in Algeria, France, Italy, Portugal), or in various enactments (as in Greece and Spain), or implicitly recognized in common law (largely so in the Anglo-Saxon countries). Strikes can also occur in public enterprises (barring certain special cases, considered later in this section) and the authorities have to defend their rights before impartial conciliators, labour courts or arbitrators like any private employer.

The freedom to strike is also embodied in several international agreements, such as the International Agreement on the Economic, Social and Cultural Rights adopted by the United Nations in 1966 (Article 8, Section 1(d)), the Universal Declaration of Trade Union Rights adopted by the World Congress of Trade Unions in 1978, and to some extent in the ILO Convention Concerning the Application of the Principles of the Right to Organize and to Bargain Collectively, No. 98, of 1949 (Articles 1 and 4).

To Marxists, strike in a capitalist society is 'one of the basic forms of the class struggle of the proletariat . . .. Strikes and lockouts under capitalism are necessary weapons for the working class, both for defence and conquest'.[1] However, their view is different in application to socialism after the proletarian revolution.

Striking in a socialist centrally planned economy is virtually a taboo on ideological, political and economic grounds. Although strikes are not necessarily explicitly prohibited by law, they are not normally tolerated in practice. It is officially assumed that as the workers own the entities (through the state) in which they are employed and the state is their own workers' state, it would obviously be self-defeating to strike against themselves and bear the consequent losses. It is further stressed that the interests of the workers, enterprises and the state are 'identical'. A Soviet jurist explained:

It is evident that in the new [socialist] society there are no socially-justified grounds for a political confrontation between the trade unions and the state and, consequently, no need for trade unions to resort to strikes and other extreme measures to protect the working people's interests . . . After all it is obvious that it is impossible to distribute and consume more than has been produced. Strikes merely reduce this availability, thereby interfering with the solution of social and economic problems in the interest of the working people. Another facet of this question is also very important. Work stoppages in enterprises, whatever their causation – as the recent events in Poland testify – play into the hands of anti-socialist elements who endeavour to give an entirely different interpretation of the industrial disputes and to steer society away from the Socialist road to development.[2]

A strike would not only prove a great ideological embarrassment to the authorities, but would also be regarded as an act of political defiance, or even a counter-revolutionary conspiracy.

Even more compelling are the economic facts of central planning. With the planned allocation of the means of production and the assumed availability of labour at the full employment level, unscheduled stoppages of work disrupt the implementation of the laid down targets, which could lead to a whole chain of unfulfilment, as outputs of some enterprises are inputs to others. Furthermore, unscheduled increases in wages and improvement in other conditions of work would place extra strain on the volume of goods and services allowed for the consumer goods market, thereby accentuating shortages and inflation. With tight planning and small or no reserves, a socialist centrally planned economy is much more vulnerable to strikes than a capitalist market economy is.

Penalties for strikes may be quite severe. In the USSR, participation in a peaceful strike (a mere refusal to work) is punishable by three years' imprisonment; but if a sit-down, demonstration or picketing are involved, the punishment is up to 15 years' imprisonment or even death.[3] A strike may be investigated by secret police and the participants may be charged with a counter-revolutionary action. In Poland, where martial law was proclaimed on 13 December 1981 to prevent strikes, many leaders of the independent trade union organization Solidarity were 'interned' (including Lech Wałęsa); thousands of arrests were made (at one stage estimated at 5000–70 000) for involvement in normal union activities or strikes and at least seven miners were killed in the course of industrial disputes.[4]

However, to the generalizations on the two systems highlighted above, we must add the following qualifications. Virtually all capitalist nations have at least some restrictions on strikes. As a rule, strikes are not allowed in essential services, especially in the armed forces, police and hospitals, and in fire prevention, sanitation, water supply and electric power services. In some countries strikes are not permitted in the public service in general (such as Austria, Colombia, the Federal Republic of Germany, Japan, Switzerland and the USA). Political strikes, strikes contravening collective agreements in force and those deliberately aimed at harming the employer are usually illegal. Governments may also intervene in other strikes, if the national interest is seriously endangered and even as a matter of political expediency.

Anti-strike legislation is mildest in Britain and most highly developed in South Africa, the Netherlands, India, the USA and many less-developed countries. Strikes are virtually banned in Argentina, Chile, India and South Africa. A very serious view of strikes is taken in a number of less-developed countries where, owing to the paucity of resources, poverty and ambitious developmental programmes, the losses consequent upon industrial disputes are more clearly perceived. Anti-strike laws and procedures in some of these countries are now more developed and stricter than under the former colonial rule.

Where there are restrictions on the freedom to strike, there are usually special provisions for handling industrial disputes in the affected services or industries, which may include compulsory arbitration. Although the government may have the power to intervene in a strike, in many cases in democratic countries it chooses not to, and similarly it may not necessarily insist on the enforcement of the penalties provided for by the law.

At the same time in the socialist bloc, the prohibition of strikes is not as tight as would first appear, as each country approaches the problem in its own way, and policies have varied from time to time. China has become most liberal on this score since the early 1970s, and the right to strike was written into the 1975 Constitution (Article 28) and reiterated in the Constitution of 1978 under Article 45. A similar but less explicit attitude has prevailed in Yugoslavia since the mid-1960s. Tito himself supported trade unions in defending workers against technocracy, and the Constitution of 1974 (Article 47) implicitly concedes the legitimacy of strikes.

It may be mentioned here that the right to strike was recognized in the East German Constitution of 1949, but it was omitted in the 1968 Constitution. The right to strike was also conceded (temporarily), in response to the pressure from liberal reform movements, in Hungary from October to November 1956, in Czechoslovakia from April 1968 to April 1969 and in Poland from October 1956 to April 1958 and again from August 1980 to December 1981.

Where the right to strike is conceded, the official view is that the work stoppage is not of a political nature, that is, the strike is a remnant of capitalism and it is directed against inflexible bureaucrats, or negligent or inefficient management – not against the socialist state or the social system in force.

The Western-style freedom to strike could be compatible with socialist economic planning, provided that plans are sufficiently liberal and investment, production targets, wage funds and prices are not tightly predetermined on a directive basis but largely left to the market mechanism. Enterprises would have to be basically guided by profit, trade unions would have to be divorced from party (or state) control and there would have to be impartial labour courts and arbitrators before which the state (that is, management) would have to be on no more than equal footing with the unions.

Freedom to strike could still be consistent with a prohibition in reasonably specified essential services and industries in which industrial disputes would have to be subject to special settlement procedures, which might include compulsory independent arbitration.

B. THE INCIDENCE OF INDUSTRIAL DISPUTES

Industrial disputes may assume a number of different forms. The best known are, of course, strikes (initiated by labour) and lockouts (by the employer). Lockouts, although not uncommon under laissez-faire capitalism up to the mid-1930s, are rare today and non-existent in the socialist countries.

A strike may be *official*, when approved and consequently supported by the union executive, and *wildcat* (or *unofficial*, or *outlaw* or *quickie*) when spontaneously staged without official union support.

The latter type may occur in capitalist countries when, *inter alia*, ordinary union members are critical of the union officials and consider them to be too conciliatory to the employers or to be giving up the class struggle. Of the major capitalist countries France, Italy and the USA appear to have the highest incidence of these strikes. In the socialist countries, where unions are part of the official establishment, virtually the only strikes that can occur are of the 'wildcat' type.

With regard to the scope of industrial disputes, they can be between individual workers and the employer, between the union and the employer, between unions (mostly 'demarcation' disputes) and between unions and the state. Of these, the last type warrants special examination.

An industrial dispute with the state may have two different backgrounds, viz. the state may be challenged as an employer or as the government. In capitalist countries as a rule, the public authority as an employer has to conform to the same rules as a private employer, it has to defend its case on an equal footing with unions before independent tribunals, industrial courts or arbitrators, and it can be sued. This is not so in the socialist countries, where the judiciary and the settlement machinery are not independent and, as a rule, the socialist state cannot be sued. There are some exceptions, whereby legal proceedings can be instituted against the management of the state enterprise if there is a clear case of breaking a 'collective' agreement or the violation of the Labour Code.

An industrial dispute may also be politically inspired as distinct from pure economic causation. The need for political motivation in strikes under capitalism is stressed by revolutionary Marxists[5] and anarcho-syndicalists.[6] Some of the major political strikes that occurred in capitalist countries in the past were: Belgium – 1893, (Tsarist) Russia – 1903, 1905, 1912, 1917, Sweden – 1912, Germany – 1920, 1922, 1948 (West Germany), Britain – 1926, 1968, France – 1934, 1968, 1969, Italy – 1968, 1969, Australia – 1969 and Japan – 1969, 1971. Some of them (such as those in Sweden in 1912, in Germany in 1920, in Britain in 1926 and in France in 1968) were in fact general strikes, that is, nationwide, which virtually paralyzed the whole economy.

Industrial disputes more often become political in many less-developed countries, where the government is usually the dominant employer who, owing to the low income levels and its developmental ambitions, lays down unpopular policies with regard to wages, working conditions and investment. Furthermore, trade unions are much closer to the state administration (than in most Western countries), especially in Africa. Under these conditions, industrial disputes cannot by-pass political involvement. As E. M. Kassalov pointed out, there is resentment amongst the low-wage earners against the high-living style of government officials, bureaucrats and politicians.[7]

Whether political strikes should be accepted as legitimate in a democratic society, is a controversial question. Although some countries prohibit them, most countries accept them as not illegitimate if economic elements are also involved. In the final analysis one could argue that in any strike both economic and political considerations are involved. This controversy assumed its most publicized form in Italy, where the Constitutional Court finally ruled that political strikes were legal, provided that they were not aimed at the overthrow of democratic law and order.

In the socialist countries, the communist regimes tend to regard all strikes as political, inasmuch as they are directed against socialized entities, including the state-appointed or at least state-approved management; strikes are also denounced as 'anti-social' because they involve losses of production, disruption in other enterprises and inconvenience to the public. But curiously enough, Mao Tse-tung considered strikes permissible *provided they were political*, viz. directed against the bureaucratic establishment (inconvenient to him); he viewed such strikes as a desirable element of the Cultural Revolution in his broader concept of the Continuing Revolution (*Pu-tuan Koming*). In Czechoslovakia in the Prague coup d'etat of February 1948, a political strike was instigated by the communist party against the democratic government in order to instal a dictatorship of the proletariat under the communist regime.

But there have also been strikes which can be described as political insofar as they were accompanied by rioting and violence, or entailed political demands, as exemplified by the following work stoppages and disturbances:

Czechoslovakia	–	Pilsen 1953, Prague 1968,
German Democratic Republic	–	East Berlin 1956,
Hungary	–	Budapest 1956,
Poland	–	Poznan 1956, Baltic ports 1970, Radom and Warsaw 1976 and all major industrial centres 1980–1,

Romania   –   Jiu Valley 1977,
USSR   –   Kemerovo 1959, Novocherkask 1962,
                       Ivanovo 1970, Riga 1976, Kiev 1981.

In Poland, in Gdansk in December 1970, the government sent tanks
which fired on the strikers and demonstrators, in the course of which at
least 49 persons were killed; in Radom in June 1976 the strikers and
sympathisers burned down communist party headquarters.

In the late 1970s there were about 32 000 reported industrial disputes
in the world annually, which involved about 40m workers and which
cost 180m working days lost.[8] Almost all these disputes occurred in the
capitalist world. The ten countries with the largest number of industrial
disputes as officially reported to the International Labour Organization
are listed in Table 9.1. The number of the workers involved and the
working days lost are also included (the data are for 1979). Finland,
France and Japan, although noted for many strikes, suffer relatively
little in terms of the workers involved and days lost, which contrasts with
Italy, Spain and the United Kingdom.

It may be generalized that in capitalist countries the level of industrial
disputes is greater the lower are the extent and degree of development
and participation of the labour movement in political and management
processes. Substantial social and economic inequality is also a contributing factor. Thus in the West, where a virtually complete freedom to
strike prevails, Australia, Britain, Canada, France, Italy, Spain and the
USA are usually more prone to strikes than the Scandinavian countries,
the Federal Republic of Germany and Switzerland.

TABLE 9.1

	Number of disputes	Workers involved	Working days lost
1. USA	4 780	1 720 000	35 467 000
2. France (in 1978)	3 206	704 800	2 200 400
3. India	2 829	2 741 320	930 300
4. Spain	2 680	5 713 190	18 416 980
5. United Kingdom	2 145	4 667 800	29 474 000
6. Australia	2 042	1 862 900	3 964 400
7. Italy	2 000	16 237 440	27 530 430
8. Finland	1 715	225 170	243 400
9. Japan	1 153	449 500	930 300
10. Canada	1 050	462 500	7 834 230

Source: Based on: *Year Book of Labour Statistics 1980* (Geneva: ILO, 1980).

Within countries, industries where workers live or work in some isolation from other groups of workers – especially in mining, on the waterfront and in transport – are more strike-prone than most others. More recently industries or services affected by rapid technological change – such as communications and engineering – have tended to display a high incidence of strikes. Jobs involving routine work (such as mail handling) are also noted for a high propensity to industrial disputation. The incidence of strikes is low in most less-developed countries owing to a lower degree of industrialization (with the consequent larger share of the economically active population engaged in agriculture and in small-scale independent craft and business, working on own account) and restrictions on strikes.

It is sometimes said that strikes are less frequent under leftist governments, as the struggle for the improvement of the conditions of the workers is partly shifted to the political arena, where it can be more effective. This assertion is only partly supported by facts.

In the socialist countries, the incidence of industrial disputes is, of course, very much smaller – not necessarily because the workers have fewer grievances, but because strikes are either prohibited, or if they are not, the whole institutional set-up militates against them. With some qualified exceptions (in such countries as China, Poland and Yugoslavia) strikes are mostly of the spontaneous type, without official union initiative and support. The duration of these work stoppages is short, in many cases only a few hours, or even less, and they are meant to be a protest to draw the management's or authorities' attention to the grievances, rather than to force the enterprise by the loss of income to meet the workers' demands. The disputes rarely extend beyond the enterprise involved. The demands are directed to the local management, and not the industrial, branch, regional, republican or federal authorities.

Of all the socialist countries, Poland and Yugoslavia have had the highest incidence of strikes, and since the mid-1960s the authorities have reluctantly come to accept them as inevitable. In July–August 1980, at least 300 000 workers struck in Poland at a particular time. The strikes paved the way for the emergence of the first independent legal trade union organization under socialism – Solidarity – and the official acceptance of the legality of strike (see Chapter 4D). Work stoppages continued on and off until martial law was imposed on 13 December, 1981. But even then several plants continued to strike, at least in the Gdansk region (a refinery), Cracow (steelworks) and Katowice (coal mines). The warning four-hour stoppage of work on 27 March 1981, called by Solidarity (with a membership of 9m at the time) was to all intents and purposes a general strike – the largest ever in any socialist country.

In Yugoslavia, the first known strikes occurred in 1958. Up to 1969 over 1900 work stoppages were recorded, and from 1973 to 1975 more than 200 occurred in Slovenia alone. Over the period 1964–69 more than 80 000 striking workers were involved.[9] China, Czechoslovakia, the German Democratic Republic, Romania and the USSR have also had many work stoppages. They were particularly widespread in China in 1975 and 1977 and they led to considerable wage increases ranging from 10 to 20 per cent.[10]

Examining the trends in the incidence of industrial disputes over the past three decades, opposite tendencies can be discerned under the two social systems. On the whole, in capitalist countries the incidence of disputes has been declining slightly, in spite of the increasing proportions of the economically active population becoming employees and in spite of the dislocations caused by accelerated technological change and the prolonged recession since the early 1970s. The trend can be attributed to the improving machinery for the settlement of industrial disputes and the declining militancy of the working class in favour of the 'peaceful parliamentary road to socialism'.

On the other hand, in the socialist countries industrial disputes have rather tended to rise. This tendency can be explained by a number of coincidental developments. There has been increasing political liberalization owing to popular pressure. Basic industrialization has been largely attained in most of these countries and the need for authoritarianism in the economic sphere is less justifiable now than in the early postwar period. The economic reforms have made the socialist countries in several respects more similar to capitalist market economies, with new industrial problems which are not unlike those under capitalism: efficiency drives, technological disruptions, the growing power of management and specialists, dismissals and the like.

C. CAUSES OF INDUSTRIAL CONFLICT

Industrial disputes are now widely recognized by the specialists in the field as complex phenomena, considering that they occur under widely varying conditions involving different occupations, industries, regions, countries and political and social systems. These conditions, furthermore, may change over time. In our discussion, focused as it is on differences between capitalist and socialist countries, we shall distin-

guish between immediate and broader causes and consequences.
The immediate causes of strikes in capitalist countries are well known.
Most of the disputes, some three-quarters, are concerned with pay in its
broadest sense – wages, penalty rates, paid holidays and other financial
benefits. Although poverty may be a very important cause of wage
strikes in less-developed countries – where income levels are low and
consequently the marginal utility of wage changes is relatively high –
this is less so in the affluent industrialized nations. In the latter case,
wage strikes can be attributed not so much to poverty but rather to
social inferiority. It is also worth noting that wage strikes are usually less
common amongst the lowest paid workers than amongst skilled and
semi-skilled workers, as the former are less union-minded and more
replaceable than the latter.

Hours of work, working arrangements, work discipline, dismissal,
union membership and the recognition of collective bargaining may
become important issues, too. To the causes listed above, we must add
the sympathetic support given to another union (which may develop
into a 'strike fever') and demarcation disagreements (arguments as to
the members of which union should perform particular jobs).

The causes of a broader nature are not necessarily spelled out in the
unions' demands, but they may nevertheless underlie the antecedents
leading to strikes and may be inferred from circumstantial indirect
evidence. First of all there is the inherent dichotomy between the haves
and the have-nots, generating gaps not only in respect of ownership but
also (even more importantly) control, power and prestige. In fact, given
the institution of private property, free enterprise and the operation of
the market, it is doubtful if this inherent conflict can ever be resolved and
removed from industrial relations.

More specific general causes which are peculiar to capitalism are rapid
technological change, essentially dictated by the private profit motive,
and the consequent disruptive effects on labour, unemployment (technological and cyclical), considerable inflation, the spread of trade union
membership, the growing effectiveness of strikes and the development of
collective bargaining (covering wider and wider areas of disputable
industrial relations). At opportune times strikes may also be promoted
by some groups (such as communists, syndicalists and anarchists)
hostile to the capitalist social system. Experience shows that small but
dedicated extremist minorities can wield a good deal of influence,
particularly if holding office in trade unions.

In the socialist countries, it is officially claimed that causes of
industrial disputes hardly exist. Indeed this is largely, but not com-

pletely, true. There is no exploitation by capitalists, no unemployment (except in Yugoslavia), no inflation on the capitalist scale (except in Yugoslavia), and demarcation disputes (between unions) and sympathy strikes are pointless. Managers do not own or control enterprises (the state does), wage rates are not set by management but by the appropriate state organs (on which workers are represented through their trade unions), standard working hours are regulated by labour legislation in the framing of which trade unions participate or are at least consulted, and workers cannot be dismissed from their jobs unless consent is obtained from the union concerned.

When industrial disputes do occur, they are officially attributed to one of the following.

(1) Differing views between management and workers on the implementation and over-fulfilment of the production plan.
(2) Over-zealous or incompetent managers or technocrats.
(3) A lack of discipline amongst the workers.
(4) Extravagant demands made by the workers.
(5) Misinterpretation of the legislation, agreements or procedures.
(6) Unexpected developments or problems for which no machinery or procedures are yet available.
(7) Provocative manipulations by 'trouble makers' (the term often used in Hungary), 'bad elements' (Chinese expression) or 'anti-socialist forces' (Soviet description).

Nevertheless, it is conceded officially that legitimate labour disputes can occur if they are caused by violations of individual rights or of collective agreements. These causes, if genuine, are acceptable even in the most authoritarian countries, such as the German Democratic Republic and the USSR, provided that they are settled within the state-imposed framework and according to laid-down procedures. But they are not supposed to involve strikes.

It must be realized, however, that socialist trade unions are not genuine champions or defenders of workers' rights and interests, but essentially instrumentalities of the socialist state (for details, see Chapter 4C). As we have demonstrated in the preceding section of this chapter, strikes do occur under socialism, legitimately or (mostly) not. Their most common immediate causes can be grouped under four headings.

(1) *Low wages.* The continued policies of consumer austerity in favour of high investment and defence spending make many workers

restless and no longer satisfied with the worn out promises of the 'communist cornucopia' in the future. The strikes in the German Democratic Republic in East Berlin in 1956 and all over China in 1976–7 were of this causation.

(2) *Oppressive working conditions.* These may embrace excessive norms of work, long working hours (including unpaid 'voluntary' work), inadequate facilities for the workers and poor working surroundings in general. The author visited a large number of workplaces in the socialist countries ('guided' and unguided) and he was surprised at the austere and depressing conditions prevailing in most of them in comparison with similar kinds of establishments in the West. The strikes in China in 1975 in protest against increased work assignments and transfers of workers to rural areas, and in the USSR in Kiev in April 1981 may be quoted as examples.

(3) *Shortages of consumer goods.* Long queues, poor quality goods, sales under the counter and special channels of distribution to privileged groups (high party officials, security organs, certain professionals) are a common occurrence. Strikes appear to be the only way of getting some action on these grievances from the indifferent or inept bureaucrats. Some of the strikes in Poland and Romania in 1980–1 were prompted by these considerations.

(4) *Price increases of consumer goods.* The public in the socialist countries is generally accustomed to price stability. Nevertheless, changing conditions may necessitate price increases and official sharp price hikes occasionally do take place (quite apart from the black market), without immediate wage increases. The strikes and riots in Poland in 1970, 1976 and 1980 bear witness to how seriously workers may react to steep price increases of basic foods.

But in addition we may mention more deep-rooted frustrations underlying the immediate causes which may precipitate strikes and riots of largely political motivation.

(1) *Authoritarianism.* Directive and inflexible management and bureaucracy and the omnipotent, ubiquitous and inexorable socialist state reduce the worker to a cog. The individuality of the worker is suppressed in favour of nebulous collectivism and the 'primacy of social interest'. Some of the strikes in Yugoslavia and most of the political strike–riots that have occurred in other socialist countries (see the preceding section) were conditioned by this factor.

(2) *State-controlled unionism.* Many workers realize that the official

unions are neither capable nor willing to fight for workers' interests. Yet in several respects the problems confronting a socialist worker are not unlike those in capitalist countries, especially since the economic reforms. The spectacular strikes in Poland in 1980, together with work stoppages in China in the same year and in the German Democratic Republic and Romania in 1981 were motivated by the objective of independent unionism.

(3) *Purely political motives.* Discontent with communist rule and particularly with Soviet domination together with the yearnings for a more liberal social system, stronger links with the West and for truly national independence, have always been present in Eastern Europe. Widespread strikes were resorted to in two major political uprisings, viz. in Hungary in October–November 1956 and in Czechoslovakia in August–December 1968.

Amongst the socialist countries, Yugoslavia is unique in that strikes there are less restricted and they are reported more freely than elsewhere in the socialist bloc. In a study carried out by a Yugoslav economist, N. Jovanov, covering 512 strikes in the late 1960s, the relative importance of different causes were established as shown in Table 9.2.

TABLE 9.2

Demands	No. of strikes	No. of workers
1. Improved basis of payment	141 (29 %)	14 968 (23 %)*
2. Higher pay	139 (29 %)	15 578 (24 %)*
3. Change of norms and basic wages	70 (15 %)	10 710 (16 %)
4. Observance of self-management rights	68 (14 %)	12 281 (19 %)*
5. Dismissal of managers	34 (7 %)	4 383 (7 %)
6. More dynamic management	21 (4 %)	2 895 (4 %)
7. Reduction of social differences in the enterprise and in society	8 (1 %)	5 054 (8 %)
TOTAL	479 (100 %)	66 869 (100 %)†
No answer	33	976*
GRAND TOTAL	512	67 845*

* Complete figures of the number of strikers are not available, the unknown components being excluded from the percentage figures.
† Percentage totals do not add up to 100 owing to rounding.
Source. The data kindly supplied by Professor D. A. Loeber, of the University of Kiel.

D. THE PRINCIPLES AND MACHINERY OF SETTLEMENT

In the modern economies, noted for the complex division of labour and interdependence, industrial disputes – especially in the form of strikes or lockouts – are treated seriously as they bring about losses to both workers and employers, and additionally to the public and society as a whole. Both capitalist and socialist countries have evolved institutions and procedures for avoiding or minimizing work stoppages and for settling them as soon as possible.

In general, the more industrialized and democratic a country, the more elaborate a system of settlement it has. The methods employed may include the development of conditions conducive to industrial peace and co-operation, informal and formal negotiations between the representatives of labour and employer(s), conciliation, mediation and arbitration. In general, governments in developed democratic countries are reluctant to intervene themselves, unless essential services are involved, in contrast to most less-developed countries and the socialist bloc, where the disruption of work, production and services are treated gravely, with a lesser concern for democratic freedoms.

There are two approaches in capitalist countries to the settlement of industrial disputes. One is prompted mainly by the desire to find a solution acceptable to both parties, with the authorities sensitive to the interests involved on each side and the emphasis on conciliation. The Scandinavian countries, Japan and the USA exemplify this philosophy. The other is preoccupied with the interest of the public and it aims at protecting the community against inconvenience and disruption. There are usually provisions for at least partial operation of essential services. Belgium, France, the Federal Republic of Germany, Italy and Portugal favour this approach.[11]

In some countries (such as Belgium, France, the USA and many less-developed countries) settlement procedures are largely established in advance, whilst in others (such as Canada, Italy and the United Kingdom) the necessary measures are largely determined on an *ad hoc* basis as the need arises. Some countries, notably Britain, several former British colonies and the USA, prefer to rely primarily on private decision-making in the settlement of industrial disputes. On the other hand, in the more authoritarian countries, especially in Latin America and the ex-French Africa, state machinery – including compulsory mediation and arbitration – are extensively resorted to.

In most capitalist countries there are special 'labour [or industrial] courts', with different degrees of jurisdiction and varied functions ranging from conciliation to adjudication and arbitration. As a rule, appeals are possible either to ordinary courts or to special higher labour courts. Industrial legislation of a number of countries provide for so-called 'cooling-off periods'. Thus, under the British Industrial Relations Act of 1971, the Secretary of State can apply to the Industrial Court for the imposition of a cooling-off period of up to 60 days before a stoppage of work can take place. In the USA under the Taft–Hartley Act of 1947, the cooling-off period is up to 80 days, during which non-union labour can be employed (and trade union officials are required to swear that they do not belong to the communist party).

Increasing attention is attached in the Western countries (more so than in the less-developed or the socialist countries) to the introduction of management methods which are more conducive to the understanding and avoidance of the causes of industrial conflicts. A novel and highly successful system has been evolved in the Federal Republic of Germany in conjunction with co-determination. It is recognized that participation in management decision-making also involves sharing in responsibilities. Neither works councils nor employers are supposed to resort to strikes or lockouts without first of all exhausting the possibilities of consultation, negotiation and mediation and the facilities provided by labour courts.

The settlement machinery and procedures are not as varied in the socialist countries. They are well established in detail and there is little left to the discretion of the disputing parties. It is conceded that disputes may arise between individual workers and management and between the trade unions and management on the observance of the labour code, the methods of the implementation of the plan and the compliance with the so-called 'collective agreement' (see Chapter 4E).

As a rule, each workplace has a 'labour disputes committee', consisting of representatives of the management and the trade union concerned. The committee's decisions are binding. But its power is limited, as wage scales, standard working hours, redundancy, pension rights and the allocation of factory housing are not within its sphere of responsibility.

Unless there is a case of an obvious violation of the law or agreement, the odds against the worker are too great for him to win, considering that trade union officials (like the managerial personnel) are usually party members and have a stake in upholding management and the state. The worker has the right of appeal directly, or via his trade union, to the 'factory committee', and if not satisfied to an ordinary court ('People's Court'). But as a Soviet source conceded, 'it does not happen often'.[12] The complainant, especially if critical of the establishment, may find himself in a lot of trouble, as his trade union may refer the case to the secret police (see Chapter 4C). Trade unions may be more successful if they take the initiative themselves. For example in the USSR in 1979, administrative charges were brought against 6000 managers who violated some regulations, of whom 146 were removed from their posts.[13]

China represents a major exception. The usual procedure is as follows. A worker may bring a complaint to the notice of his departmental or general manager or to his trade union. If the union considers the grievance reasonable and cannot get satisfaction from the management, it may refer the case to the party committee and the latter takes it up with the management. If the grievances brought up by the workers are reasonable but cannot be met at the time, the trade union has the responsibility of explaining to the workers why it is not possible. However, if the grievances are considered to be 'unreasonable', the state may take a serious view and may initiate disciplinary action. The Vice-Chairman of the All-China Federation of Trade Unions, Kang Yonghe, explained:

> If a few bad elements incite the masses to wilfully make trouble, the trade unions would explain to the hoodwinked masses that they are wrong, expose the bad elements and help the management and judicial departments take disciplinary and legal measures against these elements so as to protect the interests of the factories and all the workers.[14]

A separate discussion is warranted on the arbitration of industrial disputes under each system. Arbitration consists in the resolution of a dispute by a mutually acceptable third party with practical experience of the industry concerned, rather than by a court, with a binding effect on the parties to the dispute. Compared with the proceedings in industrial or ordinary courts, arbitration is less legalistic, costly and recriminatory, on the one hand, and speedier and more informal, on the other. Although it is usually voluntary, it may be compulsory to avoid the stoppage of work.

In the democratic capitalist countries, arbitrators are independent of the government and are preoccupied with the microeconomic interests of the disputing parties and with encouraging them to make their own bargains. On the other hand, socialist arbitration is a part and parcel of the state administration, and it is more like an expedient combination of administrative and judicial elements. Socialist arbitrators have less freedom, as they have to ensure that the requirements of the economic plan are met, and the observance or non-observance of the collective agreements must be interpreted essentially from that angle.

The fact is that most of the terms of employment are laid down in the comprehensive labour code or the labour contract, which are incapable of alteration by arbitrators. But it must be pointed out that the emphasis in socialist arbitration of industrial disputes is on comradely understanding of the broader social interest in a collectivist spirit.

The keynote of the settlement of industrial disputes is fairness and impartiality and reasonable justice to both disputing parties. A question naturally poses itself: does the worker get fair treatment compared with the employer? No definite answer can be provided to this vexed and eternal problem, owing to the inevitable subjective considerations involved, depending on ideological convictions. But the following comparative observations may be of interest.

Under laissez-faire capitalism, the settlement machinery was in fact in the employer's hands. Unemployment was high, labour was largely unorganized, strikes were illegal or could be easily matched by lockouts and an individual worker was in a hopelessly weak bargaining position in relation to his employer (see Chapter 4A). The government was either sympathetic to the employers or at least refrained from intervening.

Even under modern capitalism, it may be argued that conciliators, adjudicators, arbitrators and judges are more likely to come from, or identify with the higher social classes, either because of their social background or (usually being persons of distinguished position) because they owe their success to the social system in force. Even when they endeavour to be impartial, they cannot help understanding the employers' side better than that of the workers with whom they have less in common. One of the best developed systems for the settlement of industrial disputes in the world is that in Australia, a country which pioneered in the field, having introduced her framework (including compulsory arbitration) in 1904; there has been a good deal of public discussion of the set-up in recent years and an observer has recently presented the following critical appraisal of it:

> The Conciliation and Arbitration Commission as presently operating makes a mockery of democracy, the rule of law and separation of powers. A commissioner can make the rules, apply the rules and break the rules. It is as if an umpire could make up the rules as he went along, change them part way through the game and rewrite the scoreboard

after the match was over. A single commissioner can at his own whim and pleasure, play Santa Claus with other people's money, make orders which change the whole nature of society or infringe the most basic human liberties in a manner that no elected government would dare . . . It is time we asked just how much of our trouble stems from commissioners using their power to remake society in line with their own ideological prejudices.[15]

The situation is in fact not much different in this respect under socialism. The persons entrusted with the settlement of industrial disputes are more likely to give preference to the employer's side than to the workers'. First of all, such persons have to operate within the labour code prescribed in detail by the over-powerful state (in effect the employer), the economic plan (also imposed by the state) and the collective agreement (concluded by management, representing the state) and by the trade union (in practice an instrument of the state).

In fact it may be argued that from the legal point of view there is an incestuous relation between one party to the dispute (the state) and the arbitrators. Arbitrators are appointed by the state and are either full-time or part-time employees of the state. They are persons who have reached a distinguished status, whose position depends on the support of and by the state, and indeed who owe their position to the existing social order. Furthermore, one of the basic principles postulated in Marxist social philosophy is the 'primacy of social interest', as opposed to individual interest. As the state (that is, in fact, the party) is the interpreter of 'social interest' and as the state owns and controls the media, the workers are disadvantaged to start with. And yet one of the requirements for a just arbitration system is the equality of the disputing parties before the arbitrator and the impartiality of the latter.

RECOMMENDED FURTHER READING

1.*V. P. Androsov, 'Strike', in *Great Soviet Encyclopedia* (New York: Macmillan, 1975) vol. 9, pp. 471–74.
2. A. Brumberg, 'The Revolt of the Workers', *Dissent* (Chicago) Winter 1981, pp. 21–39.
3. R. Chermesh, 'Strikes: The Issue of Social Responsibility', *British J. Industrial Relations*, Nov. 1979, pp. 337–46.
4. F. Gamillscheg, P. Hanau and Mary McAuley, 'Labour Law and Social Insurance Law', in C. D. Kernig (ed.), *Marxism, Communism and Western Society: A Comparative Encyclopaedia*, (New York: Herder & Herder, 1973) vol. 5, pp. 47–73.

5. P. Feuille, 'Selected Benefits and Costs of Compulsory Arbitration', *Industrial and Labor Relations Rev.* (Ithaca, NY) Oct. 1979, pp. 64–76.
6. R. D. Horton, 'Arbitration, Arbitrators and the Public Interest', *Industrial and Labor Relations Rev.*, July 1975, pp. 497–507.
7. International Labour Organization, *Conciliation and Arbitration Procedures in Labour Disputes: A Comparative Study* (Geneva: ILO, 1980).
8. A. Kiralfy, 'Arbitration', in Kernig (ed.), *A Comparative Encyclopaedia* vol. 1, pp. 157–61.
9. Mary McAuley, *Labour Disputes in Soviet Russia 1957–1965* (Oxford: Clarendon Press, 1969).
10. J. M. Montias, 'Economic Conditions and Political Instability in Communist Countries: Observations on Strikes, Riots and Other Disturbances', *Studies in Comparative Communism* (Los Angeles) Winter 1980, pp. 283–99.
11. B. O. Pettman, *Strikes: A Selected Bibliography* (Bradford: MCB Books, 1976).
12. W. F. Robinson (ed.), *August 1980: The Strikes in Poland* (Munich: Radio Free Europe Research, Oct. 1980).
13. M. Shalev, 'Industrial Relations Theory and the Comparative Study of Industrial Relations and Industrial Conflict', *British J. Industrial Relations*, March 1980, pp. 26–43.
14.*S. Yershov, 'Strike Movement on the Upgrade', *International Affairs* (Moscow) 7/1979, pp. 135–37.
15. J. Zupanov, 'Two Patterns of Conflict Management in Industry', *Industrial Relations* (Berkeley, CA) May 1973, pp. 213–23.

* *Indicates contributions by writers from the socialist countries.*

10 International Migrations of Workers

A. THE EXTENT AND DIRECTIONS

International migrations have always existed in one form or another. But since about 1960 a new breed of migrants has become dominant in these movements, viz. more or less temporary workers variously described as 'foreign workers', 'guest workers', 'migratory workers', 'to-and-fro migrants', 'shuttle-migrants', 'new-style immigrants', 'temporary citizens', 'secondary-status workers', 'proletarians on loan' or 'brawn drain'. In contrast to the old-style immigrants, they are not intending or meant to be permanent settlers, but workers temporarily employed in the host countries for periods typically ranging from six months to three years and then usually returning to their home countries.

The migration of labour in this sense has received a good deal of publicity in the West European setting.[1] But in fact this phenomenon is of a much wider occurrence and it has become a noteworthy feature of the world economy. It exists not only in several parts of the capitalist world, but also in the socialist bloc. Furthermore, a two-way traffic of migrant workers has emerged across this world division.

This study examines the problem of the temporary migration of labour on a global basis and involving, as it does, different social systems. Economic, sociological and political factors are considered and special attention is given to the ideological implications of this remarkable development of our times.

The total number of foreign workers in the different parts of the world in 1980 according to one estimate was 20m.[2] This estimate appears to be on the high side and probably includes doubtful cases, too, some of whom may have turned into permanent legal or illegal residents.

In the writer's view, the total in the late 1970s was about 16m. This figure also included illegal (or 'clandestine' or 'undocumented') migrant workers, usually constituting about one-tenth of the legal total: the proportion appears to be highest in the USA (about one-half) and virtually nil in South Africa and the socialist countries.[3]

The total given above embraces only working persons, which in some cases may be family members. Although migrant workers, unlike permanent settlers, do not typically migrate with their families, many of them later bring out their spouses or even other dependants. Estimates indicate that in North-Western Europe, non-working family members represent about 80–90 per cent of the migrant workers, but in other parts of the world the proportion appears to be lower. All in all, the migrant workers' population (including their families) in the host countries in the late 1970s totalled about 20m, of whom 10m lived in North-Western Europe.

There are seven main centres of attraction to migrant workers in the world (approximate percentage shares given in brackets).

(1) North-Western Europe (37 per cent)
(2) United States (25 per cent)
(3) West Africa (20 per cent)
(4) Middle East (10 per cent)
(5) South Africa (2 per cent)
(6) Libya (2 per cent)
(7) CMEA Region[4] (1 per cent)

Further details, including the chief host and labour-supplying countries are given in Table 10.1.

Of the regions of attraction listed, *North-Western Europe* is the most interesting case study, as the recruitment, distribution and treatment of migrant workers in this area have been developed on a most systematic basis and the problems that have arisen there have, on the whole, reached the clearest and most acute forms. By 1964, the flow of migrant labour had reached impressive proportions, viz. a total of 5 270 000, when it constituted 5.5 per cent of the total labour force there. The peak was attained in 1973, viz. 7 990 000, or 8.4 per cent of the total employment in the region.[5] Owing to the recession since, the figure has been reduced by 2.0 m, so that today migrant workers constitute 6 per cent of total employment in the region. Most of them (about two-thirds) are employed in manufacturing and construction, and about one-half of the workers are skilled or semi-skilled.[6]

In the *USA*, the inflow of migrant workers, especially illegal ones, has dramatically increased since the mid-1960s.[7] Mexicans at first mostly

TABLE 10.1 *Main directions of migrant workers' movements, as of the late 1970s*

Host region (and countries*)	Number of migrant workers (millions)	Main supplying countries†
1. North-Western Europe (France, Federal Republic of Germany, United Kingdom, Switzerland, Belgium, Netherlands, Sweden, Austria, Luxemburg).	6.0	Italy, Turkey, Yugoslavia, Portugal, Spain, Algeria, Morocco, Greece, Tunisia, Finland, Austria.
2. USA	4.0	Mexico, Puerto Rico, the Carribean.
3. West Africa (Ivory Coast, Ghana, Senegal).	3.3	Upper Volta, Mali, Guinea, Togo.
4. Middle East	1.7	Pakistan, India, Egypt, Jordan, Syria, USA, Lebanon, United Kingdom, France.
5. South Africa	0.4	Transkei, Bophuthatswana, Venda.
6. Libya	0.3	Egypt, Tunisia, Syria, Yugoslavia, Turkey, Jordan, Poland, United Kingdom, Romania.
7. CMEA Region (Czechoslovakia, German Democratic Republic, USSR Mongolia, Bulgaria)	0.2	Poland, Bulgaria, Hungary, Yugoslavia, Algeria, USSR, Egypt, Turkey.
8. Other Regions	0.3	Yugoslavia, Mexico, Spain, Greece, Portugal, Turkey.
TOTAL	16.2	

* The countries are listed in the descending order of the number of resident foreign workers.
† Listed in the descending order of the number of the migrant workers found in the region.
Sources. Author's estimates based on a variety of widely differing official statistics and private estimates.

worked in agriculture as unskilled labourers, but more recently they (and many others) have made their mark in manufacturing and certain services as well. They represent no more than 5 per cent of total employment.

The international migration of workers in equatorial *West Africa* is of long standing, but it has increased in intensity in recent years. The migratory workers are mostly unskilled, are chiefly employed in agriculture, mining and services and they represent about one-fifth of local employment.

Whilst the oil crisis has restricted the flow of migrant workers to North-Western Europe since 1973, it has boosted up their movement to the *Middle East* and *Libya*. By the late 1970s their number had increased to 2.0m, a ten-fold increase over the preceding decade. Construction is the main industry for migrant employment, followed by services, commerce and agriculture. Migrant labour now represents one-tenth of total employment, but in the case of Kuwait and Qatar the proportion is three-quarters, and in the case of the United Arab Emirates it is nine-tenths. It is noteworthy that amongst the migrant workers are highly skilled personnel from Western and Eastern Europe and the USA.[8]

Labour migrations to South Africa are of long standing, and traditionally black workers were recruited from the surrounding South African, British and Portuguese dependencies (including Angola, Botswana, Lesotho, Malawi, Mozambique, Namibia and Swaziland). Since the late 1970s the total number has settled at about 350 000, almost wholly received from the newly created 'independent' states of Bophuthatswana, Transkei and Venda. These workers are black, mostly unskilled and are largely employed in mines, where they constitute some two-thirds of total employment.[9]

The international movements of workers have also emerged in the socialist bloc, viz. amongst some *CMEA countries*.[10] No complete statistics are published officially,[11] but some private researchers within the region and outside have produced several (rather fragmentary) studies.[12] These movements began in the early post Second World War period, when they mostly involved Bulgarian, Hungarian and Polish workers moving to the depopulated Czechoslovakia. In 1973 the number involved in the CMEA was 100 000 and in 1975, between 200 000 and 205 000.[13] It appears that, since that time, the total has remained at the latter level or has perhaps increased slightly.[14]

Only some CMEA countries are significant host countries. Czechoslovakia and the German Democratic Republic lead the way, with some 60 000–70 000 foreign workers each in 'high' years, mainly from Bulgaria, Poland, Hungary, the USSR, Algeria, Egypt and Turkey. The USSR is next, with some 50 000, mainly from Bulgaria, Poland, Czechoslovakia and the German Democratic Republic. Hungary and Mongolia also have significant numbers of foreign workers, their numbers varying from year to year; in Mongolia, one-third of all the construction work is done by Soviet labour.[15] Most of the foreign workers in the CMEA region are skilled and are engaged in the construction or operation of joint enterprises, the training of specialists or are participating in scientific and technical projects of one kind or another. Foreign workers represent a very small proportion of total employment in the CMEA – only 0.1 per cent (the highest proportion applies to Czechoslovakia – for example, 0.25 per cent was reported[16]). The relative role of migrant workers in the most important host and labour-supplying countries is shown in Table 10.2.

There are now also flows of workers between the capitalist world and the socialist bloc, although the numbers involved are relatively small. Highly skilled British, Dutch, French, German, Italian and Japanese workers are often engaged in the construction and modernization of plants in virtually all the socialist countries. In China, Bulgaria, Poland, Romania, Vietnam and Yugoslavia skilled Western personnel participate in the operation of joint ventures, not to mention the offices of capitalist banks and other firms that operate in almost all the socialist countries. Moreover, unskilled and semi-skilled labour has been recruited by Bulgaria, Czechoslovakia and the German Democratic Republic in Algeria, Egypt and Turkey. The estimated number of these different types of workers engaged in the socialist bloc in the late 1970s was 15 000–20 000.

Similarly, the socialist countries are increasingly interested in supplying their workers to capitalist nations, usually on short or medium-term contracts. With the exception of Yugoslavia, no socialist country allows permanent emigration (except in some cases to rejoin families). These workers are mostly professionals or skilled tradesmen engaged in the construction of various industrial projects, roads and communications, or acting as advisers, or operating various types of business ventures.[17]

The total number of the workers from the socialist countries engaged on these bases in the capitalist world in the late 1970s was about 30 000.[18] To this figure, we must add 700 000 or so Yugoslavs working in Western Europe. In 1979 the Chinese Government made offers to several Western governments and multi-national corporations to supply contract labour for the construction of various public works and industrial projects.[19]

B. PRINCIPLES AND MECHANISMS

The international movements of workers are a complex process shaped by a variety of factors, largely (but not completely) reflecting the social

TABLE 10.2 *Leading labour-importing and labour-exporting countries, as of the late 1970s*

Labour-importing countries			*Labour-exporting countries*		
Country	*Number of migrant workers*	*Percentage of total employment*	*Country*	*Number of migrant workers*	*Percentage of total employment*
USA	4 000 000	5	Mexico	4 500 000	22
France	1 900 000	10	Italy	1 400 000	9
Federal Republic of Germany	800 000	3	Turkey	900 000	8
United Kingdom	800 000	3	Yugoslavia	850 000	17
Saudi Arabia	800 000	40	Portugal	600 000	18
Ivory Coast	700 000	27	Spain	550 000	5
Switzerland	400 000	15	Algeria	550 000	25
South Africa	350 000	5	India	400 000	2
Libya	300 000	33	Greece	350 000	8
Belgium	300 000	7	Morocco	350 000	8
United Arab Emirates	250 000	90	Egypt	350 000	4
Kuwait	250 000	75	Pakistan	250 000	2
Ghana	250 000	8	Tunisia	200 000	7
Netherlands	200 000	5	Guinea and Guinea–Bissau	200 000	10
Sweden	200 000	5			
Austria	200 000	6	Finland	120 000	13
Iran	200 000	2	Togo	100 000	13
Senegal	150 000	8	Upper Volta	100 000	5
Oman	80 000	65	Austria	100 000	3
Czechoslovakia	60 000	n*	Jordan	80 000	7

* n – negligible, less than 0.5 per cent.
Sources. Author's estimates. based on a variety of sources.

system in force – a fact to which researchers devoted little attention in the past.

In the capitalist world, fundamentally, the migrations of workers are conditioned by the existence of unemployment and low living standards in the labour-exporting areas and by job opportunities and higher wages in the labour-attracting countries, and these movements are essentially shaped by the market forces. The direction, size and composition of migrant labour are essentially determined by individual workers and employers, the initiative in some cases being taken by the former and in (most) others by the latter. This mechanism operates in its most spontaneous form not in the highly competitive market economies of North-Western Europe and the USA, but in fact in the equatorial West Africa, where there is little, if any, government intervention.

The labour markets in capitalist host countries now typically consist of two segments – primary and secondary. The *primary labour market* is in a sense an exclusive domain largely reserved for the native citizen workers. These workers have first choice of where and in what capacity they will work. The best qualified (or connected) ones get into a more exclusive inner super-primary labour market, noted for opportunities for further advancement, attractive superannuation or pension schemes, fringe benefits and the like.

The *secondary labour market* is largely residual, normally noted for unpleasant, heavy, dangerous or unhealthy work, of low social prestige and usually requiring lower or no skills. It is also noted for apathy, absenteeism, high labour turnover and even anti-social attitudes and behaviour.

The migrant worker – disadvantaged as he is by his alien status, language, his lack of knowledge of local conditions, no connections, no or unrecognized skills, racial appearance and low bargaining position in general – is usually reduced to the secondary labour market. Yet from the point of view of his employer, he may be highly desirable – hardworking, eager to please, uncomplaining and even grateful for the opportunity to work. But he is kept there because of prejudice of one sort or another, or convenience.

In the last decade or so, another phenomenon has emerged which can be described as a consequential *tertiary labour market*. It exists in the countries which both export and (largely in consequence) import labour, viz. Austria, Greece, Italy, Portugal and Spain. Thus in 1975, there were 99 000 Austrians working abroad (78 000 in the Federal Republic of Germany and 21 000 in Switzerland), but at the same time there were over 185 000 foreign workers employed in Austria (132 000 Yugoslavs,

26 000 Turks, 2000 Italians and 25 000 other nationalities).[20] Greece was employing at least 35 000 black and Arab Workers, and similarly Italy and Spain had significant numbers of migrant workers from north Africa, and Portugal – from Cape Verdi.[21]

The migrant labour market is generally considered to be elastic in periods of boom and prosperity, but rather inelastic in recessions. During upswings, the native drift from the secondary to the primary market is accentuated, employers become desperate and keen to fill the unwanted vacancies, whilst supply in the labour-exporting countries appears to be always plentiful, and workers are attracted by the ease of finding jobs and higher (and rising) wages. But experience since the early 1970s, especially in North-Western Europe, indicates that neither the demand for, nor the supply of, migrant labour respond downwards in a recession. Citizen workers prefer to be unemployed rather than displace foreign workers in the secondary market, and foreign workers prefer and tend to stay longer than originally envisaged by all the parties concerned.

The movements of workers amongst the socialist countries, where they occur, are not prompted by unemployment in the labour-supplying countries. In fact they now suffer from shortages of labour.[22] The intra-CMEA migrations of workers essentially derive from the national economic plans, further prompted by the drive to integrate the member countries into a more viable economic bloc. Two Czechoslovak economists rationalized this process as follows:

> They [the intra-CMEA movements of labour] are increasingly necessary to establish international project teams . . . to carry out major targets in the field of science, engineering, technology and the training of new personnel, with a view to achieving maximum economies in the outlay of social labour . . . Manpower exchanges are becoming an integral element of the development of the international Socialist division of labour.[23]

These movements, better described as 'planned transfers', are a consequence of inter-governmental bilateral or multilateral agreements, within the framework of which the relevant state entities (enterprises and institutions) negotiate the details of the engagements.

The CMEA countries have embarked on far-reaching co-operation in the area of labour and social questions since the mid-1960s, at first on a bilateral and since 1970 also on a multilateral basis. By the decision of the CMEA Executive Committee in 1974, the 'Conference of the Heads of State Labour Organs of the CMEA Member-Countries' was established as a permanent institution.

The movements of workers between the socialist and capitalist countries take place virtually on conditions strictly determined by the former, in both directions. As a rule, the socialist governments do not allow permanent emigration.[24] The temporary workers sent to Western Europe or less-developed countries are still embraced by the state plans embodying export and foreign aid commitments, including the construction of projects, the marketing of products, the operation of the socialist-owned business ventures, training programmes, and so on. Additionally, teams of specialists may be sent to less-developed countries to carry out agreed medical, scientific or agricultural schemes, or to advise on and promote the 'socialist road' to economic and social development.

The migrations of workers to the socialist countries are also carefully planned, by the host governments. It is even more essential than in the other direction, as it necessitates the provision of housing, additional supplies for the consumer goods market and various expenditures affecting the balance of payments, at least partly involving hard currencies.

As far as the workers going to the socialist countries are concerned, they may be prompted by two different considerations. Those from the industrialized West are usually sent by their companies which pay their employees the usual salaries and allowances (in hard currencies). On the other hand, workers from the Third World are attracted by assured jobs, better material conditions (than in their home countries) and perhaps by the ideological attraction of observing 'socialism in practice.' Evidence indicates that secondary labour markets of sorts have also emerged in some socialist countries, and foreign workers are channelled to them, especially in Czechoslovakia and the German Democratic Republic.[25] But the difference between primary and secondary markets is not as pronounced as in capitalist countries and wages do not become depressed by the market pressure.

Although the operation of the market prevails in the capitalist world and state direction in the socialist countries, the following exceptions must be noted. With the qualified exception of West Africa, the movements of migrant workers in the capitalist world are largely organized and controlled by the state. The general terms of employment and residence are negotiated between the governments of the host and the labour-supplying countries, the former being the dominant party laying down conditions from a 'position of strength.' In fact there is usually regulation of migrant labour in the host countries, at least in the first year of employment.

Its extreme form is administered in South Africa, where the state strictly regulates the whole process from start to finish. State labour bureaus recruit foreign workers in their 'homelands' according to strict requirements, and these workers are not free to choose their employer or place of employment. Thus an increase in the market demand for labour in a particular area, industry or occupation in South Africa and the operation of the market on the supply side in the 'homelands' are of no consequence unless the South African state acknowledges them and decides to act accordingly.[26] On the supply side, the prohibition by the Angolan, Mozambiquan and Zimbabwean governments, since the late 1970s of labour migration to South Africa, has led to the virtual discontinuation of the flow, in spite of the willingness of many local workers and of the acute shortages of labour in South Africa. In Western (including southern) Europe governments have restricted the number of immigrant workers since 1973 by more than 2.5m, in spite of the opposition on the part of the employers and workers concerned.

On the other hand, in the socialist countries the market mechanism does operate to some extent. In Yugoslavia, the directive system of planning and management has been replaced (especially since the mid-1960s) by 'market socialism' and movements of workers out of the country and their re-entry are virtually unrestricted. In several other socialist countries, the appearance of quasi-secondary labour markets and illegal and semi-legal emigration attest to at least some operation of the market mechanism.

C. ECONOMIC BENEFITS

The most obvious initial beneficiaries of the international migrations are the workers themselves, as otherwise they would not move. This generalization certainly applies to migrations from non-socialist countries. A large proportion of them would otherwise be unemployed or under-employed, and their wages would be lower.[27] *Per capita* incomes in the host countries are typically much higher than in the labour-exporting countries. For evidence see Table 10.3.[28] In North-Western Europe and in the CMEA countries foreign workers, in general, enjoy the same economic rights and privileges as citizen workers, as long as they have valid work and residential permits.[29]

In Western Europe, the USA and the Middle East workers earn hard currencies and in many cases accumulate considerable savings, which are partly remitted home. The average amount of cash remittances alone (that is, not including the purchases of durables and savings retained) is usually much higher than the *per capita* GNP in the home country, as is illustrated in Table 10.3.

In the CMEA countries, foreign workers are accorded preferential treatment in the allocation of housing, often to the resentment of the native workers who may have to wait for a flat or apartment for 6–8 years.[30] Migrant workers there also benefit from a complete health cover and other social services without extra cost to them.

Migrant workers may acquire skills and further their experience in the industrial advanced countries. But it appears that the socialist countries are more genuinely interested in assisting foreign workers, including those from non-socialist countries, than is usual in the capitalist world. Moreover, if the worker is brought out by his prospective employer or sent by the state (in the case of the socialist countries), his travelling costs are borne by the sponsor and the worker has an opportunity of travelling abroad and broadening his outlook, without having to pay for it.

To the employers in the host countries, migrant workers usually represent a cheap, mobile, conscientious and even docile labour force. In most of these countries, many of the essential services (such as garbage

TABLE 10.3   *Remittances received by selected labour-exporting countries in 1975*

Recipient country	Total received (US $m)	Average per migrant worker (US $)	Per capita GNP (US $)
Algeria	466	1 096	780
Egypt	367	611	310
Jordan	167	549	460
Morocco	533	1 925	470
Syria	55	785	660
Tunisia	146	1 327	760
Turkey	1 312	1 609	860
Arab Republic of Yemen	221	690	210
People's Democratic Republic of Yemen	56	799	240

Sources. Based on: R. P. Shaw, 'Migration and Employment in the Arab World: Construction as a Key Policy Variable', *Int. Lab. Rev.* (Geneva) Sept.–Oct., 1979, p. 596. *Europe Year Book 1978*, vol. I, (London: Europe Publications, 1978) pp. xvii–xxi.

collection, urban transport, the maintenance and repair of public utilities), farm work, mining and construction would be neglected or more costly without foreign workers, as there are not enough willing native workers. The remarkably rapid and successful modernization and transformation of the economies in North-Western Europe and the Middle East in the last decade or two would have hardly been possible without these new-style immigrants.

But there are also other, broader advantages to the countries involved. A clearly evident benefit to the labour-exporting country are the migrants' remittances and in particular their contribution to the balance of payments. The net flow of the remittances (excluding those in kind and sent through unofficial channels) to the less-developed countries alone amounted to $4600m in 1972, to $8100m in 1975, and it has increased considerably since.[31]

Remittances from Europe alone to the six major labour-exporting countries (Algeria, Greece, Morocco, Tunisia, Turkey and Yugoslavia) accounted for more than 25 per cent of the value of their visible exports and met about 14 per cent of their import bill in 1976.[32] In 1977 in the case of Morocco, Egypt, Jordan and Democratic Yemen, the remittances received represented the following percentages of these countries' exports of goods: 44, 66, 186, and 352, respectively; and in the case of the Arab Republic of Yemen, the percentage was 5449, or more than 50 times the country's export of goods.[33] In Southern Africa in the 'Black Homelands', 40 per cent of their Gross Domestic Product (GDP) is derived from their migrant workers' remittances, and some 75 per cent of the state budgets is obtained from the South African state.[34]

In some cases, the labour-exporting country may share in the output produced by its labour in the host country. This is the case with Bulgarian–Soviet co-operation, whereby Bulgarian workers are employed by the Soviets in the exploitation of forests at Komi; the Bulgarian Government is supplied with lumber at the average cost (as of mid-1970s) of 18–20 roubles (about $20) per cubic metre (compared with the world market price of $130).[35] Similar assured supplies of raw materials (minerals, metals, fuels, fish) and even manufactures (textiles, chemicals) are obtained by Czechoslovakia, the German Democratic Republic, Hungary and Poland, from joint production ventures operated with some Asian, Middle Eastern and African countries.[36] The personnel supplied by the socialist countries to their joint and other ventures help create profits, a proportion of which is then repatriated to the parent countries or reinvested in the host countries.

Most host countries benefit substantially from not having to provide housing, education and various social amenities to the extent necessary for their citizen population to marshall the same number of workers. In effect investment resources do not have to be diverted from the production sector for social overheads. In South Africa the investment economies of this nature in 1970 were estimated to be in the order of 8 per cent of the GDP.[37]

These savings are quite large in the USA in the case of illegal immigrant workers, for whom virtually no tax-supported social services are provided. In reflecting on the overall benefits of the illegal migration of workers to the USA, N. Hansen concluded:

> The informal illegal migration system continues to function because it benefits all parties concerned, at least so long as each party looks only at its own situation and what it would be if illegal immigrants were strictly curtailed.[38]

D. ECONOMIC AND SOCIAL PROBLEMS

For many years the policy-makers and theoretical writers were preoccupied with the immediate benefits to various parties involved. But more recently risks, unfulfilled hopes and unexpected costs have been recognized, both in the host and the labour-exporting countries.

(a) The Host Countries

Most host capitalist countries have suffered from considerable unemployment, especially since the early 1970s, and the presence of foreign workers accentuates the problem.[39] The availability of willing foreign workers is in many cases a contributory factor to the persistence of low wages in the affected occupations, industries or regions, to the detriment of competing citizen labour. A number of specialists in the field maintain that because of the specific situations that have arisen, migrant workers have a 'primitivizing' effect on the affected industries. Cheryl Benard summed it up as follows:

> Cheap and plentiful imported labour slows down the rationalization of industry, undercuts the incentive to achieve technological advance and regional decentralization of production, accustoms the economy to labour-consuming production, damages the ecology by concentrating industry in central areas, neglects agriculture, prevents the

substitution of labour by capital and permanently deforms the national labour market.[40]

M. Castells went further by insisting that:

immigrant workers do not exist because there are "arduous and badly paid" jobs to be done, but rather arduous and badly paid jobs exist because immigrant workers are present or can be sent to do them . . . If immigrant labour were to disappear, *depending on the balance of power of the labour movement*, the building industry would be reconverted and modernized.[41]

Many migrant workers have turned out to be more permanent residents than originally envisaged and desired by the host countries, especially in North-Western Europe. These workers soon began to bring out their families and have children, with the consequent pressure on housing, schooling and other public amenities and social service benefits, representing unforeseen costs to the employers, local authorities and central governments. Some specialists believe that 'the extension of welfare benefits to migrants reduce the wage of the domestic workers to such an extent that the utility level of domestic workers may not even be affected by the transfer.'[42]

The migrant workers' remittances, which have reached substantial proportions, are a drain on the host countries' foreign exchange reserves and may contribute to their balance-of-payments difficulties.

The movements of labour out of and into the socialist countries introduce complications into economic planning and may produce disruptive effects, especially in the case of the outflow of workers, considering the prevalent shortages of labour.

(b) Migrant Workers and Their Home Countries

From the standpoint of the migrant workers and the labour-exporting countries the following problems must be noted. First, these countries, at least temporarily, lose some of their most valuable and needed labour. Migrant workers are on the whole better educated, more enterprising than the average worker and are typically in the most productive age bracket.[43] A familiar element of this outflow is the 'brain drain'.[44] In consequence, wages of skilled workers in short supply may go up, impeding local development.

Second, the migrant workers' earnings are usually much lower than those of the citizen workers. Even where there is anti-discrimination legislation, as in North-Western Europe and the USA, in practice foreign workers experience unfair occupational grading and placement on the lowest rung of the wage scale and, furthermore, they do not enjoy the equality of opportunity in the choice of jobs and advancement.

Several studies have demonstrated that in the USA, largely as a result of Mexican workers, wages and working conditions along the Mexican border have been depressed to unduly low levels, especially in the case of blue-collar workers. Thus, according to one study, the annual real income in these areas is $684, or 8 per cent, lower than in comparable unaffected areas.[45] According to another, more recent investigation, Mexican workers – concentrated as they are in the secondary labour markets – receive only two-thirds of the wages prevailing in the primary markets.[46] In South Africa, by the mandatory 'job reservation system' (operating since 1911), most of the skilled and better-paid jobs are reserved for the whites. The black migrant workers receive only about one-tenth of the wage earned by the whites.[47]

Third, migrant workers suffer from an inferior political and social status. Being foreigners, they are subject to the usual political restrictions applicable to aliens, have no citizen rights and are precluded from resorting to political pressure to improve their position. In the Federal Republic of Germany, for example, they have no right to free assemblage, to move freely about the country, to choose their jobs, places of employment and schools; they cannot bring out their spouses or families until they have worked for 1–3 years; they can be instantly deported for drunken driving or for establishing a de facto relationship with a German woman, and there are cases of discrimination against them in restaurants and in local councils' residential ordinances.[48]

Foreign workers also suffer from what has become known as the 'psychotherapy of transplantation', they are usually reduced to the lowest social strata and in many cases they are socially rejected by the host population (also see Section E of this chapter). This also applies to the well-educated refugee workers from the socialist countries and, furthermore, they are often an object of contempt and attack by left-wing elements.

Fourth, migrant workers suffer from instability of employment and are most likely to be dismissed in recession, when their work as well as residential permits can be revoked. The unemployment problem in Western Europe since the early 1970s has been partly tackled by sending these workers home and reducing their recruitment. Thus their numbers between 1973 and 1977 were reduced in the Federal Republic of

Germany by 1 900 000 (from 2.6m to 0.7m)[49] and in Switzerland by 250 000[50] and during 1977–8, 2.0m foreign workers lost their jobs in North-Western Europe.[51]

Fifth, the labour-exporting countries are used as a cushion for absorbing economic fluctuations in the labour-importing countries. In effect, the brunt of cyclical risk is shifted to the poor countries who can least afford it.

Sixth, the expected transfer of skills and technology to the labour-exporting countries has proved disappointing. First of all, much of the migrant labour force is employed in unskilled or semi-skilled capacities (such as garbage-collection, heavy labouring on construction sites, cleaning and dishwashing and repetitive routine tasks in factories). Neither employers, nor trade unions, nor governments in the host countries are interested in training these workers – on the contrary, in most cases they have a vested interest in keeping them unskilled and uncompetitive. At any rate, their high labour-turnover impedes the acquisition of any but the most rudimentary skills, and those which are acquired are usually irrelevant to the needs of their home countries. The more successful workers tend to stay or migrate elsewhere. It appears that the socialist countries are more interested in providing training and experience of developmental value to the labour-exporting countries.

Seventh, the contribution of labour migration to the development of the labour-exporting countries has been minimal or negative. These countries lose some of their most productive workers. The migrant worker's savings are mostly used to buy a family home, imported luxuries or perhaps a small shop or cafe, and are not necessarily available for investment in productive industries of developmental consequence. The migrant workers from rural areas do not necessarily return to their villages to modernize farming, but rather drift to the cities, often joining the urban pools of unemployed and under-employed. The theorizing about 'economic development through migration' that was churned out by some enthusiasts in the 1960s and early 1970s has proved barren, judging by practical results.

Finally, the migrant workers' remittances have proved to be an unstable element of the balance of payments and a co-liability. Their inflow is irregular, highly susceptible to the number of the workers, the size of their families with them and above all the state of economic activity in the host countries. At the same time, the remittances generate imports, mostly of Western luxuries. The vulnerability of the balance of payments of the labour-exporting countries is illustrated by the serious difficulties experienced by Turkey over the period 1974–8, when remittances declined by 80 per cent.[52] In the socialist countries, foreign workers are paid, as a rule, in soft local currencies, even if they come from the capitalist world, which reduces the effective value of their savings, if any. But there are now exceptions to this rule.[53]

(c) Migrant Workers and Trade Unions

One would expect that workers' grievances should be taken up by trade unions. The ILO insists on the effective equality of opportunity and treatment with the national workers in respect of:

> The membership of trade unions, exercise of trade union rights and eligibility for office in trade unions and in labour-management bodies, including bodies representing workers.[54]

As is well known, migrant workers face many special problems and all-pervasive discrimination, in some cases deliberately intended, in others unintentioned, but nevertheless real and grossly iniquitous. But the trade unions' capacity and willingness to understand and to rectify these problems have in most cases proved limited. Although the unions want foreign workers as members, they appear to be interested more in these workers' membership dues and in preventing possible competition and action in the labour market than in providing genuine protection and remedies.

Owing to unfavourable local conditions and their own backgrounds, the inclination of the migrant workers to join trade unions is, as a rule, weak.[55] Disenchanted with indifference, the lack of understanding or even plain hostility on the part of the existing trade unions, migrant workers have made efforts in some host countries (especially in the United Kingdom) to organize their own ethnic unions. Most native trade union establishments have opposed the formation of distinct ethnic unions, prompted by racial and social prejudice, animosity to any special treatment and the fear of undermining the unity and cohesion of the existing trade union movement.

However, the attitudes of the national trade union bodies appear to be increasingly understanding and liberal, even though in many cases condescending, especially in Belgium, Britain, France, the Federal Republic of Germany, the Netherlands and Sweden. In some cases, migrant workers reach positions of some influence in trade unions. In the Federal Republic of Germany, the Trade Union Federation has separate nationality bureaus, manned by the nationals concerned.[56] In most North-Western European countries (Belgium, Britain, France, the Federal Republic of Germany, Luxemburg, the Netherlands) foreign workers can now be elected to bodies representing the workers (under workers' participation). But evidence indicates that migrant workers are under-represented on such bodies.[57]

Some co-operation is developing between the national trade union bodies of the host and labour-exporting countries, such as between the Federal Republic of Germany, Luxemburg, the Netherlands) foreign Yugoslavia on the other. There are possibilities for further international co-operation in this sphere under the auspices of the International Confederation of Labour.

E. MIGRANT WORKERS AND MARXISM

The inferior position and vulnerability of the migrant worker were recognized more than a century ago by Marx, who himself spent most of his adult life in exile amongst refugees (1843–83, in France, Belgium and England); Engels and Jenny Marx (Marx's eldest daughter) also took a keen interest in the problem. Between them, over the period 1843–94, they wrote over 145 contributions on the 'Irish question'.[58]

Although the circumstances and conditions of modern migrant workers are vastly different from those Marx and Engels witnessed in the latter part of the 19th century, it is possible to give them a Marxist or neo-Marxist interpretation.

(a) Uneven Capitalist Development and Labour

In *Capital*, vol. II, Marx insisted that capitalism in its higher stages necessarily leads to the *concentration and centralization of capital and production* in the hands of larger and larger firms controlled by fewer and fewer capitalists, leading to monopolies. This idea was further applied to the regional distribution of industries within each country and on the international scale between different countries, and has been elevated by Marxists to one of the 'laws of uneven capitalist development'.[59]

Concentration and centralization enable massive investment and technological progress, which may lead to new employment opportunities, the exhaustion of the *industrial reserve army of workers* and shortages of labour, especially in the periods of upswing. On the other hand, in the stagnant and impoverished less-developed countries, exploited through *non-equivalent exchange*, the reserve army of workers is ever present, depressing wages to bare subsistence levels. At the same time, owing to the political liberation of the former dependencies, investment capital can no longer move easily and safely to cheap labour. Hence the recruitment or attraction of cheap labour by the rich industrialized countries. As usual, capital takes the initiative and labour – to survive – has no option but to follow.

(b) A New Source of Capital Accumulation

The turn to cheap foreign labour by the employers in the industrialized capitalist countries can be regarded as an effort to arrest the *declining profit rate*.[60] The postwar period in North-Western Europe was marked by large capital inflows from the USA, rapidly advancing technology and productivity and at the same time depressed living standards of the masses. But by about 1960 population growth had begun to fall and wages to rise. The super-exploitation of foreign labour (see the section below) has enabled sustained capital accumulation and has in fact accelerated it. An American Marxist writer has concluded that 'the great international movements of labour constitute something akin to a form of development aid given by the poor countries to the rich'.[61]

(c) Super-Exploitation

The central feature of Marxian ideology is the exploitation of the working class by capitalists to the extent of the *surplus value*. Marx maintained that under normal conditions in the capitalist society the wage-earner does not receive the full value he creates but only a living wage. This wage tends to gravitate to the subsistence level, that is, the cost of maintaining the worker in a good working condition, raising an average family and of educating and training his offspring to be able to take up work.[62] Later, Marx added that the level of this wage depended on the stage of economic development and what was generally regarded as an acceptable subsistence level. By modern standards, it would include such social services as maternity allowance, child endowment, education, vocational training, long service leave, widows' pension, old age pension, funeral expenses and the like.

But in the case of modern migrant workers the *degree of exploitation* is much greater than the original Marxian model implied. Their exploitation can be interpreted to be threefold, viz. to the extent of: (1) the primary surplus value (as prevailing in the traditional primary labour markets), (2) the depressed wages and working conditions in the secondary and tertiary labour markets, (3) the non- (or limited) availability of social service benefits to the foreign workers.

(d) The Sub-Proletariat

As has been shown throughout this study, migrant workers are in an inferior position to native workers in almost every respect – wages, conditions of work, entitlements to social services, political rights and consequently, their overall social status and esteem.

Migrant workers have come to be described as an 'under-class', a social 'sub-stratum' or 'sub-proletariat',[63] and its members as 'second-rate humans', 'twentieth century slaves', 'proletarians on loan' or 'undomesticated proletarians', and the recruiting drives for these workers as 'slave trade' or even 'slave raids'.

The worst occupations or workplaces in the host countries have been denuded of native labour ('de-nationalized') and instead mostly filled with migrant workers. The host societies have, in effect, become sub-stratified with these workers, typically 'marginalized' as socially incongruent but economically indispensable appendages. Some observers in fact doubt if migrant workers represent free labour, even though they sign contracts and receive the same wages as citizen workers for the same jobs. In all important respects, their status is rather 'comparable to peonage or slavery'.[64]

This sub-stratum is separated by an embarrasingly wide and segregated 'social distance', especially in Britain, France, the Federal Republic of Germany, Switzerland and the USA. To this situation, Barbara E. Schmitter has applied the concept of *structural distance*, denoting 'the relative absence of linkages between host country institutions and immigrant groups'.[65]

(e) The Native Aristocracy of Labour

The existence of the primary (as contrasted with secondary and tertiary) labour markets in the host countries, together with the rather indifferent and self-seeking trade unions, recreate what Marxists call an 'aristocracy of labour.' This concept was widely discussed by revolutionary Marxists in the latter part of the 19th century, referring to some well-paid workers and bureaucrats. A number of exclusive craft unions (see Chapter 4A), as well as officials in some other unions, were similarly categorized. These groups were accused of siding with the bourgeoisie rather than the lower proletariat in order to protect their privileged position, and they were opposed to class struggle and revolution. Like their predecessors, the privileged native labour interests in the host countries today are opposed to the proletarian revolution and instead favour social democracy and the 'parliamentary road to socialism'. They are similarly accused by revolutionary Marxists of opportunism and revisionism.

(f) Neo-Alienation

Marx described alienation (in *Paris Manuscripts* and *Capital*) as the estrangement or de-humanization of the worker in relation to the goods he produces and the exploiting capitalist employer. Although in absolute material terms the migrant worker today is better off than he would be in his home country, he is soon clearly aware of his inferior status in almost every respect compared with the native working class. He is conscious of various forms of discrimination, super-exploitation and social rejection. There is evidence that he is no longer meek and passive but gives vent to his frustrations and predicament in anti-social attitudes and actions – such as breaking or circumventing bureaucratic regulations, doing the least possible work in the longest possible time, participating in or even initiating strikes, pilfering from factories and the like.[66]

(g) A Potential Revolutionary Force?

Many employers and authorities in the host countries have found that migrant workers are not as tame and submissive as originally expected. As they become familiar with local conditions and become a more or less permanent fixture, they begin to press for equal economic and social opportunities, and even equal political rights. On several occasions, for example in Britain, the Federal Republic of Germany and South Africa, they have resorted to public protests and strikes.

The potential for revolutionary movement and action by migrant workers has been speculated upon from two different angles with a converging conclusion. Certain right-wing and ultra-nationalist elements view the ethnic workers' groups as alien and hostile enclaves in the host societies and accuse them of being easily infected with Marxist and other radical ideas.

At the same time, revolutionary Marxists conceive the exploited and disenchanted migrant sub-proletarians as the real potential revolutionary spearhead in the industrialized host countries, where the working classes have been bought off by affluence and comfortable working conditions, partly at the expense of foreign labour. Thus M. Castells pointed out a few years ago:

> immigrant workers constitute both in the reality of their daily oppression and in their potential for social revolt, one of the most important and least known stakes in the newly emerging class struggles of advanced capitalism.[67]

According to Castells, the 'resurgence of social struggles in France since 1968 has had a profound effect on immigrant workers' and there has been 'Maoist penetration' among foreign workers.[68]

Migrant workers may also become a powerful force for social unrest and in revolutionary movements in their home countries. It is known that many workers, such as Italians, returning home join the Communist Party.[69] In the socialist countries, foreign workers from the capitalist world, of course, have all the opportunities to learn about Marxism and carry its precepts to their homelands.

The black liberation movement in Southern Africa, which is strongly influenced by Marxism and co-operates with Marxist groups, is opposed to the migrant labour system in South Africa (and against the puppet states which only help perpetuate the system). According to J. Loxley, the creation of the three 'independent' Bantu states by the South African Government in the late 1970s was dictated by its determination to 'preempt rising class consciousness' and instead to divert their attention towards tribalism and Bantu nationalism.[70] He concluded that: 'The Soweto uprising [of June 1976] furnishes further evidence of the progressive possibilities of using the migrant labour system as a vehicle for forging class alliance and class unity.'[71] The Marxist (or at least left-wing) governments in Angola, Malawi and Mozambique took steps between 1974 and 1976 to restrict the flow of migrant workers to South Africa.

However, the impediments to the revolutionary capacity of the migrant workers must be recognized. They after all represent different nationalities, languages, religions and standards of education and social consciousness. They are preoccupied with earning maximum income and are too interested in the sort of comfortable life and security which they observe in the host countries. They live in highly organized and efficient societies which they do not necessarily understand how to undermine. But most importantly, they are extremely vulnerable, as they can lose their jobs and be deported, and perhaps, further, may have to answer to their own governments.

(h) Socialist Neo-Imperialism?

The critical view held in the socialist countries of the migration of labour in its modern form in the capitalist world is well known, as is exemplified by the following verdict spelled out in a Polish source:

> The contemporary migration of labour . . . is one of the most repugnant phenomena in the new international economic order, precipitating as it does the ever-widening gap between poor and rich countries . . . In consequence, millions are alienated and families are deprived of fathers. At the same time, in the host countries masses of proletariat emerge, consisting of foreign workers.[72]

As is also known, Marxism is opposed to colonialism and imperialism, including foreign investment. They are regarded as inevitable by-products of developed capitalism in search of cheap raw materials and markets for its mass-produced manufactures, profit maximization (in view of the 'declining profit rate') and political influence.[73]

Yet the socialist countries themselves have greatly extended their economic involvement and political influence in the Third World. The socialist bloc's share in the Third World's foreign trade rose from less than 2 per cent in the early 1950 to more than 5 per cent in the late 1970s.[74] In their search for cheaper raw materials and larger markets for their manufactures, they have made substantial investments there by establishing wholly-owned subsidiaries and joint ventures. They have also been sending their workers to operate these companies and engage in various other projects (*see p. 199, especially note 17*). An Indian writer, reflecting on the many facets of the socialist involvement in his country, commented a few years ago:

> India's economic relations with the USSR and other communist countries have virtually converted this country in[to] a captive colonial economy. . . . But to mortgage our national interests in the name of socialist ideology is to invite a new form of slavery after having won our political independence.[75]

Furthermore, some socialist countries themselves, especially Czechoslovakia and the German Democratic Republic, have recruited labour in the Third World.

RECOMMENDED FURTHER READING

Also see Notes and References to this chapter.
1. K. Damaher, 'South Africa, U.S. Policy, and the Anti-Apartheid Movement', *Rev. Radical Political Economics* (New York) Fall 1979, pp. 42–59.
2. A. C. Evans, 'European Community Law and the Trade Union and Related Rights of Migrant Workers', *International and Comparative Law Q.* (London) July 1979, pp. 354–66.
3. Therese J. F. A. Gerold-Scheepers and N. M. J. van Binsbergen, 'Marxist and Non-Marxist Approaches to Migration in Tropical Africa', *African Perspectives* (Leiden) 1/1978, pp. 21–35.
4. Rosalinda M. Gonzalez and R. A. Fernandez, 'U.S. Imperialism and Migrations: The Effects on Mexican Women and Families', *Rev. Radical Political Economics* (New York) Winter 1979, pp. 112–22.
5. F. Mehl and Sandra E. Rapaport, 'Soviet Policy of Separating Families and Their Right to Emigrate', *International and Comparative Law Q.* (London) Oct. 1978, pp. 876–89.
6.* A. Fyodorova, 'The "Brain Drain" – an Imperialist Policy', *International Affairs* (Moscow) Nov. 1981, pp. 60–67.
7. A. Portes and R. L. Bach, 'Immigrant Earnings: Cuban and Mexican Immigrants in the United States', *International Migration Rev.* (New York) Fall 1980, pp. 315–341.
8. G. Renshaw (ed.), *Employment, Trade and North–South Co-operation* (Geneva: ILO, 1981).
9. R. C. Rist, 'Guestworkers and Post-World War II European Migrations', *Studies in Comparative International Development*, (New Brunswick, NJ) Summer, 1979, pp. 28–53.
10. Saskia Sassen-Koob, 'The Internationalization of the Labor Force', *Studies in Comparative International Development*, Winter 1980, pp. 3–25.
11. M. Slater, 'Migrant Employment, Recessions, and Return Migration: Some Consequences for Migration Policy and Development', *Studies in Comparative International Development*, Fall–Winter 1979, pp. 3–22.
12. H. Wolpe, 'Capitalism and Cheap Labour-Power in South Africa: From Segregation to Apartheid', *Economy and Society* (Henley-on-Thames) Nov. 1972, pp. 425–56.

* *Indicates contributions by writers from the socialist countries.*

Notes and References

CHAPTER 1: LABOUR AND THE SOCIAL SYSTEM

1. The designation is applicable to the countries ruled by the communist (or Marxist) regimes. In the Marxist terminology, two stages of communism following the proletarian revolution are distinguished – the 'lower' (or transitional) phase, also called 'socialism', during which some elements of capitalism are still retained, and the 'higher' phase, described as 'communism' or more explicitly 'full communism', when society will reach its ideal stage free from the vestiges of capitalism. All the Marxist countries, including the oldest of them (the USSR), describe themselves officially as 'socialist' (not 'communist') as they are still in the lower phase.

2. Social ownership in these countries assumes either of the two forms: (i) *state ownership* – it is predominant and applies to the most important industries and public services, the labour employed are in effect wage earners, and profits and losses are absorbed by the state in one form or another; (ii) *co-operative* (or *collective*) *ownership* – it is found in agriculture, small-scale industry and consumer services and the enterprises or farms are owned, managed and operated by clearly defined groups of members, who share in the income of the entity concerned (after taxes, investment provision and other laid-down deductions). The distinction has important implications for industrial relations – the entities in the former category are in several respects like firms in capitalist countries with the industrial conflict being more clearly apparent, whilst in the latter the dichotomy of interests is not so obvious.

3. The descriptions applied by different thinkers are: the 'industrial society' (R. Aron), the new 'industrial state' (J. Galbraith), the 'post-industrial society' (D. Bell), the 'post-bourgeois society' (R. Dahrendorf), the 'post-capitalist society' (K. Boulding), the 'post-civilization society' (H. Kahn), the 'super-industrial society' (A. Toffler), the 'technotronic age' (Z. Brzezinski), 'the self-service society' (J. Gershumy) and the 'optimum regime' (J. Tinbergen).

4. For details, see R. Aron, *The Opium of the Intellectuals* (Garden City, NY: Doubleday, 1957); D. Bell, *The End of Ideology* (Glencoe, Ill: Free Press, 1960) and *The Coming of Post-Industrial Society* (New York: Basic Books, 1973); Z. Brzezinski, *Between Two Ages: America's Role in The Technotronic Era* (New York: Viking Press, 1970); J. K. Galbraith, *The New Industrial State* (Boston: Houghton Mifflin, 1967); J. Tinbergen, *The Theory of the*

Optimum Regime (Rotterdam: NEH, 1959); A. Toffler, *Future Shock* (London: Bodley Head, 1970).

5. The features of the full communist society were incidentally discussed by Marx, *Critique of the Gotha Programme* (written in 1875), Marx and Engels, *German Ideology*, (1845–6), Lenin, *The State and Revolution* (1916) and Trotsky, *Literature and Revolution* (1925). Also see L. Eastman, 'Mao, Marx and the Future', *Problems of Communism* (Washington) May-June 1969, pp. 21–6.

6. For summaries and further references, see H. V. Perlmutter, 'Emerging East-West Ventures: The Transideological Enterprise', *Columbia J. World Business* (New York) Sept.–Oct. 1969, pp. 39–50; A. Meyer, 'Theories of Convergence', in C. Johnson (ed.), *Change in Communist Systems* (Stanford: Stanford University Press, 1970); L. Gouré *et al., Convergence of Communism and Capitalism: The Soviet View* (Washington: University of Miami, 1973).

7. The origin in fact goes back to prehistoric times and is reflected etymologically. The Indo-European root *ortho* meant a 'poor child', 'orphan', 'servant' or 'slave', and it gave rise to *Arbeit* (German), *labor* (Latin), *lavoro* (Italian), *rab* (Russian) and *robota* (Polish) – all meaning 'labour'. Similarly, in at least several other languages labour or work at least originally carried depreciative or degrading implications. In Greek *ponos* originally meant 'toil', 'suffering' and, in Hebrew, *abodah* meant 'servant work'. The French *travaille* and Spanish *trabajo* are derived from vulgar Latin *trabs* denoting 'draught animals'.

8. Marx, *Grundrisse der Kritik der politischen Oekonomie* (translated by M. Nicolaus as *Foundations of Political Economy* (Harmondsworth: Penguin, 1973)).

9. M. Michalik, *Moralność pracy* [Work Morality] (Warsaw: IW CRZZ, 1977) pp. 226–7.

10. Ibid., pp. 109–10.

11. Ibid., p. 218.

12. The initial exposition of this theory is embodied in Engels, 'Part Played by Labour in the Transition from Ape to Man' (written in 1876) and which later appeared in his *Dialectics of Nature*).

13. Marx, *Capital*, vol. I (1867); Engels, *Dialectics of Nature* (1873–83).

14. Marx, *Capital*, vol. I and III.

15. The ideas along these lines were first developed by Engels in *The Origin of the Family, Property and the State* (written in 1884).

16. R. Hyman, 'Inequality, Ideology and Industrial Relations', *British J. Industrial Relations*, 2/1974, p. 183.

17. C. Crouch, *Class Conflict and the Industrial Relations Crisis* (London: Heinemann, 1977) pp. 4, 21, 23.

18. D. D. Martin, 'Does Nationalization Hold Any Promise for the American Economy?', *J. Economic Issues*, 2/1977, pp. 327–38.

19. A. Herman and Marianna Strzyżewska-Kamińska, ['Ownership as the Basis of the Contemporary Economic Systems'], *Ekonomista* [The Economist] (Warsaw) 3/1978, p. 585.

20. Also colloquially and cynically labelled as the 'bilateral monopolistic struggle for power'.

21. For details, see J. Wilczynski, *Profit, Risk and Incentives under Socialist Economic Planning* (London: Macmillan, 1974) especially pp. 20–49, 126–56.
22. There are some exceptions regarding employment in certain essential services (such as fire brigades, hospitals, police, the armed forces) where the employees may not be allowed to strike. But they can submit their grievances to independent arbitration.
23. A series of practical studies carried out at the Hawthorne plant of Western Electric Co. near Chicago by a group of Harvard researchers over the period 1927–32. To their surprise, they found that the most important factor determining the productivity of labour were not so much equipment and techniques of production, but personal relationships in the work team and relations with management, especially at the lower and middle level (foremen in particular).
24. J. Purcell and M. J. Earl, 'Control Systems and Industrial Relations', *Industrial Relations*, Nottingham, Summer 1977, p. 54.

CHAPTER 2: EMPLOYMENT, UNEMPLOYMENT, MOBILITY

1. The more reliable measures are percentage ratios in which: (i) the labour force is related to total population above the school-leaving age (for example, 14 or 15); (ii) the labour force to the working population (say, men 15–65; women 15–60); (iii) the labour force in a given age bracket to the same working-age bracket (for example 15–20, 20–4, 24–60); (iv) the male *or* female labour force to the same male *or* female age bracket; (v) the single *or* married labour force to the single *or* married population.
2. Thus national practices traditionally differed as to the treatment of the armed forces, inmates in institutions, persons living on reservations, persons seeking work for the first time, seasonal workers, persons engaged in part-time economic activities and family members assisting in joint economic pursuits. However, owing to the efforts by the ILO, the comparability of the national data has been improving.
3. *Year Book of Labour Statistics 1980* (Geneva: ILO, 1980) pp. 15–31.
4. Other generalizations that may be briefly noted are. (i) Of men in the 20–64 age bracket, the rate is over 90 per cent throughout the world and this proportion has remained steady over a long period. (ii) The rate for women is lower, roughly less than a half the male rate (but it is rising), and it is lower in less-developed countries and higher in industrialized countries. (iii) The rates for young people (the 14–20 age bracket) have tended to decline, especially in the affluent nations, owing to the extension of education and prosperity. (iv) The rates for old people (60 and over) have tended to decline, especially in the rich countries owing to affluence and early retirement. (v) In less-developed countries the rates tend to decline further as living standards improve – more young people continue their education beyond the elementary level, fewer people continue working beyond the normal retiring age and more women limit themselves to household work; however, in the long run the decline may be reversed if industrialization proceeds along the typical capitalistic lines.

5. V. Kostakov, ['Employment under the Conditions of the Intensification of Production'], *Voprosy ekonomiki* [Problems of Economics] (Moscow) 4/1974, p. 37.
6. For different views on the subject, see A. Berry and R. H. Sabot, 'Labour Market Performance in Developing Countries: A Survey', *World Development* (Oxford) Nov.–Dec. 1978, pp. 1199–1242; W. Driehuis, 'Labour Market Imbalances and Structural Unemployment', *Kyklos* (Basle) 4/1978, pp. 638–61; E. Ginzberg (ed.), *Jobs for Americans* (Englewood Cliffs, NJ: Prentice-Hall, 1976); L. Squire, *Labor Force, Employment and Labor Markets in the Course of Economic Development* (Washington: World Bank) Staff Working Paper No. 336, June 1979.
7. For example see J. Bramham, *Practical Manpower Planning* (London: Institute of Personnel Management [IPM], 1975); Thakur Manab, *Manpower Planning in Action* (London: IPM, 1975); O. Mehmet, 'Benefit-Cost Analysis of Alternative Techniques of Production for Employment Creation', *Int. Lab. Rev.* (Geneva) July–Aug. 1971, pp. 37–50.
8. Margaret Schroeder, 'Labor Planning in the USSR', *Southern Econ. J.* (Chapel Hill) July 1965, p. 65.
9. Cs Vertes, ['Realities and Problems'] *Figyelö* [Economic Observer] (Budapest) 14 Dec. 1977, pp. 1, 2.
10. M. Ya. Sonin, ['Utilize Labour Resources Effectively'], *Ekonomika i organizatsiya promyshlennogo proizvodstva* [The Economics and Organization of Industrial Production] (Novosibirsk) April 1977, pp. 10–12.
11. J. Mincer, 'Labour Force Participation', in *International Encyclopedia of the Social Sciences* (New York: Macmillan, 1968) vol. 8, pp. 474, 479; *Year Book of Labour Statistics 1980* (ILO) p. 21.
12. A. Biryukova, 'Socialism and Women's Social Role', *International Affairs* (Moscow) May 1977, p. 30.
13. F. Engels, *The Origin of the Family, Private Property and the State*, (Chicago: Ch. H. Kerr, 1902) pp. 79, 91 and 99.
14. Shulamith Firestone, *The Dialectic of Sex* (New York: W. Morrow, 1970) pp. 8–9, 232–3.
15. Paddy Quick, 'The Class Nature of Women's Oppression', *Rev. Radical Political Economics* (New York) Fall 1977, p. 42.
16. Albania, Bulgaria, Czechoslovakia, the German Democratic Republic, Hungary, the Democratic People's Republic of Korea, Mongolia, Poland, Romania, the USSR and Vietnam; Yugoslavia has an associate status.
17. Batya Weinbaum, 'Women in Transition to Socialism: Perspective on the Chinese Case', *Rev. Radical Political Economics*, Spring 1976, p. 54.
18. Maria Metzler, 'Overt and Disguised Discrimination against Women in Collective Agreements: Findings of an Austrian Survey', *Int. Lab. Rev.*, March–April 1980, pp. 243–53.
19. G. Nikolayev, 'Unemployment – the Scourge of Capitalism', *International Affairs*, Nov. 1979, pp. 36–7.
20. Biryukova, op. cit., pp. 31–2.
21. Ibid., p. 30.

22. Quoted from: *Ekonomicheskie nauki* [Economic Studies] (Moscow) 11/1975, p. 34.
23. Biryukova, op. cit., p. 52.
24. *Sotsialisticheskii trud* [Socialist Labour] (Moscow) Sept. 1979, p. 76; A. Biryukova, op. cit., p. 52; *Soviet Weekly* (London) 11 Aug. 1979, p. 13.
25. Carma Hinton, 'Women: The Long March Toward Equality', *New China* (New York) Spring 1975, p. 29.
26. Hinton, loc. cit.; Weinbaum, op. cit., pp. 52–3.
27. A. P. Biryukova, ['Yes, the USSR Needs a Woman Action Programme'], *Ekonomika i organizatsiya promyshlennogo proizvodstva*, April 1974, pp. 116–17.
28. Hinton, op. cit., p. 32.
29. Weinbaum, op. cit., p. 51.
30. Quick, op. cit., p. 48.
31. Hinton, op. cit., p. 31; N. Shishkan, ['Women's Participation in Social Production'], *Ekonomicheskie nauki*, 11/1975, p. 36.
32. For example, H. B. Connell, 'Special Protective Legislation and Equality of Employment Opportunity for Women in Australia', *Int. Lab. Rev.*, March–April 1980, p. 199; Ruth Nielsen, 'Special Protective Legislation for Women in the Nordic Countries', *Int. Lab. Rev.*, Jan.–Feb. 1980, p. 80.
33. Under Article 9 of the Declaration on the Equality of Opportunity and Treatment for Women Workers, adopted by the Sixtieth Session of the International Labour Conference in 1975 (see *Women Workers and Society* (Geneva: ILO, 1976) pp. 202–3).
34. Thus, according to the data compiled by the ILO and published in the *Year Book of Labour Statistics 1979* and *1980*, the (percentage) rates for selected countries in the 1970s were as follows: Upper Volta – 2, Bangladesh – 3, Libya – 4, Egypt – 6, Iran – 9, Mexico – 14, Brazil – 21, Israel – 24, Australia, France and the Federal Republic of Germany – 32, the United Kingdom – 35, Canada – 36, Japan – 37, the USA – 39, Finland – 43, Denmark – 44, Sweden – 45. But a few unexpected exceptions may be noted: the Netherlands – 22, Italy – 25, New Zealand – 27 on the one hand, and Thailand – 46, Bermuda – 47 and Niger – 51 on the other.
35. For these four countries the rates, in that order, were 37 per cent, 41 per cent, 45 per cent and 30 per cent.
36. Shishkan, op. cit., p. 32.
37. Biryukova, op. cit., p. 51.
38. *Rocznik statystyczny 1980* [Statistical Yearbook 1980] (Warsaw: Central Statistical Office of Poland, 1980), p. 57.
39. *Hospodářské noviny* [Economic News] (Prague) 27 July 1979, p. 4.
40. *Sotsialisticheskii trud*, 9/1979, p. 76.
41. Biryukova, op. cit., p. 52.
42. A. C. Harberger, 'On Measuring the Social Opportunity Cost of Labour', *Int. Lab. Rev.*, vol. 103, 1971, p. 560.
43. Y. Sabolo, 'Employment and Unemployment 1960–1990', *Int. Lab. Rev.*, Dec. 1975, p. 408.
44. United Nations *Monthly Bulletin of Statistics* (New York) Nov. 1981, pp. 17–20.
45. Sabolo, *loc. cit.*

46. Marx, *Capital*, vol. I (1867), especially chs. XV, XXIV and XXV.

47. V. S. Goilo, ['Unemployment'] in *Bolshaya Sovetskaya Entsiklopediya* [Great Soviet Encyclopedia] 3rd edition (Moscow: ISE, 1970), p. 87.

48. For details, see N. C. Barth, 'Market Effects of a Wage Subsidy', *Industrial and Labour Relations Rev.* (London) July 1974, pp. 572–85; J. Burton, 'Employment Subsidies – the Case for and against.' *National Westminster Bank Quarterly Rev.* (London) Feb. 1977, pp. 33–43; A. R. Prest, 'The Role of Labour Taxes and Subsidies in Promoting Employment in Developing Countries,' *Int. Lab. Rev.*, vol. 103, 1971, pp. 315–32.

49. For example, see Mahbub al Haq, *The Poverty Curtain: Choices for the Third World* (New York: Columbia University Press) 1971, especially p. 42.

50. A. S. Bhalla, 'The Role of Services in Employment Expansion', *Int. Lab. Rev.*, May 1970, pp. 193–4, 197.

51. Not uncommon in Japan. According to one estimate the unemployment rate there of 2.5 per cent in the late 1970s would have been 'around 6 per cent, had there been US labour market practice'. M. Deppler and K. Regling, 'Labour Market Developments in the Major Industrial Countries', *Finance and Development* (Washington) March 1979, p. 27.

52. E. Yemin, 'Job Security: Influence of ILO Standards in Recent Trends', *Int. Lab. Rev.* Jan.–Feb., 1976, pp. 30–31.

53. M. Kalecki, 'Political Aspects of Full Employment', *Political Q.* (London) 3/1943, pp. 322–31.

54. J. Timar, 'The Level of Employment and Its Equilibrium in Socialism', *Acta oeconomica* [Economic Papers] (Budapest) 2/1969, p. 173.

55. CMEA, or popularly known as Comecon, is the Council for Mutual Economic Assistance established in 1949 with its headquarters in Moscow. It now embraces 10 full member countries, viz. Bulgaria, Cuba, Czechoslovakia, the German Democratic Republic, Hungary, Mongolia, Poland, Romania, the USSR and Vietnam (in addition Angola, Mozambique and Yugoslavia, plus Finland, Iraq and Mexico have kinds of associate status).

56. *Statisticheskii ezhegodnik stran-chlenov Soveta Ekonomicheskoi Vzaimpomoshchi 1980* [Statistical Yearbook of the CMEA Countries 1980] (Moscow: Statistika, 1980) p. 9.

57. *Rocznik statystyczny 1978*, p. 461.

58. *Magyar hirlap* [Hungarian Bulletin] (Budapest) 6 Sept. 1977, p. 7; *Rocznik statystyczny 1980*, p. 62; *Trud* [Labour] (Moscow) 17 July, 1979, p. 2.

59. Taxes in the form of interest rate (ranging from 3 to 6 per cent p.a. in different countries), levied on assets in the possession of (mostly industrial) enterprises and payable, as a rule quarterly, to the state budget. For further details see J. Wilczynski, *Socialist Economic Development and Reforms* (London: Macmillan, 1972) pp. 176–80.

60. 15 per cent in Poland, 15–20 per cent in Czechoslovakia, 25 per cent in the USSR. *Izvestiya Akademii Nauk SSSR: Seriya ekonomicheskaya* [Communications of the Academy of Sciences of the USSR: The Economic Division] (Moscow) Nov.–Dec., 1977, pp. 70–71; *Nowe drogi*, 2/1978, p. 125.

61. Based on: *Statisticki godišnjak Jugoslavije 1980* [Statistical Yearbook of Yugoslavia 1980] (Belgrade: Federal Statistical Office, 1980) pp. 80, 135;

United Nations, *Monthly Bulletin of Statistics,* Nov. 1981, p. 20.
62. *Zycie gospodarcze* [Economic Life] (Warsaw) 1 March, 1981, p. 2.
63. I. G. Ushakov, ['Material Incentives and the Rationalization of Employment in the CMEA Countries'] *Izvestiya Akademii Nauk SSSR* . . . , Jan.–Feb. 1978, pp. 74–5.
64. J. Loxley, 'Labour Migration and the Liberation Struggle in Southern Africa', paper presented at the Seminar on International Labour Issues, McGill University, Montreal, 10 April, 1980, p. 7.
65. W. Teckenberg, 'Labour Turnover and Job Satisfaction: Indicators of Industrial Conflict in the USSR', *Soviet Studies* (Glasgow) April 1978, p. 198.
66. A. Kotlyar, 'Problems of Younger Workers in the USSR', *Int. Lab. Rev.,* April 1974, p. 369.
67. J. Penc, ['Social Policy and the Reduction of Working Hours'], *Ruch prawniczy, ekonomiczny i socjologiczny* [Developments in Law, Economics and Sociology] (Poznan) no. IV, 1978, p. 261.
68. M. Ya. Sonin, ['Towards an Effective Utilization of the Labour Force'], *Ekonomika i organizatsiya promyshlennogo proizvodstva,* 4/1977, p. 4.
69. *Das Volk* [People] (Erfurt) 18 Oct. 1977, p. 3.

CHAPTER 3: WORK DISCIPLINE AND CONDITIONS OF WORK

1. M. Weber, *The Protestant Ethics and the Spirit of Capitalism* (1904–5); R. H. Tawney, *Religion and the Rise of Capitalism* (1926).
2. M. Michalik, *Moralność pracy* [Work Morality] (Warsaw: IW CRZZ, 1977) p. 98.
3. Ibid., p. 126.
4. Marx, *Capital* (New York: International Publishers, 1967) vol. I, p. 356.
5. *Beijing Rev.* (Peking) 17 Nov., 1980, pp. 4–5.
6. For example, the proceeds from the 1980 *Subbotnik* totalled 250m roubles which by the decision of the Council of Ministers in consultation with the All-Union Central Council of Trade Unions, were apportioned as follows: 50m r. for the construction of convalescent homes for mothers and children, 85m r. for pre-school institutions and 112m r. for hospitals. *Izvestiya,* 11 Nov., 1980, p. 2.
7. *Słownik wiedzy obywatelskiej* [The Dictionary of Civic Knowledge], (Warsaw: PWN, 1970) pp. 97–8.
8. Michalik, op. cit., pp. 95, 99.
9. J. Maziarski, ['Attitudes to Work'], *Nowe drogi* [New Paths] (Warsaw) 11/1977, pp. 84–5.
10. *Népszabadság* [People's Daily] (Budapest) 10 Feb., 1980, p. 3.
11. For details see, for example, G. Grossman, 'Notes on the Illegal Private Economy and Corruption', in US Congress, Joint Economic Committee, *Soviet Economy in a Time of Change* (Washington: GPO, 1979) vol. I, 10 Oct., pp. 834–55; Ch. A. Schwartz, 'Economic Crime in the USSR: A Comparison of the Khrushchev and Brezhnev's Eras', *Int. Comp. Law Q.* (London) April 1981, pp. 281–96; S. J. Staats, 'Corruption in the Soviet Union', *Problems of Communism,* Jan.–Feb. 1972, pp. 40–47.

12. For example see Ji Zhe, 'China's National Capitalists: Past and Present', *Beijing Rev.*, 28 April, 1980, p. 19; A. Lubowski, ['Where Are Those Milliards Gone?'], *Życie gospodarcze* [Economic Life], 3 May, 1981, p. 1.
13. For details, see S. Rosefielde, 'An Assessment of the Sources and Uses of Gulag Forced Labour, 1929–56', *Soviet Studies* (Glasgow) Jan. 1981, pp. 51–87; S. G. Wheatcroft, 'On Assessing the Size of Forced Concentration of Camp Labour in the Soviet Union', *Soviet Studies*, April 1981, pp. 265–95.
14. Marx, *Capital* (New York: International Publishers, 1967) vol. I, p. 530.
15. *European Industrial Relations Rev.* (London) Jan. 1978, p. 7, Sept. 1978, p. 6, July 1981, p. 3 and Sept. 1981, p. 7; *Życie gospodarcze*, 24 Feb., 1981, p. 1.
16. *Business Eastern Europe* (Geneva) 27 March, 1981, p. 98.
17. *Życie gospodarcze*, 29 March, 1981, p. 2.
18. For example, see J. de Givry, 'The ILO and the Quality of Working Life. A New International Programme: PIACT', *Int. Lab. Rev.* (Geneva) May–June 1978, pp. 261–71.
19. Michalik, op. cit., p. 146.
20. For example, Marx, *Poverty of Philosophy* (written in 1846–7).
21. In *Paris Manuscripts* (written in 1844) and in *Capital*, vol. I (1867).
22. Ch. Dufour, 'Unpleasant or Tedious Jobs in Industrialized Countries', *Int. Lab. Rev.*, July–Aug. 1980, p. 421.
23. W. Teckenberg, 'Labour Turnover and Job Satisfaction: Indicators of Industrial Conflict in the USSR', *Soviet Studies*, April 1978, pp. 195–6.
24. *The Canberra Times*, 23 May, 1980, p. 3.
25. I. J. Balint, ['Productivity and the Manpower Situation as Reflected in Statistics'], *Társadalmi szemle* [Social Review] (Budapest) April 1978, p. 34.
26. Reported in A. Dadashev, ['Losses of Working Time Caused by Absenteeism'], *Trud* [Labour] (Moscow) 30 Aug., 1979, p. 2.
27. M. Kabaj, ['In Search of the Lost Time'], *Nowe drogi*, Sept. 1980, p. 114.
28. A. Dadashev, loc. cit.
29. For example, see R. N. Ottaway, *Humanising the Workplace* (London: Croom Helm, 1978).
30. Mainly in: Marx, *Paris Manuscripts* (1844), *Capital*, vol. I (1867) and *The Critique of the Gotha Programme* (1875); Engels, *Part Played by Labour in the Transition from Ape to Man* (1876).
31. K. R. Szymanski, ['The Humanization of Work and Its Programmes of Implementation in Enterprises'], *Ekonomika i organizacja pracy* [The Economics and Organization of Labour] (Warsaw) May 1979, pp. 1–4.
32. For example, Alicja Kozdrój, ['The Humanization of Work – Twenty Years of Polish Experience'], *Gospodarka planowa* [Planned Economy] (Warsaw) May 1980, pp. 275, 277.
33. The creation of the ILO was postulated in the Versailles Treaty under Article XIII (prepared by Samuel Gompers, who subsequently became the first President of the ILO). Although the USA was a leading foundation member of the ILO, paradoxically she never ratified the Treaty itself.
34. One of the items concerned was: E. Pletnev and R. Kossolapov, 'Lenin and Social Progress', *Int. Lab. Rev.*, April 1970, pp. 317–30 (the lead article).
35. For example, see Yu. Romanov, ['Victory for Reactionaries – Why the USA Withdrew from the International Labour Organization'], *Izvestiya* (Moscow) 5 Nov., 1977, p. 5; J. Białocerkiewicz, ['Legal and Political

Aspects of the ILO Membership'], *Sprawy miedzynarodowe* [International Affairs], (Warsaw) Feb. 1978, pp. 119–22.

36. In this vein, for example Poland in 1977 proposed a Convention on the Right to Work and on Employment Policy. Although the proposal was supported by other socialist countries, too, it was not adopted by the ILO as most capitalist countries opposed it.

37. Those which are still operative are concerned with merchant shipping, viz.: No. 53 (Masters' and Mates' Competency Certificates) of 1936, No. 55 (Liabilities of Shipowners in Case of Sickness, Injury or Death of Seamen) of 1936, and No. 74 (Certification of Able Seamen) of 1946. On the other hand, the USSR ratified 43 Conventions.

38. V. Mrachkov, 'International Labour Conventions and Bulgarian Legislation', *Int. Lab. Rev.*, March–April 1979, pp. 215–6.

39. Ibid, p. 218.

40. For example, see Białocerkiewicz, op. cit., p. 117.

CHAPTER 4: TRADE UNIONS AND COLLECTIVE BARGAINING

1. For example, F. Engels, *The Conditions of the Working Class in England* (originally written in 1845); K. Marx, *The Poverty of Philosophy* (1846–7); Rosa Luxemburg, *The Mass Strike, Political Party and the Trade Unions* (1906); V. I. Lenin, *What Is To Be Done?* (1901–2).

2. V. I. Lenin, *Collected Works* (Moscow: FLPH, 1961) vol. 5, pp. 413–36.

3. V. I. Lenin, *Collected Works* (Moscow: Progress Publishers, 1964) vol. 22, p. 301.

4. E. Bernstein, *Strike: Its Nature and Operation* (originally published in 1906); K. Kautsky, *The Social Revolution* (1902).

5. The term originated in France (*syndicats jaunes*) in 1887, when during a strike at Montcean-Les-Mines employers contrived to organize a labour union to break the strike. The union met in a hall in which windows (previously broken by the striking workers) were patched with yellow paper.

6. Lenin, op. cit., vol. 32, pp. 20–21.

7. Umoh James Umoh, 'Long History of Unions' Divisions', *West Africa* (London) 2 June, 1980, p. 964.

8. Quoted from: F. Deppe, 'Trade Unions', in C. D. Kernig (ed.), *Marxism, Communism and Western Society: A Comparative Encyclopaedia* (New York: Herder & Herder, 1973) vol. 8, p. 224.

9. Emily C. Brown, *Soviet Trade Unions and Labor Relations* (Harvard University Press, 1966) p. 1.

10. Thus, in the USSR, the 130m trade unionists, constituting about 97 per cent of the working population, are organized in 2.5m union groups consisting of 700 000 local trade unions with 500 000 workshop union committees. The whole structure is headed by the All-Union Central Council of Trade Unions, A. S. Shibayev (a member of the Politburo) being its chairman. *Kommunist* (Moscow) 5/1977, p. 10.

11. *Beijing Rev.* (Peking) 8 June, 1979, p. 11.

12. *Soviet News* (London) 28 Aug., 1979, p. 276.

13. *Peking Rev.*, 8 Dec., 1978, p. 5.

14. In Sweden trade unions also administer unemployment insurance and benefits for about one-half of the country's employees (the funds being derived from the members' contributions and state grants). Similar responsibilities are also discharged by unions in some less-developed countries.

15. J. L. Porket, 'Participation in Management in Communist Systems in the 1970s', *British J. Industrial Relations*, Nov. 1975, p. 380.

16. *A Chronicle of Human Rights in the USSR* (New York) Jan.–March, 1977, p. 77.

17. *Munka* [Work] (Budapest) 3/1979, p. 1.

18. W. Adamski, ['Solidarity in the Eyes of Public Opinion'], *Kultura* [Culture] (Warsaw) 22 March, 1981, pp. 7, 8.

19. *Kultura*, 21 June, 1981, p. 2.

20. *Pravda*, Moscow, 11 Feb., 1981, p. 4.

21. V. Chalidze, 'A Workers' Movement in the USSR?', *Chronicle of Human Rights*, Jan.–March, 1978, p. 41.

22. For further details, see *Chronicle of Human Rights*, Jan.–March, 1978, pp. 37–51; July–Sept., 1979, pp. 10–11.

23. *Chronicle of Human Rights*, January–March, 1979, pp. 13–14; *A Chronicle of Current Events* (London) 51/1979, p. 186.

24. *The Free Labour World* (Brussels: ICFTU) July–Aug., 1980, pp. 4–5.

25. Reported in *The Australian*, Sydney, 30 Jan., 1981, p. 4.

26. *Australian Financial Rev.*, Sydney, 10 Nov., 1981, p. 35.

27. *East Europe* (New York) June, 1969, p. 17; *Int. Lab. Rev.* (Geneva) March–April, 1979, p. 208.

28. Of the 165 sovereign countries in the world, 143 are members of the ILO, and of these 91 have ratified Convention 87, and 108, Convention 98. Of the capitalist countries, the democratic USA is conspicuous by not having ratified either Convention 87 or 98 (which, in a sense paradoxically, contrasts with her rival, the authoritarian USSR which has ratified both).

29. But it may be mentioned here that in the Dominican Republic the employer is obliged to negotiate only if the trade union represents at least 60 per cent of the workers' involved. See, A. S. Bronstein, 'Collective Bargaining in Latin America: Problems and Trends', *Int. Lab. Rev.*, Sept.–Oct. 1978, p. 588.

30. Capitalist countries, conspicuous by their omission, include Canada, Chile, India, Iran, Mexico, the Netherlands, New Zealand, South Africa, Switzerland and the USA. On the socialist side, only Afghanistan, Kampuchea, Laos, Mozambique and Somalia have not ratified it (Albania, China and the Democratic People's Republic of Korea are not ILO members at present). Nevertheless, collective bargaining still plays a very important part in many of these countries, especially in Canada, Mexico and the Netherlands.

31. E. Cordova, 'A Comparative View of Collective Bargaining in Industrialised Countries', *Int. Lab. Rev.*, July–Aug., 1978, p. 424.

32. *Soviet News*, 28 Aug., 1979, p. 278.

33. Based on V. Zhmakin and L. Pisareva (eds), *Kollektivnoe dogovory v sotsialisticheskikh stranakh* [Collective Agreements in the Socialist Countries] (Moscow: Profizdat, 1976).

34. Bronstein, op. cit., p. 583.
35. E. R. Livermash, 'Collective Bargaining', in D. L. Sills (ed.), *International Encyclopedia of the Social Sciences* (New York: Macmillan, 1968) vol. 8, p. 499.
36. However, in some countries (such as Finland, Italy, Poland, Sweden, the United Kingdom and the USSR) collective agreements may extend to the whole industry, covering non-unionized workers as well.
37. Porket, op. cit., p. 381.
38. Pope John Paul II is well known for his sympathetic attitude to the working class and his concern for the elimination of poverty and discrimination throughout the world. He was born to a humble family in Poland, where even under the communist rule, four-fifths of the population are practising Catholics (to the exasperation of the communist regime). His election to the Papacy in October 1978 created a world sensation, as he is the first non-Italian pope since 1522, the first pope from Poland and indeed the first pope from the socialist bloc. He is incidentally the first pope to visit a socialist country (viz. Poland in June 1979). He is opposed to Marxism as a solution to social problems and some observers see his appointment as heralding a new era for Christian churches in Eastern Europe and perhaps for East–West relations. He has given moral support to the independent trade union organization Solidarity and received Lech Wałęsa when the latter was on a visit to Rome in January 1981.
39. The Marxist term 'yellow' is applied to working-class organizations giving up the class struggle in favour of co-operation with employers and the propertied classes in general (for the derivation of the term 'yellow', see Chapter 4, Note 5). Lenin described the Bern International (founded in Bern in February 1919 by social-democratic parties as a successor to the Second International) as the 'Yellow International' (in *Collected Works*, vol. 29, p. 42).
40. For example, see H. Hartmann, 'Trade Union Organization and the European Economic Community', *Studies in Comparative International Development* (New Brunswick, NJ) 3/1978, pp. 41–58.
41. For evidence, see *Flash* (WCL, Brussels) 20 Oct., 1980, p. 2; 15 March, 1981, pp. 2–3; 1 May, 1981, pp. 4–5; 15 Sept, 1981, p. 1; 7 Jan., 1982, p. 1. *Free Labour World*, July–Aug., 1980, p. 4. *International Trade Union News* (ICFTU, Brussels) 3 Sept., 1980, p. 2; 5 Dec., 1980, p. 2; 15 Dec., 1980, p. 2; 16 March, 1981, p. 1; 30 March, 1981, p. 2; 29 Sept., 1981, p. 2; 17 Dec., 1981, pp. 1–2.
42. For details, see J. Wilczynski, *The Economics and Politics of East–West Trade* (London: Macmillan, 1968) pp. 146–90.
43. *Rynki zagraniczne* [Foreign Markets] (Warsaw) 4 April, 1974, p. 5.
44. For further details, see F. Levcik and J. Stankovsky, *Industrial Co-operation between East and West* (White Plains, NY: M. E. Sharpe, 1979); J. Wilczynski, *The Multinationals and East-West Relations* (London: Macmillan, 1976); L. Żurawicki, *Multinational Enterprises in the West and East* (Alphen aan den Rjin, Netherlands: Sijthoff & Noordhoff, 1979).
45. See some of his relevant publications on the subject: *International Trade Unionism* (London: George Allen & Unwin, 1972); *A Concrete Trade Union Response to the Multinational Company* (Geneva: ICF, 1974); *Vodka-Cola*

(London and New York: Gordon and Cremonesi, 1978).
46. D. Warburton, 'Imported Redundancies and East-West Trade', *Free Labour World*, Jan.–March, 1980, pp. 7–8.
47. *Chronicle of Human Rights*, Jan.–March, 1977, pp. 82–3.
48. Ibid., p. 82.
49. Reported in T. Bartoszewicz, ['Trade Unionism and Protectionism'], *Handel zagraniczny* [Foreign Trade] (Warsaw) 3/1979, p. 26.
50. Ibid., p. 27.
51. D. Marković, 'Multinational Corporations, the Working Class and Trade Union Strategy', *Rev. International Affairs* (Belgrade) 1 Sept., 1980, p. 13.
52. Ibid., p. 15.

CHAPTER 5: INDUSTRIAL DEMOCRACY AND WORKERS' PARTICIPATION

1. *Great Soviet Encyclopedia* (New York: Macmillan, 1975) vol. 9, p. 369.
2. Other names used more or less synonymously are: workers' participation, co-determination, co-decision making, shop-floor democracy, the humanization of work relations, the democratization of control, the integration of workers into decision-making, and people's approach to management.
3. The first systematic analysis of the problem was given by Engels in *The Origin of the Family, Private Property and the State* (1884).
4. Initially documented in such pioneering works as A. A. Berle and G. C. Means, *The Modern Corporation and Private Property* (New York: Macmillan, 1932); J. Burnham, *The Managerial Revolution* (New York: John Day, 1941).
5. J. Schregle, 'Co-determination in the Federal Republic of Germany: A Comparative View', *Int. Labour Rev.* (Geneva) Jan.–Feb. 1978, p. 85.
6. The practice of allocating shares to employees is best developed in France and the Federal Republic of Germany. The EEC authorities are in favour of extending this form of workers' participation further. See *Worker Participation in the European Community* (Brussels: Commission of the European Communities, 1977) pp. 10, 14, 31.
7. The latter two firms were near-bankrupt companies taken over by the workers.
8. T. Clarke, 'Industrial Democracy: The Institutionalized Suppression of Industrial Conflict?', in T. Clarke and L. Clements (eds), *Trade Unions under Capitalism* (Hassocks, UK: Harvester Press, 1978) p. 377.
9. L. Héthy and Cs. Makó, 'Workers' Direct Participation in Decisions in Hungarian Factories', *Int. Lab. Rev.*, July–Aug. 1977, p. 21.
10. For further details, see Schregle, op. cit., pp. 81–98.
11. For further details, see *Worker Participation in the European Community*, op. cit.
12. H. Hartmann, 'Trade Union Organization and the European Economic Community', *Studies in Comparative International Development* (New Brunswick, NJ) 3/1978, pp. 51–2.
13. P. G. Gyllenhammar, 'How Volvo Adapts Work to People', *Harvard Business Rev.*, July–Aug, 1977, pp. 102–13.

14. Schregle, op. cit., pp. 97–8.
15. Commonly abbreviated in English to BOAL or *OOUR* in Serbo-Croat (for *Osnovna Organizacija Udruženog Rada*).
16. A. Whitehorn, 'Yugoslav Workers' Self-Management – A Blueprint for Industrial Democracy?', *Canadian Slavonic Papers* (Ottawa) Sept. 1978, pp. 421–8.
17. Héthy and Makó, op. cit., p. 11.
18. Quoted from *Życie gospodarcze* [Economic Life] (Warsaw) 10 Oct., 1980, p. 2.
19. A. Smith, 'Romania's Economic "Reforms",' in NATO, Economic Directorate, Information Directorate (eds), *Economic Reforms in Eastern Europe and Prospects for the 1980s* (Oxford: Pergamon, 1980) p. 52.
20. N. Caragea, ['Workers' Self-Management: An Ingenious Idea with Far-Reaching Implications for the Development of Our Socialist Democracy'] *Revista economica* [Economic Review] (Bucharest) 16 Nov., 1979, p. 2.
21. Clarke, op. cit., p. 378 (emphasis in the original).
22. Ibid., p. 362.
23. Schregle, op. cit., p. 98.
24. *Soviet Weekly* (London) 1 Sept., 1979, p. 9.
25. *Soviet News* (London) 28 Aug., 1979, p. 280.
26. Héthy and Makó, op. cit., p. 13.
27. CMEA is the Council for Mutual Economic Assistance, originally created in 1949 and now embracing 10 full member countries: Bulgaria, Cuba, Czechoslovakia, the German Democratic Republic, Hungary, Mongolia, Poland, Romania, the USSR and Vietnam (in addition Angola, Mozambique and Yugoslavia, plus Finland, Iraq and Mexico have kinds of associate status). Although the grouping has achieved a remarkable degree of economic integration, especially in industrial production, little has been done in the sphere of industrial relations.
28. For evidence from different countries, see, for example, Gyllenhammar, op. cit., p. 106; Héthy and Makó, op. cit., p. 13; Schregle, op. cit., pp. 83, 90; Whitehorn, op. cit., p. 426; E. J. Vaughan, 'Some Observations Upon the Logic of Participative Management', *J. Industrial Relations* (Sydney) Sept. 1976, pp. 226–7.
29. Héthy and Makó, op. cit., p. 13.
30. For example, see D. Bell, *The Coming of Post-Industrial Society* (New York: Basic Books, 1973) p. 119; J. Ellui, *L'illusion politique* [Political Illusion] (Paris: Laffont, 1965) p. 159; N. Bujdolu and A. Deniforescu, ['Workers' Participation in Decision-Making'], *Era Socialista* [The Socialist Era] (Bucharest) 20 April, 1980, pp. 8–9; Héthy and Makó, op. cit., p. 14; Alicja Kozdrój, ['The Humanization of Work – Twenty Years of Polish Experience'], *Gospodarka planowa* [Planned Economy] (Warsaw) 5/1980, p. 274.
31. Vaughan, op. cit., p. 226.
32. Clarke, op. cit., p. 375.
33. Ibid., pp. 376–7.
34. L. Szamuely, 'Industrial Democracy in Western Europe: Effects and Contradictions', *Acta oeconomica* [Economic Papers] (Budapest) 4/1978, pp. 346, 352, 356.

35. Ibid., p. 341.
36. Héthy and Makó, op. cit., pp. 18–19.
37. Bujdolu and Deniforescu, op. cit., p. 9.
38. M. Djilas, *The New Class: An Analysis of the Communist System* (London: Thames & Hudson, 1957); *Unperfect Society: Beyond the New Class* (New York: Harcourt, Brace and Jovanovich, 1969).
39. V. Holesovsky, *Economic Systems: Analysis and Comparisons* (New York: McGraw-Hill, 1977) p. 453.

CHAPTER 6: TECHNOLOGY AND LABOUR

1. Marx, *Capital* (New York: International Publishers, 1967) vol. I, pp. 371–507; vol. III, pp. 142–53.
2. For example, see K. Engelhard, 'Strategy of the War Monopolies', *World Marxist Rev.* (Toronto) 7/1970, pp. 68–72; Gus Hall, *Imperialism Today* (New York: International Publishers, 1972) pp. 101–5, 126ff; F. Schmid, *Der Militär-Industrie-Komplex* [The Military–Industrial Complex] (Frankfurt: Verlag Marxistische Blätter, 1972).
3. This thinking can be traced back to the ideas first put forward by T. Veblen (*The Engineers and the Price System*, 1921), developed in the 1930s (especially in the USA) and further confirmed by the exponents of managerialism such as J. Burnham (*The Managerial Revolution*, 1941).
4. *Quotations from Chairman Mao Tse-tung* (Peking: Foreign Languages Press, 1966) p. 239.
5. Ch. Dufour, 'Unpleasant or Tedious Jobs in the Industrialized Countries', *Int. Lab. Rev.* (Geneva) July–Aug. 1978, p. 416.
6. Lenin, *Collected Works* (Moscow: Progress Publishers, 1965) vol. 29, p. 427 (emphasis in the original). 'Pood' was a Russian measure of weight equal to 36.1 lbs or 16.4 kg.
7. M. Michalik, *Moralność pracy* [Work Morality] (Warsaw: CRZZ, 1977) pp. 88–9.
8. For further details, see J. Wilczynski, *Socialist Economic Development and Reforms: From Extensive to Intensive Growth under Central Planning in the USSR, Eastern Europe and Yugoslavia* (London: Macmillan, 1972) pp. 25–46.
9. Yu. Yakovets, ['Indicators and Incentives for Economizing Labour'], *Sotsialisticheskii trud* [Socialist Labour] (Moscow) 1/1979, p. 109.
10. Ibid., p. 109, 112.
11. For example, see J. Balint, ['The Statistics of Productivity and the Labour Force'], *Társadalmi szemle* [Social Review] (Budapest) 4/1978, pp. 30–31; Z. Karpisek, M. Pick and K. Vyhnalik, ['Are We Searching for Viable Solutions?'], *Hospodářské noviny* [Economic News] (Prague) 7 Oct. 1977, p. 8.
12. Balint, op. cit., p. 23.
13. Ibid., p. 24.
14. Ni Chi-fu, 'Basic Principles for Trade Union Work in the New Period', *Peking Rev.*, 3 Nov., 1978, p. 12.
15. A. S. Bhalla, 'Technology and Employment: Some Conclusions', *Int. Lab.*

Rev., March–April 1976, pp. 189–203; Y. Sabolo, 'Employment and Unemployment 1960–1990,' *Int. Lab. Rev.*, Dec. 1975, pp. 401–17.

16. J. de Givry, 'The ILO and the Quality of Working Life. A New International Programme: PIACT', *Int. Lab. Rev.*, May–June 1978, p. 270.

17. K. Gill, 'Technological Progress and the Crisis of Capitalism', *World Marxist Rev.* (London) June 1980, pp. 45–46.

18. E. Jonsson, 'Labour as a Risk-Bearer', *Cambridge J. Economics*, Dec. 1978, pp. 373–80.

19. G. Nikolayev, 'Unemployment – the Scourge of Capitalism', *International Affairs* (Moscow) 11/1979, p. 42.

20. E. Manevich, ['Ways of Improving the Utilization of Manpower'], *Voprosy ekonomiki* [Problems of Economics] (Moscow) 12/1973, p. 28.

21. *Magyar hirlap* [Hungarian Bulletin] (Budapest) 6 Sept., 1977, p. 7.

22. I. G. Ushakov, ['Material Incentives and the Rationalization of Employment in the CMEA Countries'], *Izvestiya AN SSSR: Seriya ekonomicheskaya* [Communications of the Academy of Sciences of the USSR: Economics Division], (Moscow) Jan.–Feb. 1978, pp. 74–5.

23. M. Bornstein, 'Unemployment in Capitalist Regulated Market Economies and Socialist Centrally Planned Economies', *Amer. Econ. Rev.*, May 1978, p. 40.

24. *Workers' Participation in the European Community* (Brussels: Commission of the European Communities, 1977) p. 5.

25. *Soviet News* (London) 17 Jan., 1978, p. 24.

26. M. Ya Sonin, ['Utilize Labour Resources Efficiency'], *Ekonomika i organizatsiya promyshlennogo proizvodstva* [The Economics and Organization of Industrial Production] (Moscow) 4/1977, pp. 8–9.

27. L. S. Degtyar, ['Financial Incentives in the Promotion of the Efficiency of the Use of Labour'], *Izvestiya AN SSSR*, Nov.–Dec. 1977, pp. 71–2.

28. R. Batkayev, ['Economic Conditions for the Implementation of the Shchekino Scheme'], *Sotsialisticheskii trud*, May 1979, pp. 30–36; G. Bogomolov, ['Socialist Competition and the Shchekino Scheme'], *Sotsialisticheskii trud*, April 1979, pp. 39–43; K. Cherednichenko, ['Lessons of the Shchekino Scheme'], *Kommunist* (Moscow) 11/1979, pp. 37–47.

29. J. Malačić, ['Yugoslav Economists on Unemployment in Yugoslavia'], *Ekonomska revija*, [Economic Review] (Ljubljana) 3–4/1975, p. 636.

CHAPTER 7: WAGES, INCENTIVES AND LIVING STANDARDS

1. M. Dobb, *Wages* (London: Nisbet, 1928).

2. c = *constant capital* (past labour, as embodied in fixed assets, raw materials, components, semi-finished products), v = *variable capital* (wages), s = *surplus value* (rent, interest, profit).

3. Marx, 'Wage Labour and Capital', written in 1849 (can be found in Marx and Engels, *Selected Works* (Moscow: FLPH, 1962) pp. 74–97; Lenin, 'On the So-Called Market Question' (written in 1893) in *Collected Works* (Moscow: FLPH, 1963) vol. 1, pp. 106–7.

4. Marx, *Critique of the Gotha Programme* (written in 1875).

5. E. L. Manevich, 'Wages – Socialism', in *Great Soviet Encyclopedia* (New York: Macmillan, 1975) vol. 9, p. 510.
6. J. Jonczyk, ['Work Discipline Today and Tomorrow'], *Nowe drogi* [New Paths] (Warsaw) 4/1976, p. 126.
7. It includes the following six branches of the economy contributing to the Marxist-defined national income ('net material product'): industry, construction, agriculture and forestry, transport and communications, trade, other minor activities (research and development, non-domestic laundrying, and so on). The services other than those specified above are considered to be non-productive; in the Western-defined national income these services constitute about one-fifth of the total national income.
8. It may be mentioned here that in the developed capitalist countries the share of total personal income going to labour is about 75 per cent (the rest going to capital) and this proportion has remained virtually unchanged since the Second World War.
9. E. M. Kassalov, *Trade Unions and Industrial Relations* (New York: Random House, 1969) p. 241.
10. Marx, *Capital* (New York: International Publishers, 1967) vol. 1, pp. 628–48, 745–49.
11. Chin Chi-chu, 'What the Workers and Cadres Say About Bonus', *Beijing Rev.* (Peking) 25 Aug., 1978, p. 32.
12. In the USSR up to the early 1930s higher distinctions (medals, titles) had been awarded only to groups of workers, but since that time they have been conferred on individuals as well.
13. M. Michalik, *Moralność pracy* [Work Morality] (Warsaw: PWE, 1977) p. 105.
14. T. Rudolf, ['Fraternal Co-operation'], *Ekonomicheskoe sotrudnichestvo stran-chlenov SEV* [Economic Co-operation amongst the CMEA Countries] (Moscow) 1/1978, p. 47.
15. Chin Chi-chu, op. cit., p. 23; *News Bulletin* (Australia–China Society, Melbourne) Dec. 1978, p. 4.
16. Chen-mei Fan and Liang-shing Fan, 'Some Recent Developments in Chinese Incentive Schemes in Agriculture', *Canadian J. Agric. Economics* (Guelph, Ont.) July 1980, pp. 85–6.
17. H. Mehnke, ['Effects of Incentives on Technological Development'], *Prace a mzda* [Work and Wages] (Prague) 10/1978, p. 538.
18. *Życie gospodarcze* [Economic Life] (Warsaw) 29 March, 1970, p. 8.
19. R. Batkayev, ['Economic Conditions for the Implementation of the Shchekino Method'], *Sotsialisticheskii trud* [Socialist Labour] (Moscow) May 1979, p. 31.
20. M. V. Kokhanova, ['The Determination and Utilization of Self-Supporting Material Incentive Funds at the Present Stage (the USSR, Bulgaria, Poland and Czechoslovakia)'], *Vestnik Moskovskogo Universiteta: Ekonomika* [Reports of the Moscow University: Economics] (Moscow) July–Aug. 1978, pp. 66–8; V. Houzvicka, ['The Appraisal of Material Incentives for Technical and Organizational Development'], *Prace a mzda*, 1/1979, p. 13.
21. *Figyelö* [Economic Observer] (Budapest) 29 Oct., 1969, p. 3; *Ekonomika i organizacja pracy* [The Economics and Organization of Labour] (Warsaw) Jan. 1970, p. 43.

22. Urszula Wojciechowska and T. Sawczuk, ['Principles Governing the Formation and Utilization of the Funds in the Socialist Countries'], *Gospodarka planowa* [Planned Economy] (Warsaw) 12/1978, p. 626.
23. Thus to illustrate by reference to the USSR. In the 1970s the *average* incentive payments on the macro-scale fluctuated in different years from 4.7 to 13.9 per cent of the national wage fund. *Finansy SSSR* [Soviet Finance] (Moscow) 6/1976, p. 58 and 1/1979, pp. 3–11.
24. R. Hyman, 'Inequality, Ideology and Industrial Relations', *British J. Industrial Relations*, 2/1974, p. 172.
25. Wu Jian and Wang Dachao, 'Living Conditions of the Working Class in Developed Capitalist Countries', *Beijing Rev.*, 6 April, 1981, p. 19.
26. Hyman, op. cit., pp. 178, 186.
27. Marx, *Critique of the Gotha Program* (Moscow: FLPH, 1947) especially p. 27.
28. J. Kleer, ['Observations on the Principle of Distribution'], *Nowe drogi*, 9/1968, p. 93.
29. A. Guber, 'What Do You Mean by "Living Standard"?', *Soviet Weekly*, (London) 14 July, 1979, p. 5.
30. The following sources of non-labour income may be noted: interest on government bonds and on savings bank deposits (about 3 per cent p.a.), income from private enterprise where it is still tolerated (private farms, individual plots, personal services, catering, crafts), social service benefits, remittances from abroad, plus black marketing, embezzlement, pilfering in factories and on socialized farms).
31. In the USSR personal income figures were not published from the mid-1930s up to the mid-1960s as they were treated as state secrets.
32. *Annuarul statistic al Republicii Socialiste România 1980*, p. 123.
33. P. Wiles, *Distribution of Income East and West* (Amsterdam: North-Holland, 1974) pp. 1–25.
34. J. Cromwell, 'The Size Distribution of Income: An International Comparison', *The Review of Income and Wealth* (New Haven, USA) Sept. 1977, pp. 294, 304–5.
35. *China Trade Report* (Hong Kong) Oct. 1980, p. 4.
36. *Beijing Rev.*, 16 Nov. 1979, p. 13.
37. B. Fick, ['The Differentiation of Wages'], *Nowe drogi*, 11/1969, p. 4; *Rocznik statystyczny 1968* [Statistical Yearbook 1968] (Warsaw) GUS, 1968, p. 548.
38. *Polityka* [Politics] (Warsaw) 20 June, 1981, p. 2.
39. Falus K. Szikra, 'On High Personal Incomes in Hungary', *Acta oeconomica* [Economic Papers] (Budapest) 1–2/1980, p. 82.
40. Consisting of the following maximum loadings: occupational skill – 2.80 (above the basic rate of 1.00), regional conditions – 2.00, the difficulty of work – 1.33, personal effort – 1.20, and the social importance of the work – 1.15. Y. Gromberg, ['Some Problems of the Theory of Wages under Socialism'], *Voprosy ekonomiki* [Problems of Economics] (Moscow) Dec. 1968, p. 57.
41. *Statistički godišnjak Jugoslavije 1980* [Statistical Yearbook of Yugoslavia 1980] (Belgrade: Federal Statistical Office, 1980) pp. 140–41.
42. For example, in the 1970s the percentage of personal income of collective farms represented by income from personal ('subsidiary') plots was: in the

USSR (in 1976) – 26 per cent, in Bulgaria (1975) – 28 per cent, in Hungary (1976) – 40 per cent and in Mongolia (1972) – 50 per cent. G. Shmelev, ['Subsidiary Plots in the CMEA Countries'], *Voprosy ekonomiki*, July 1978, p. 120.

43. K. Laski, 'The Problems of Inflation in Socialist Countries', *Eastern European Economics* (White Plains, NY) Summer 1979, p. 20.

44. For details, see R. Krzyżewski, *Konsumpcja społeczna w gospodarce socjalistycznej* [Social Consumption in the Socialist Economy] (Warsaw: PWN, 1968) pp. 115–20. Also see: M. Kaser, *Health Care in the Soviet Union and Eastern Europe* (London: Croom Helm, 1976); B. Mieczkowski, *Personal and Social Consumption in Eastern Europe* (New York: Praeger, 1975).

45. *Soviet News*, 14 July, 1979, p. 5.

CHAPTER 8: INFLATION AND LABOUR

1. M. Mieszczankowski, ['On Some Causes of Secular Inflation'], *Życie gospodarcze* [Economic Life] (Warsaw) 28 March, 1976, p. 11.

2. *Soviet News* (London) 3 Aug., 1976, p. 284.

3. *Pravda* (Moscow) 8 Feb., 1977, p. 3.

4. *Statistisches Jahrbuch der Deutschen Demokratischen Republik 1980* [Statistical Yearbook of the German Democratic Republic 1980] (East Berlin: Staatsverlag der DDR, 1980) p. 265.

5. I. Konnik, *Dengi v period stroitelstva kommunisticheskogo obshchestva* [Money during the Period of Communist Construction] (Moscow: Finansy, 1966) pp. 148–9.

6. Based on *Rozwój gospodarczy krajów RWGP 1950–1968* [Economic Development of the Comecon Countries, 1950–1968] (Warsaw: Central Statistical Office, 1969) pp. 38–9. B. Csikós-Nagy, ['Consumer Prices in 1975'], *Figyelö* [Economic Observer] (Budapest) 8 Jan. 1975, pp. 1, 3, also ['Price Measures for 1976'] *Népszabadsag* [People's Daily] (Budapest) 3 Dec. 1975, p. 10.

7. Katharine H. Hsiao, *Money and Monetary Policy in Communist China* (New York: Columbia University Press) 1971, p. 232, 235.

8. Reported in *The Australian Financial Rev.*, 6 May, 1980, p. 18.

9. Hsiao, loc. cit.

10. Based on: *Rocznik statystyczny 1975* [Statistical Yearbook 1975] (Warsaw: Central Statistical Office, 1975) pp. 405–06.

11. A. Zwass, 'Inflation in Planned Economies', *Eastern European Economics*, (White Plains, NY) Spring 1978, p. 7.

12. Z. Fedorowicz, ['The Mechanism of Inflationary Pressure in the Socialist Economy'], *Ekonomista* [The Economist] (Warsaw) 5–6/1980, p. 1202.

13. J. Wilczynski, *East–West Banking and Finance and Their Relevance to Australian and Canadian Interests* (Ottawa: Institute of Soviet and East European Studies, Carleton University, Feb. 1978) p. 22; *The Economist*, (London) 11 July 1981, p. 33; *Życie gospodarcze*, 4 Dec. 1980, p. 1 and 26 Feb. 1981, p. 3.

14. Based on UN *Monthly Bulletin of Statistics* (different issues).

15. Zwass, op. cit., p. 13.
16. M. Korosić, ['Inflation and Income Distribution'], *Ekonomska politika* [Economic Policy] (Belgrade) 12 Aug. 1974, p. 18.
17. Fedorowicz, op. cit., p. 1206.
18. B. Csikós-Nagy, 'Inflation and Anti-Inflationary Policy', *Acta oeconomica* [Economic Papers] (Budapest) 3–4/1977, pp. 304–5 (emphasis in the original).
19. S. Nikitin and S. Pronin, 'What Causes Inflation?', *World Marxist Rev.* (Toronto) July 1976, pp. 110–11.
20. Ibid., p. 111.
21. O. Bogomolov, S. Gorbunov, 'Inflation in the West: Its Causes, Mechanism and Consequences', *International Affairs* (Moscow) April 1979, p. 53.
22. Ibid.
23. B. Burkitt, 'Wage Restraint and the Inflationary Barrier', *Rev. Radical Political Economics* (New York) Spring 1979, pp. 49–51.
24. Korosić, op. cit., p. 19.
25. Fedorowicz, op. cit., p. 1206.
26. Korosić, op. cit., p. 20.
27. *Business Eastern Europe* (Geneva) 15 Jan. 1982, p. 17; *World Currency Report* (different numbers); *Życie gospodarcze*, 1 March, 1981, p. 5.
28. E. Drabowski, ['The Acceleration of Inflation in the Capitalist Economy'], *Nowe drogi* [New Paths] (Warsaw) 8/1974, p. 86.
29. Fedorowicz, op. cit., pp. 1205–6.
30. For example, in Poland food subsidies to maintain low prices for *domestic* consumption amounted to 267 490m, 309 280m and (planned) 300 700m zlotys in 1980, 1981 and (planned) 1982, respectively – representing as much as 21, 24 and 21 per cent of the total budgetary expenditure in the respective years. *Życie gospodarcze*, 4 Oct., 1981, p. 5.
31. Susanne Beckmann, ['The Contribution of Price Advisory Boards to the Stability of Consumer Prices'], *Sozialistische Finanzwirtschaft* [Socialist Financial Management] (East Berlin) 1 July, 1975, pp. 48–50.
32. For details, see J. Wilczynski, *Comparative Monetary Economics* (London: Macmillan and New York: Oxford University Press, 1978) p. 238.
33. In the classic article, A. W. Phillips, 'The Relation between the Rate of Change of Money Wage Rates and the Level of Unemployment in the United Kingdom, 1861–1957', *Economica*, Nov. 1958, pp. 283–99.

CHAPTER 9: INDUSTRIAL DISPUTES

1. *Great Soviet Encyclopedia* (New York: Macmillan, 1975) vol. 9, pp. 471, 472.
2. M. Baglai, ['Problems of the Theoretical Assumptions behind Trade Unionism under Socialism'], *Pravda* (Moscow) 26 Dec. 1980, p. 2.
3. *A Chronicle of Human Rights in the USSR* (New York) Jan.–March 1977, p. 79.
4. Reported in *The Canberra Times*, 16 Dec. 1981, p. 1, 17 Dec. 1981, p. 1, 23 Dec. 1981, p. 1, and 19 Feb. 1982, p. 5.
5. Especially see V. I. Lenin, *What Is To Be Done?* (originally written in 1901–

2); Rosa Luxemburg, *The Mass Strike, the Political Party and the Trade Unions* (written in 1906).

6. For example, G. Sorel, *Reflections on Violence* (first published in 1908).

7. E. M. Kassalov, *Trade Unions and Industrial Relations: An International Comparison* (New York: Random House, 1969) pp. 315–16.

8. Based on *Year Book of Labour Statistics 1980* (Geneva: ILO, 1980) pp. 627–40.

9. *Ekonomska politika* [Economic Policy] (Belgrade) 22 Aug., 1977, p. 7; *Vjesnik* [Herald] (Zagreb) 10 June, 1978, pp. 18–19; plus data supplied by Professor D. A. Loeber of the University of Kiel.

10. Audrey Donnithorne, 'The Control of Inflation in China', *Current Scene* (Hong Kong) April–May 1978, p. 6.

11. A. Pankert, 'Settlement of Labour Disputes in Essential Services', *Int. Lab. Rev.* (Geneva) Nov.–Dec., 1980, pp. 731–2.

12. *Soviet News* (London) 28 Aug., 1979, p. 276.

13. Baglai, loc. cit.

14. Kang Yonghe, 'China's Trade Unions', *Beijing Rev.* (Peking) 8 June, 1979, p. 13.

15. P. F. Hercus, 'Arbitration Makes a Mockery of the Law', *The Weekend Australian* (Sydney) 10 Nov., 1979, p. 22.

CHAPTER 10: INTERNATIONAL MIGRATION OF WORKERS

1. For example, for some recent publications see, Cheryl Benard 'Migrant Workers and European Democracy', *Political Science Q.* (New York) Summer 1978, pp. 277–99; W. R. Böhming, 'International Migration in Western Europe: Reflections on the Past Five Years', *Int. Lab. Rev.* (Geneva) July–Aug. 1979, pp. 401–14; G. Minet, 'Spectators or Participants? Immigrants and Industrial Relations in Western Europe', *Int. Lab. Rev.*, Jan.–Feb. 1978, 21–35; R. C. Rist 'Guest Workers and Post-World War II European Migration', *Studies in Comparative International Development*, (New Brunswick, NJ) Summer 1979, pp. 28–53.

2. *Rynki zagraniczne* [Foreign Markets] (Warsaw) 5–8 April 1980, p. 4.

3. Organized schemes for importing foreign workers with a view to their illegal employment have existed for many years in several parts of the world, especially in Western Europe, and some of them have been uncovered by authorities in such countries as Belgium, France, the Federal Republic of [West] Germany, Italy, Switzerland, the United Kingdom and the USA. For example, see Commission of the European Communities, *Clandestine Immigration* (Brussels, 1975) Doc. SEC (75) 1705; W. Fogel, 'Illegal Alien Workers in the United States', *Industrial Relations* (Berkeley) Oct. 1977, pp. 243–63; R. de Grazia, 'Clandestine Employment: A Problem of Our Times', *Int. Lab. Rev.*, Sep.–Oct. 1980, pp. 550–52.

4. Member countries of the Council for Mutual Economic Assistance, originally established in 1949, now embracing Bulgaria, Cuba, Czechoslovakia, the [East] German Democratic Republic, Hungary, Mongolia, Poland, Romania, the USSR and Vietnam.

5. N. Hansen, 'Europe's Guest Worker Policies and Mexicans in the United

States', *Growth and Change* (Lexington, KY) April 1979, p. 4.

6. For further details, see references indicated in Note 1.

7. Their total number in the mid-1970s, according to different estimates, ranged from 4m to 12m, mostly Mexicans (J..A. Bustamante, 'Immigrants from Mexico: The Silent Invasion Issue', in R. S. Bryce-Laporte (ed.), *Sourcebook on the New Immigration* (New Brunswick, NJ: Transaction Books, 1980) p. 139). Some of them came as permanent settlers and some are not workers but family members or adventurers. The author's estimate of the *migrant workers* (in conformity with the concept specified at the outset of this chapter in the late 1970s was 4.0m.

8. For further details see, J. S. Birks and C. A. Sinclair, 'International Labour Migration in the Arab Middle East', *Third World Q.* (London) April, 1979, pp. 87–99; R. P. Shaw, 'Migration and Employment in the Arab World: Construction as a Key Policy Variable', *Int. Lab. Rev.*, Sep.–Oct. 1979, pp. 589–605.

9. Further details can be found in Jill Nattrass, 'Migrant Labour and South African Development', *South African J. Economics* (Bramfontein) March 1976, pp. 65–83; M. Burawoy, 'Functions and Reproduction of Migrant Labor: Comparative Material from Southern Africa and the United States', *Amer. J. Sociology* (Chicago) March 1976, pp. 1050–87; J. Loxley, 'Labour Migration and the Liberation Struggle in Southern Africa', paper presented to Seminar on International Labour Issues, McGill University, Montreal, 10 April, 1980 (37 pp.).

10. There were several thousand Soviet engineers, technicians, scientists and economic advisers in China in the 1950s, but they were withdrawn suddenly after 1958, prompted by the Sino-Soviet dispite.

11. To this writer's knowledge, only Czechoslovakia and Hungary have published some, incomplete, official figures.

12. The most comprehensive and reasonably recent ones are: M. Virius and J. Balek, ['The Exchange of Workers amongst the CMEA Countries'], *Zahraniční obchod* [Foreign Trade] (Prague) no. 9, 1976, pp. 4–8; F. Levcik, 'Migration and Employment of Foreign Workers in the CMEA Countries and Their Problems', in US Congress, Joint Economic Committee, *East European Economics Post Helsinki* (Washington: GPO, 25 Aug. 1977) pp. 458–78.

13. Virius and Balek, op. cit., p. 6.

14. According to some estimates, the total may be over 2.0m. Thus a Finnish source recently claimed that in Czechoslovakia alone the number was between one and two million. *Suomen Kuvalehti* [Finnish Magazine], (Helsinki) 9 Dec. 1977, p. 63 (but it gave no sources on which it based its estimate). Levcik (op. cit., p. 466) gave a figure for Czechoslovakia for 1975 of 37 000–40 000 and Virius and Balek (op. cit., p. 6) gave no more than 50,000. The Czechoslovak statistical yearbook for 1979 (*Statistička ročenka Československé socialistické republiky 1980* (Prague: SNTL, 1980) p. 180), gave the following figures: 1970 – 14 288, 1974 – 21 687, 1975 – 19 442, 1976 – 16 523, 1977 – 13 096, 1978 – 11 238 and 1979 – 12 220; however, these figures appear to cover only a particular category of workers. This writer is inclined to accept the figures by Virius and Balek and assume 200 000 workers for the CMEA in the late 1970s.

15. Virius and Balek, op. cit., p. 5.
16. Ibid., p. 8.
17. At the end of 1978, there were 359 companies in the OECD countries and 185 in the developing countries, wholly or partly owned by the CMEA countries, with invested capital totalling at least $724m. These subsidiaries operate in the fields of banking and finance, resource development, marketing, manufacturing and transport (roughly in that order of importance). For further details see, C. H. McMillan, 'Growth of External Investments by the Comecon Countries', *The World Economy*, (London) Sep. 1979, pp. 363–86.
18. Of whom in 1975 at least 18 000 were Poles, 3000 were Romanians, 2000 Bulgarians, Czechoslovaks and Hungarians (each), and the balance was represented by the Soviets, East Germans and others. Z. Ecevit and K. C. Zachariah, 'International Labor Migration', *Finance and Development*, (Washington) Dec. 1976, p. 35; Levcik, op. cit., p. 466.
19. The offer was made by China's Ministry of the Metallurgical Industry, which has 30 engineering organizations divided into 200 enterprises, comprising 400 000 engineers, technicians, semi-skilled and unskilled workers. *Sydney Morning Herald*, 4 Dec. 1979, p. 5; *Rynki zagraniczne*, loc. cit.
20. Ecevit and Zachariah, op. cit., p. 33.
21. Hansen, op. cit., p. 5.
22. Under capitalist regimes, the present socialist countries were noted for high levels of unemployment (up to 25 per cent) and underemployment. Unemployment had been eliminated in the USSR by 1930, in Eastern Europe by the early 1950s and in China by 1960. Some hidden underemployment is, however, found in certain regions or enterprises. The shortages of labour have recently become acute owing to the slowdown in the growth of the working-age population and insufficient importance attached to labour-saving innovations. In the late 1970s, labour shortages in Bulgaria, Czechoslovakia, Hungary and the USSR represented 2–3 per cent of the existing employment and in Poland there were eight vacancies for each job seeker. *Magyar hirlap* [Hungarian Bulletin] (Budapest) 6 Sep. 1977, p. 7; *Rada narodowa gospodarka administracja* [Local Economy and Administration] (Warsaw) no. 25, 1978, p. 27; *Trud* [Labour] (Moscow) 17 July 1979, p. 2.
23. Virius and Balek, op. cit., p. 4.
24. However, over the period 1945–70 over 7.5m left Eastern Europe illegally or semi-legally (the German Democratic Republic – 2 287 000, Poland – 577 000, Hungary – 172 000, Czechoslovakia – 144 000), mostly to Western Europe, and some of them to North America, Australia and New Zealand (Levcik, op. cit., p. 460–61). Yugoslavia and Vietnam are the only socialist countries allowing permanent emigration.
25. *Suomen Kuvalehti*, loc. cit.
26. Loxley, op. cit., p. 6.
27. Thus, according to a survey of Yugoslav migrant workers, in 1970 their net monthly earnings (which averaged US $264) were 2.5 times higher than net earnings of workers in Croatia. L. A. Kosinski 'Yugoslavia and International Migration', *Canadian Slavonic Papers* (Ottawa) Sep. 1978, p. 325.

28. This generalization also holds in the case of the countries noted for the consequential tertiary markets, but not necessarily in the case of skilled workers from the West on temporary engagements in the socialist or less-developed countries.

29. There have been several efforts by international bodies to protect the migrant workers' rights, including the equality of treatment in respect of wages, conditions of work, social benefits and participation in trade unions and workers' representation. The most important instruments are the Conventions of the International Labour Organization, viz.: *Migration for Employment Convention (Revised)*, 1949 (No. 97); *Migrant Workers (Supplementary Provisions) Convention*, 1975 (No. 143); *Migrant Workers Recommendation*, 1975 (No. 151). The European Economic Community has a *Code of Conduct on Migrant Labour*. However, these documents identify the problems and indicate what abuses should be removed rather than remove them. There is no effective machinery for the enforcement of the conventions and recommendations.

30. Virius and Balek, op. cit., p. 7; *Suomen Kuvalehti*, loc. cit.

31. Ecevit and Zachariah, op. cit., p. 36.

32. Ibid.

33. Shaw, op. cit., p. 596.

34. Loxley, op. cit., p. 16.

35. Virius and Balek, op. cit., p. 5.

36. McMillan, op. cit., pp. 378–82.

37. Loxley, op. cit., p. 9.

38. Hansen, op. cit., p. 5.

39. In late 1981 total unemployment, (and rates in brackets), in some of the leading host countries were: Belgium – 500 000 (14.4 per cent), France – 1 910 000 (the rate not available), the Federal Republic of Germany – 1 260 000 (5.4 per cent), the Netherlands – 410 000 (9.7 per cent), the United Kingdom – 3 000 000 (13.7 per cent) and the USA – 7 760 000 (7.2 per cent). United Nations *Monthly Bulletin of Statistics* (New York) Dec. 1981, pp. 17–20.

40. Benard, op. cit., p. 293.

41. M. Castells, 'Immigrant Workers and Class Struggles in Advanced Capitalism: The Western European Experience', *Politics and Society* (Chicago) vol. 5, no. 1, 1975, p. 54 (emphasis in the original).

42. M. B. Krauss and W. J. Baumol, 'Guest Workers and Income Transfer Programs Financed by Host Governments', *Kyklos* (Basel) vol. 32, no. 1–2, 1979, p. 36.

43. Thus about two-thirds of the migrants entering North-Western Europe are classed as skilled or semi-skilled. In South Africa, 90 per cent of foreign workers are male and 80 per cent are below the age of 40. Ecevit and Zachariah, op. cit., p. 34; Loxley, op. cit., p. 3.

44. For recent details see, J. N. Bhagwati, 'International Migration of the Highly Skilled: Economics, Ethics and Taxes', *Third World Q.* (London) July 1979, pp. 17–30; W. A. Glaser, 'International Flows of Talent', in Bryce-Laporte (ed.), op. cit., pp. 59–67.

45. B. Smith and R. Newman, 'Depressed Wages along the U.S.–Mexico Border: An Empirical Analysis', *Economic Inquiry* (Long Beach, CA), Jan. 1977, p. 63.

46. A. Portes and R. C. Bach, 'Immigrant Earnings: Cuban and Mexican Immigrants in the United States', *International Migration Rev.* (New York) Fall 1980, p. 334.
47. Loxley, op. cit., p. 11.
48. Benard, op. cit., pp. 281–4, 295.
49. *Das Volk* [People] (Erfurt) 23 Aug. 1978, p. 3.
50. *Int. Lab. Rev.*, Nov.–Dec. 1978, p. 73.
51. Böhming, op. cit., p. 401.
52. *Rynki zagraniczne*, loc. cit.
53. For example, Bulgaria and Czechoslovakia agreed to pay the Egyptian workers engaged in the early 1970s in US dollars, and similarly later Czechoslovakia undertook to pay Yugoslav workers in hard currency. *Delo* [Work] (Ljubljana) 11 Feb. 1972, p. 5; Levcik, op. cit., p. 473.
54. ILO, *Migrant Workers Recommendation*, Geneva, 1975, No. 151, Paragraph 2.
55. Thus, in the late 1970s, the following percentages of foreign workers were union members (in brackets, of citizen workers): in Belgium – 45 per cent (75 per cent), France – 10 per cent (23 per cent), the Federal Republic of Germany – 30 per cent (35 per cent), the Netherlands – 35 per cent (40 per cent), Sweden – about 80–85 per cent (also 80–85 per cent), Minet, op. cit., p. 22.
56. Ibid.
57. Ibid., pp. 29–31.
58. They can be found in a collected, edited form in Marx and Engels, *Ireland and the Irish Question: A Collection of Writings* (New York: International Publishers, 1972).
59. For example, see E. Mandel, 'The Laws of Uneven Development', *New Left Rev.* (London) Jan. 1970, pp. 19–38.
60. Marx formulated the thesis of the declining profit rate in *Capital*, vol. III, and it has been accepted by Marxists as one of the most fundamental *laws* of capitalist development. The profit rate declines owing to the increasing *organic structure of capital* (capital–labour ratio), as labour alone (not capital) can create value and profit.
61. Elizabeth McL. Petras, 'Towards a Theory of International Migration: The New Division of Labor', in Bryce-Laporte (ed.), op. cit., p. 445.
62. The Marxian formula for value is: c (*constant capital*, that is, the depreciation of durable-use and single-use producer goods) $+ v$ (*variable capital*, that is, wages) $+ s$ (*surplus value*, that is, profit, rent, interest). The worker receives v, equal to the value of his *labour-power* (determined by his bargaining power), contributed in the *necessary labour-time*; s, appropriated by the capitalist(s), is equal to the value created by the worker in his *surplus labour-time*; s/v is the *rate of surplus value* – 'an exact expression of the degree of exploitation of *labour-power* by capital'. Marx, *Capital* (New York: International Publishers, 1967) vol. I, pp. 177–243.
63. The designation 'sub-proletariat' is preferable to the Marxian term *lumpenproletariat* (deliberately idle, engaging in criminal activities, demoralized and prepared to succumb to bourgeois bribes in betrayal of the militant and proud working class). Although by the latter Marx meant the lowest layer of the proletariat, he was contemptuous of it and considered it

to be of little revolutionary value. He would regard modern migrant workers (judging by his attitude to the Irish workers in England) with sympathy and understanding and as representing a revolutionary potential.

64. Benard, op. cit., pp. 278–9.
65. Schmitter, op. cit., p. 180.
66. Benard, op. cit., p. 297.
67. Castells, op. cit., p. 33.
68. Ibid., p. 61.
69. Benard, op. cit., pp. 296–7.
70. Loxley, op. cit., p. 13.
71. Ibid., p. 35.
72. *Rynki zagraniczne*, loc. cit.
73. See especially V. I. Lenin, *Imperialism: The Highest Stage of Capitalism* (originally published in 1917); K. Nkrumah, *Neo-Colonialism: The Last Stage of Imperialism* (London: Nelson, 1965).
74. Based on the United Nations *Monthly Bulletin of Statistics*.
75. M. R. Pai, 'Is India a New Economic Colony?', *East-West Relations*, (The Hague) vol. VII, no. 1, 1973, pp. 34, 37.

Index